The Defence School of
100 years of military photog

"Legends and Heroes"
The stories of those who made a difference

"Behind the Lens"
A lifetime in military photography

---

by
Dave Humphrey

RB
Rossendale Books

Published by Lulu Enterprises Inc.
3101 Hillsborough Street
Suite 210
Raleigh, NC 27607-5436
United States of America

Published in paperback 2014
Category: History/Memoirs
Copyright Dave Humphrey © 2014
ISBN : 978-1-291-98410-1

Dedication

To Carole; my mentor, financial advisor, health coach and fun manager.
A life without regrets is a life lived to the full.
Thank you Carole from the bottom of my heart

Foreword
by
Mr Jon Jarvis MA BA FBIPP
Officer Commanding
The Defence School of Photography

It is with great honour that I accepted the invitation from Mr. Humphrey to write a short foreword to this book. I have known Dave for some 30 years and have witnessed his passion and commitment to the photographic branch and associated training first hand; a consummate professional, who always gives of his best. His enthusiasm and dedication towards the creation, and now reincarnation, of the military photographic museum was ably supported by two other DSOP 'legends'; Mr. Dave Jenkins (my first instructor) and Mr. Jack Eggleston.

In his acknowledgement to the compilation of the stories he has put together, Dave recognises those who are taking over museum responsibilities and, in turn, they too are fully aware of the 'large shoes' they have to fill (and the scrutiny their efforts will be exposed to - no pun intended!)

As the 44th Commanding Officer of the photographic school, I am conscious that a significant milestone will occur in 2015. In this year, the Defence Photographic School will reach its Centenary and the narratives provided by Dave in this book, provide a distinct and distinguished insight, recognising the National Service provided by those who have completed military photographic training. I hope you enjoy the read as much as I did.

About the author

David served 45 years with the Ministry of Defence, 22 years as a photographer with the Royal Air Force, followed by 23 years as an Instructional Officer with the Defence School of Photography.

He appeared on the BBC TV programme "Inside Out" and the Channel 4 TV documentary series "Time Watch" featuring a missing wartime photo reconnaissance pilot. He has also appeared on similar documentaries for the American Discovery channel series "Spies in the Sky" and the Australian Discovery channel programme "Last Plane out of Berlin".

Born in Birmingham in 1940 and educated at St Phillips Grammar School, he joined the RAF in the late fifties to "see the world". He managed to spend half of his career living abroad in Europe, the Mediterranean and the Middle East. He has also served with ships of Royal Navy as the principle photographer to the Commander-in-Chief of NATO in Malta. He

David demonstrates the F24 camera to the late Lord Lichfield

also worked with Royal Marine and Army units as a reconnaissance and surveillance operator in the Middle East.

He became an Associate Member of the British Institute of Professional Photography in 1972. David continued his association with the Ministry of Defence as an Instructing Officer training over a thousand servicemen and women at the Defence School of Photography.

He retired in November 2004, having nursed the training through the early stages of the digital revolution. He holds a keen interest in the history of military photography, being the founder and curator of the Museum of Military Photography, opened by the late Lord Lichfield, in June 2000.

Contents

Page

The Defence School of Photography
Centenary 1915 – 2015

*The story of the unique
photographic training establishment,
founded by the Royal Flying Corps*

In the beginning....

The current home of the Defence School of Photography is the largest purpose built training school for photography in Europe. Since the origins of its foundation in 1915, it is now the oldest established photographic training facility with a continuous history.

The background to Aerial reconnaissance

The story of aerial reconnaissance really goes back to the efforts to gain information from use of the high viewpoint and tethered balloons in particular. The advent of the photographic process used in the field began to create a great influence on the amount of information which was permanent accurate and recordable, rather than dependant on the eyes of an observer. Initial experiments were made difficult because of the long exposure times required to record the image onto the slow sensitive glass plates together with the time taken for subsequent processing.

During the many conflicts during the 19th century, including the American Civil War, photography became increasingly important to present images of persuasion, both for and against the consequences and brutality of war. It was also recognised as an essential advantage to provide accurate intelligence gathering.

However, it was not until the aeroplane emerged as an ideal controllable camera platform that the full power of aerial photographic reconnaissance was proven to the sceptics of the British high command. The turning point for acceptance of its value came in the battle for Neuve Chapelle in March 1915. In the February of 1915, the pioneer photography work of Nos. 2 and 3 Squadrons gave Sir Douglas Haig a detailed picture of the area, including the hidden intricacies of the enemy defences. This information ensured that the battle casualties were far less than expected under previous conditions and confirmed the value of aerial photography from that moment on. Despite the previous experiences of some army units such as the Royal Engineers and the photographic surveys completed in Canada and other parts of the world in the latter part of the 19th century, the need to train many more soldiers in the skills of the photographic process became essential to keep pace with the increasing demand for aerial photographs. The School of Photography was therefore founded by the Royal Flying Corps at South Farnborough to fulfill this primary objective. In the following years to come the School of Photographic Interpretation and the School of Military Survey also became interlinked to form the nucleus of British Military Intelligence.

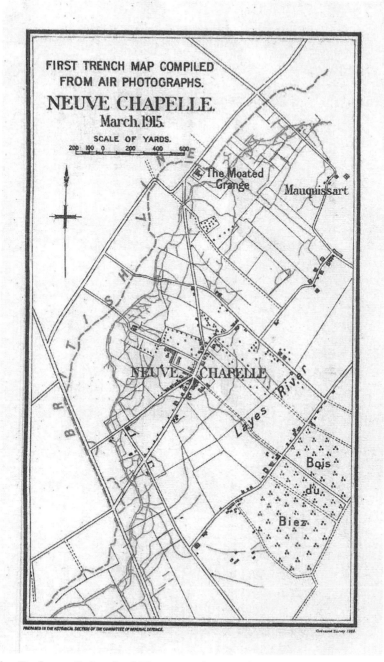

FIRST TRENCH MAP COMPILED
FROM AIR PHOTOGRAPHS.

NEUVE CHAPELLE.
March. 1915.

SCALE OF YARDS.

200 100 0   200   400   600

The Moated Grange

Mauquissart

NEUVE CHAPELLE

Layes River

Bois du Biez

PREPARED IN THE HISTORICAL SECTION OF THE COMMITTEE OF IMPERIAL DEFENCE.

Ordnance Survey 1926.

The Royal Flying Corps
WW1 1914 – 1918

"Necessity is the mother of invention"

In September 1914 the Royal Flying Corps (RFC) took its first air photographs of the war over enemy positions at the battle of the Aisne. The results were sufficient to encourage the formation of an experimental photo

section attached to the RFC. In January 1915 Lieutenant Moore-Brabazon (the late Lord Brabazon), commanded the section at Pinehurst near Farnborough set up to investigate the most suitable cameras and methods for obtaining air photographs. As air photography progressed during the early stages of World War 1, the increasing number of prints required soon overwhelmed the few enlisted photographers and although many more were trained in the field it soon became evident that some form of organised training needed to be introduced. In the summer of 1915 formal training began at Pinehurst and at the Regent Street Polytechnic. During the two years that followed, air photographs became indispensable to intelligence and the demands for photographs seemed insatiable. It was during this time that a Sergeant Major Laws (the late Group Captain Laws), with the British Expeditionary Force, was busy forming, equipping and organising the running of photographic sections at the various Wings in France. Laws was sent back to the UK to deal with the photographic training at Farnborough. Matters seemed to have progressed slowly at first and it was not until 11th September 1915, that a Lieutenant Campbell was able to report that "Sgt Major Laws is now at this station and training is proceeding on sound lines. About 6 men are sufficiently advanced to send to a Wing." Shortly after, on the 7th November 1915, Sgt Major Laws was granted a commission in the Lincolnshire Regiment and seconded to the Royal Flying Corps as the Officer Commanding the School of Photography. The primitive accommodation for the school consisted of two packing cases known as BE huts and was later commented on by Captain Porri: "At present our limited accommodation hardly enables the supply to meet the demand for trained photographers. The men have to be rushed through their course, which should last 3 weeks or a month, in about 10 days, and are then posted away, a fresh lot of recruits then taking their places. Consequently, we are unable to keep a pool of trained men with the present accommodation. There is however, ample room in our proposed new buildings, to enable us to keep this pool of 50 trained men and enable another 20 to be in course of training. Our present permanent staff of 25 NCOs and men required for the production, instruction and experimental section's work, would require augmentation, and at least 5 further NCOs and men as instructors would be required". The new buildings, specially constructed by German POWs, came into use in 1917 when the school became No 1 School of photography at Farnborough. It was the only permanent building erected for the Royal Flying Corps during the 1914 — 1918 war. Early air reconnaissance soon showed that air photography posed very different problems to those of general photography.

The aeroplane was a vibrating platform subjected to "air pockets" and buffeting, from which the camera operator worked in the teeth of a howling gale often freezing in the process. Apart from the effects of vibration and haze, there were many other problems including hostile enemy action — in at least one instance an operator had to interrupt his photography to shoot down an enemy plane. Cameras, at first hand held, were soon mounted on the side of the fuselage. Longer focal length lenses were developed; plate magazines with mechanical changes were fitted, and followed by complete camera installations fitted inside the fuselage. The School not only kept pace with the numerous developments in training, but helped solve many of the problems involved. It also learned from first hand experiences that the unique problems and limitations of aerial photography called for very specialised training to produce photographers capable of coping with it. On 1st April 1918 the Royal Flying Corps became the Royal Air Force and at the 11th hour on the 11th day of November 1918, Armistice Day, hostilities ceased. The "war to end all wars" was over.

Between the wars
1918 – 1939

A period of training stagnation followed the end of hostilities but in 1920 the School started a regular programme of peacetime training which progressed smoothly until 1925. An event occurred which revolutionised air photography and caused dramatic changes in the training of photographers. This was the introduction into the Royal Air Force of the first air cameras to take roll film instead of plates. Soon afterwards enormous strides were made in the techniques of both air reconnaissance and map making (survey) photography.

Large numbers of exposures could be made on a single flight (sortie) and large areas could be covered. The long lengths of film raised a hoard of problems in processing and printing and necessitated a vast amount of new equipment. The School had the difficult task of familiarising itself with all this new equipment and of revising syllabuses and training methods. All this was accomplished with little disruption to the training programme. In 1935 the clouds of war began to gather over Europe once more and the RAF began to expand to meet this threat. At the School the expansion of training though gradual at first was rapidly intensified, once it became apparent to those in high places that air photography would play a prominent role in the event of war. The graph for training output rose steeply, the staff increased and extra accommodation had to be provisioned.

Royal Air Force School of Photography
WW2 1939 – 1945

The outbreak of the second World War is a matter of record. As the enemy occupied more and more of Western Europe in 1940, the use of air reconnaissance became very extensive, and the photographers were completely swamped. It was vitally important to train more photographers and at greater speed. In August 1940 therefore, a second school was started in Blackpool, using a hastily converted technical college. The training of airwomen photographers began in 1941 at Blackpool and soon afterwards it was reported that the consumption of materials had increased by some 15%. The need for economy demanded an investigation which showed that to their credit, the increase was entirely due to the increase in recruitment of young airwomen. They proved to have better manual dexterity and were able to complete intricate manual tasks more quickly so produced more volume of work. At both Schools training was streamlined to the maximum and intakes were as large and frequent as space allowed. This was a period of intense activity in air photography and gave rise to an enormous gain in experience.

The development of cameras, new installations and new techniques progressed alongside the development of aircraft which flew ever faster and higher. Partly to minimise enemy intervention, photo reconnaissance sorties were flown very low down where image movement was a problem, or very high up where long focus lenses were necessary for adequate image scale. Both conditions gave rise to acute problems in the resolution of fine detail needed for intelligence. In addition to its reconnaissance uses, air photography was extremely useful for recording weapon strikes, both on operations and in aircrew training. The introduction of night photography with its special complications added to the ever growing list of tasks. To help in coping with the miles of film exposed and the millions of prints required, continuous film processing and multiprinting machines were introduced. Air photography became a vast organisation and the intelligence it produced was vital to the progress of the war. Not only were the two Schools faced with the task of training the numbers of photographers needed to feed this organisation, they had to continually adapt instruction to embrace new equipment and new techniques and yet strive for higher standards in training (without increasing training time) to meet the increasingly exacting demands made on photographers in the field. Together the Schools trained a total of 6,510 photographer personnel during the war.

This crest was granted Royal Approval by King George VI in November 1939

Post WW2 1945-1965

After the return to peacetime training in 1945, the School unfortunately had to move from Farnborough into improvised accommodation at Farnham, only to suffer a second move in 1948 to Wellesbourne Mountford in Warwickshire. There is remained until October 1963, when it moved to temporary accommodation at RAF Cosford (joining the "Photographer Boy Entrant" training which had been there since 1956). The construction of a new purpose built school building was soon to be completed there. Since the war dramatic changes in aircraft performance and the wide coverage obtainable with multiple camera installations brought about far reaching changes in air photography. New sophisticated equipment and techniques increased the complexity. It follows that the training courses became more comprehensive and intense to enable students to achieve the required skills and knowledge

On the 3rd December 1965 the new building for the School of Photography was formally opened at RAF Cosford by Air Chief Marshal Sir Alfred Earle, KBE CR. Sir Alfred Earle was a former student back in 1930 and 1934. He had also been the Deputy Chief Instructor at the School and it was during that time he started the "Boy Entrant" training scheme and the SNCO's Instruction Course. He flew most of the SNCO's attending those courses in the School's Avro Anson aircraft — up and down the southern railway taking overlap photography. He later became the Officer commanding, No 2 School of Photography at Blackpool. The site for the new School was made ready by clearing an old hangar called "Hinaidi East". There was a great deal of careful planning to enable the latest equipment to be incorporated and it became the largest, most advanced photographic school of its kind in Europe. The first courses to be trained at the new School were of one year's duration for "Craft Apprentices" in photography. The skills included air film processing, printing and management of air camera systems. The students were also expected to be very competent with general photography including studio work, public relations tasks, exterior and technical subjects using sensitometric quality controls. The training syllabuses were aligned   to civilian examination requirements. In 1968 a "single skill" Training Policy was introduced. A basic "Air Photography Operator" course was devised to last 17 weeks and produce a tradesman capable of operating air film processing machinery including electronic printing machines and installing air cameras into aircraft under supervision. Advanced courses were made available to tradesmen when they had qualified to Senior Aircraftsmen, in the skills of "Air Camera Fitter' and "Ground" general photographer. "Air Photography Operators" who had been promoted to Corporal, were eligible for the advanced training course titled "Photographic Processing Analyst".

The Joint School of Photography

The closure of the Royal Naval Air Station, HMS Ford, at Lossiemouth in 1972 brought about the formation of the Joint School of Photography at RAF Cosford when the School took on the additional tasks of training the Royal Navy and Army basic students formerly trained at Lossiemouth. It was perhaps inevitable that further rationalisation would take place as a Tri Service School. In 1978 the air photography training was again revised to become a 16 week basic course and titled "Air Photography Processor 2". This came about due to the sophisticated air cameras now requiring specialised skills given over to the electronics training of the Air Radar Fitter who was made responsible for the "optical sensors". The "APP 2" tradesman could apply for the advanced "Air Photography Processor 1" course (13 weeks long) when they became selected for advancement to Corporal.

An additional course was held at RAF Hereford which covered Service disciplines and management aspects which they must attend before promotion to JNCO. The promotion to Sergeant followed a similar pattern with the advanced course for the "Photographic Processing Analyst" (10 weeks long) and the Service management training course at RAF Hereford for SNCO's. The general or "Ground" photographer underwent a very intense course of 27 weeks duration covering all the aspects of studio, public relations, architectural, technical, portraiture, copying and an excellent colour phase. Some "Ground" photographers were also responsible for staffing Lithographic printing shops therefore all students were given a basic litho course, followed by an advanced course if and when they are required to fill such a post. Advanced courses were also available together with specialist colour courses. All students were given the opportunity as part of their course to qualify for the City and Guilds Certificates relevant to their trade. The photographic Processing Analysts could apply for membership of the British Institute of Professional Photography (BIPP) as Associate members. All other students could apply to the BIPP, the Master Photographers Association and the Royal photographic Society through the normal qualifying procedures. It is a reflection on the training and their personal endeavours that many ex students reached Fellowship standard in these organisations. The specialist

Officer training courses gave an appreciation of management skills required for administering complex photo litho establishments both at home and abroad. There were also commitments to train foreign students of many nationalities during this time. In the 1980's and the 1990's, Video production and media operations became an essential part of the tri service needs as many International conflicts became highly sensitive to public information. The role was taken to very high standards by experienced Instructors whose enthusiasm and skills were reflected by the achievements of their ex students. The media became heavily reliant on their productions when the operational areas became too dangerous to permit normal coverage by National media reporters.

The Defence School of Photography

The digital revolution changed the face of training and the timescales beyond recognition in a very short space of time and placed tremendous demands on the skills and adaptability of the training staff. They rose to the challenge, achieving remarkable increases in students practical and creative standards in a time scale previously thought impossible. The greatest challenge was to keep current training realistic, relevant and valid to the rapidly changing requirements of the digital equipment and software.

The Defence Training Review brought about the re naming of the school. On June 6th 2004 the School was renamed again as the Defence School of Photography under the control of the Defence Intelligence Services Centre (DISC) at Chicksands. A wide variety of specialist training courses, to (around 36 in all, including complete video production) became available to many government and local civil organisations including a local fire service, police, DHSS and HMRC. From July 2004, students from all three services attending the basic photography training were placed on the same course known as the Defence Photographers course.

This principle of training became the prototype and flagship of tri service training amalgamation at Cosford particularly in aircraft engineering. The RAF Cosford base became the Defence College of Aeronautical Engineering and a massive expansion programme estimated at over 200 million pounds was announced in September 2005.

A summary of accomplishments

In the first 50 years of its history the School trained more that 20,000 photographers, including those from 20 different countries. Many well known personalities attended the School either in command or as pupils. Mention has already been made of Group Captain F C V Laws who had so much to do with its origins and was Officer commanding the School in 1924 as a Squadron Leader and later in 1933 as a Wing Commander. Reference has also been made to Air Chief Marshal Sir Alfred Earle and the following should also be mentioned. These include Air Marshal Sir Ronald Rees and Group Captain J Bussey, a first World War pilot. He took the long course successfully in 1921 and later became the Chief Instructor. One of the famous Beamish brothers, Flying Officer G Beamish was a student in 1927. Perhaps the least known student was a remarkable airman known as Aircraftman Ross, who was better known as the legendary Colonel Lawrence of Arabia. Sadly his stay at Farnborough was short lived due to the hounding of newspaper reporters and he was forced to leave the Service before completing the course. He re-enlisted as Aircraftman Shaw and contributed much to the development of marine craft in the Marine Branch. The first war sortie of World War 2 was a photographic operation, made on the day war was declared. Since that day much has been demanded of the Air Camera, and also of the men and women on whom its success so greatly depended. I include this article of an appreciation of the photographers by Bomber Command. It echoes my driven ambition to re-instate the Military Photography Museum as a tribute to their memory:

"Shall history forget the photographers ... they toiled unceasingly and year by year the task increased; in squadron camera rooms, in the multiplying aircraft and in the darkrooms, as the first handful of F24 cameras increased to a grand total of 3,000 and the miniature cameras for the radar numbered 600. The first of the 1,000 bomber raids in mid 1942 found them "ready "at the operational and training units. Colour photography, with its exacting demands for skills and care in all stages of the long process, was tackled successfully by our photographers who had no previous experience of this work. Radar photography, requiring entirely separate treatment increased the flow of work by numerous miniature films. And finally, the daylight offensive of the heavy bombers which came about as an addition to the night attacks and was on the same great scale, rising to a force of 1,107 aircraft between the 6 Operational Groups alone. The skill, patience, ingenuity and endurance of all photographers had indeed been worthy of the highest praise".

School of Photography Commanding Officers

WW1 - The Royal Flying Corps
1915 2nd Lt F C V Laws RFC
1917 Lt C Porri RFC
1917 Maj P R Burchall RFC

Between the wars - The Royal Air Force
1920 Sqn Ldr A R Cooper
1922 Sqn Ldr W J Guilfoyle OBE MC
1924 Sqn Ldr F C V Laws OBE
1930 Wg Cdr A H Steele-Perkins OBE
1932 Wg Cdr H M Probin DSO
1932 Wg Cdr R H Neville OBE MC
1933 Wg Cdr F C V Laws OBE
1933 Wg Cdr G Bowman DSO MC DSO
1934 Wg Cdr M L Taylor AFC
1936 Wg Cdr C Porri
1938 Sqn Ldr J Silvester

WW2 - The Royal Air Force
1939 Sqn Ldr R C Sturgiss
1940 Wg Cdr H G Barrett
1941 Wg Cdr J B Newman MBE
1941 Wg Cdr A E Taylor
1942 Wg Cdr P R Burchall OBE
1943 Sqn Ldr W H Dunton (No 2 School)
1945 Wg Cdr C G R Lewis

Post war - The Royal Air Force
1947 Wg Cdr H C Westwood OBE
1950 Wg Cdr E T Scott
1953 Wg Cdr G J Buxton MBE
1955 Sqn Ldr S Hoskin
1955 Sqn Ldr J W Berry
1959 Sqn Ldr P R Mayle
1961 Sqn Ldr F R J Richardson DFM
1964 Sqn Ldr J E Bellingham AFC
1968 Sqn Ldr K M Hall

Joint School of Photography Commanding Officers

1972 Sqn Ldr W H P Brown
1974 Lt Cdr T Marriott RN
1974 Sqn Ldr A A Blain
1976 Sqn Ldr G P Proctor
1978 Sqn Ldr G C Ashman
1982 Sqn Ldr G J Brown
1985 Lt Cdr M H Larcombe RN
1989 Sqn Ldr B A Broad
1991 Lt Cdr C L Hamlin RN
1993 Sqn Ldr V Kinnin
1996 Sqn Ldr S Ivory
1998 Mr J D Ness

Defence School of Photography Commanding Officers

2000 Mr G H Sellars
2010 Mr J Jarvis

The Military Photography Museum

Within DSOP there was a very unique Military Photography Museum, located at RAF Cosford. In 1999 it was transferred for public view in the old parachute packing room specially converted under the direction of John Francis, the then Director of the RAF Museum at Cosford. The Earl of Lichfield performed the official opening ceremony on the 6th of June 2000. It housed a collection of many items of cameras, equipment and remarkable photographs covering the history of military photography from the turn of the last century to modern conflicts. The collection was the most comprehensive of its kind. David Humphrey, David Jenkins and Jack Eggleston, were all former Instructors and museum curators when it was previously housed within the School building. They worked for many months in their own time during the transition to the new site, to ensure the contents and their unique historical value would be freely available to the public and students of both photography and military history. It was during the opening of the Military Photography Gallery at the RAF Museum, Cosford on 16th June 2000 that the late Lord Lichfield also included a visit the training facilities at DSOP.

S/Sgt Giles Penfound RLC, S/Sgt Steve Prendergast RLC, and Lt Jan Greene RN with Lord Lichfield at DSOP

The interior of the Military Photography Gallery
at the RAF Museum, Cosford
opened by the late Lord Lichfield in June 2000

Jack Eggleston, Dave & Ollie Jenkins,
Lord Lichfield (centre) at DSOP
Dave Humphrey, Carole Ludlow-Smith, Ronnie Payne

Lord Lichfield opens the Military Photography Gallery
Dave Jenkins, Jack Eggleston, Lord Lichfield, Dave Humphrey

Facts are stubborn things...

"The results of aerial photography attained at the present time are so surprising in their excellence that if the comparative infancy of the subject is taken into account the future possibilities are vast and various."
  Captain W. E. De B. Whittaker, the Kings Regiment, 1915

In the prelude to WW2, General Werner Von Fritsch, presided over a briefing with his fellow staff officers in 1938 and made the following prophesy: -

"The military organisation with the best aerial photo-reconnaissance, will win the next war".

And to the next 100 years ...

UAVs: MQ9 – Reaper – the new generation

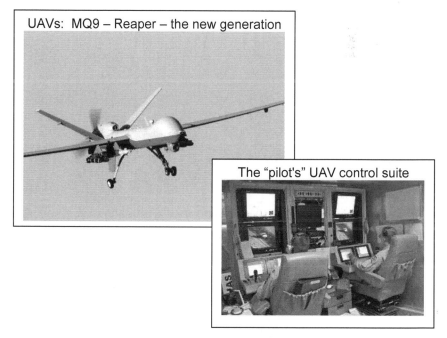

The "pilot's" UAV control suite

"Legends and Heroes"

Why I wrote 'Legends and Heroes'

A collection of stories about those who made a difference

During my good fortune to enjoy such a fortuitous career, I came across stories of people who made a remarkable contribution to the outcome of both world wars through the photographic process and its impact on the history of world conflicts for ever.

Their achievements have been placed on record but sadly their stories seemed to me to have lost the impact they deserved with the passage of time. Some of them are closely linked and some of them bore the brunt of controversy, scandal and dismissal, despite their gargantuan efforts. However they all have one thing in common, they made a difference and because of them we are here today enjoying the lives we hold so dear ...it could have been all so very different.

My eternal gratitude to those wonderful authors who provided the books and articles which gave me the insight to re examine the events we can now perceive with so much clearer definition.   Enjoy!

Dave Humphrey February 2014

Authors Introduction

by Dave Humphrey

The stories behind aerial photo reconnaissance are of outstanding bravery, legendary heroes, political intrigue and controversy, most of which has been little known to the public. It had a massive impact on the successful outcome of WW2, and not for the first time! Along with the advent of the aeroplane in WWI, it changed the face of military conflict forever.

The earliest efforts of "aerial" reconnaissance were recorded during the Napoleonic wars and the American Civil war; tethered balloons being used as observation platforms. As far back as the 1850's, military photography was conducted by the Royal Engineers. In 1860 by Captain Henry Shaw, the Chief Instructor of the Royal Engineers School of Photography from 1858-64, describes one of the most common uses of photography from travels and campaigns. Yet, just over 100 years ago, the introduction of the flying machine and aerial photo reconnaissance were dismissed. In 1910 General Hague informed his staff officers;

"I hope none of you gentlemen is so foolish as to regard the aeroplane as a useful instrument of war. There is only one way to gather reconnaissance... and that is by use of the cavalry!"

In the prelude to WW2, General Werner Von Fritsch, presided over a briefing with his fellow staff officers in 1938 and made the following prophesy: - *"The military organisation with the most efficient reconnaissance, will win the next war".*

The standards achieved by the photographers and pilots of the Royal Air Force photo reconnaissance units, supplied the photographic interpreters with the military intelligence to close the chapter on the German General's predictions. In 1962, during the cold war deadly gamble over the Cuban missile crisis, aerial photo-reconnaissance provided undisputed evidence to support the prevention of an outbreak of WW3. The role of aerial and terrestrial reconnaissance in all its forms continues to play a vital role in the theatre of military conflict and will continue to do so in an ever increasing capacity for the future.

Legends and Heroes

Contents

Chapter 1

Victor Laws   In the beginning ...

"The Father of Photo Reconnaissance"

Group Captain Frederick Charles Victor Laws OBE

Victor Laws (the name he preferred to be known by) was born in 1887 and joined the Army on 1st February 1905. Before the Great War, Laws was an amateur photographer who on his own initiative experimented with photography from lighter-than-air aircraft. He set up his own darkroom to augment his pay by taking photos and selling them to the officers of his Battalion. His military career began in the Coldstream Guards and the Royal Engineers, and he served in Egypt and the Anglo-Egyptian Sudan as well as in the Camel Corps. His enthusiasm with photography and the potential value of aerial photography prompted his determination to influence the senior officers with his ideas.

In 1908 he used his photographic skills to record the detail of Woolwich Arsenal with his camera aboard the airship Beta 2, to prove how much detailed information could be recorded. Laws discovered that vertical photos taken with 60% overlap could be used to create a stereoscopic effect when viewed in a stereoscope, thus creating a perception of depth that was an aid in cartography and in intelligence derived from aerial images. Laws took similar photos from kites, Bleriot and Farman aircraft and other types just completed by the Royal Aircraft Factory at Farnborough. He also conducted camera experiments at the second RFC site at Salisbury Plain. As dirigibles were allocated to the Royal Navy in 1912, Laws was chosen to help form an aerial reconnaissance unit of fixed-wing aircraft, at that time consisting in part of B.E.2 biplanes from the Royal Aircraft Factory. This No. 2 (Aeroplane) Company became No. 3 Squadron in the RAF, the first heavier-than-air British unit. As a young Staff Sergeant in the Guards, he volunteered to transfer to the Royal Flying Corps, when it was formed on 13th April 1912. He was able to illustrate the detailed information available from aerial pictures when assessed by experts as to the content and potential intelligence available. It was not an easy road however as many senior officers were not in accord with new ideas, especially the advocate of aerial flight by the frail structures of the early 1900's. In fact the famous General Haig commented to his staff officers on the subject: "I hope none of you gentlemen is so foolish as to consider the aeroplane as a useful instrument of warfare. There is only one way to gather reconnaissance and that is by use of the cavalry"!

In 1914, the British entered into aerial reconnaissance in World War I with no credible heavier-than-air capability. The shortage was in optics and cameras as well as aircraft and pilots. Laws and his collaborators first created the A-camera, then later the L-camera (for Laws), which became the standard British airborne camera, usually fixed on the side of the fuselage pointing down. With Lt. Moore-Brabazon, the later Lord Brabazon, another aviation pioneer, Laws built the L/B camera for special situations, introduced late in the war. Laws demonstrated the ability to have a permanent, accurate and reproducible medium which could be distributed to as wider circulation as necessary. The HQ building of the Royal Flying Corps had a small room under the stairs which he quickly took over and adapted as his darkroom and workplace. His endeavours impressed Moore-Brabazon and he encouraged Victor Laws to continue his pursuits. He took it upon

Laws as a young
RFC officer - circa 1915

himself to promote the principles to higher command and so began the birth of aerial photo reconnaissance. Laws soon became a Sergeant Major and was the first NCO in charge of photography in the RFC being attached to No 1 Squadron. In 1914, Laws went to France with RFC No. 3 squadron and organized the air reconnaissance sections. He was later commissioned in the field in November 1915.

Between them, Laws and Major Moore-Brabazon developed and improved the design of aerial cameras in collusion with Colin Williamson, a brilliant engineer and head of the Williamson manufacturing company. The later designs overcame a number of problems including changing the glass plate negatives automatically by a mechanised gearbox and lever system. The freezing cold had made it difficult to changing the coated glass plates by hand so this solution and the 18 plate capacity of the camera magazine increased the number of images which could be recorded during one flight (sortie). The Williamson manufacturing company became a major contributor to the design and production of many air cameras and photographic support equipment equipment for the Royal Flying Corps and the Royal Air Force in later years.

The turning point for wider acceptance of aerial photo reconnaissance in those early years came after a particularly successful operation was launched from the lines of the deadly trench warfare. At this time there had been growing public outcry because of the ever rising casualty lists. On this occasion however the planners and commanders made full use of the accurate information from aerial reconnaissance photographs over the target area. The resultant number of casualties was dramatically reduced as a direct result. Perhaps political pressure added to the demand for greater use the amount of intelligence gathered from quality aerial photo reconnaissance.

By this time the demand for many aerial photographs became essential. Although many of the conscripts had skills from their civilian experiences, such as carpentry, metal worker, fabricating and engineering, photography was a rare skill by comparison in numbers. This then became a training priority for the establishment of the first technical school in the Royal Flying Corps. Its objective: to teach the skills of photography to suitable conscripts and so it was in the summer of 1915 with the founding of the first technical training school known then as the School of Photography at South Farnborough. The first primitive accommodation consisted of two packing cases known as "BE" huts. Initially, the training courses had to be compressed into a ten-day time scale due to the required numbers of trained men. New buildings were later constructed by German POWs and came into use in 1917 (the only permanent building erected for the Royal flying Corps during the war). The value of aerial photography had changed the concepts of reconnaissance and intelligence gathering forever. The early student members were taught by experienced photographers who became the first instructor staff. The air camera magazines needed to be loaded with the light sensitive glass plates. The main objectives were to enable the students to work in total darkness and encourage the manipulative skills necessary to work by the senses of touch. The cameras were then fitted to aircraft ready for their operation sorties. On return to base the camera and its magazine were unloaded from the aircraft. The glass plate negatives were then removed from the camera magazine in total darkness and processed by hand to an exact "recipe" (consisting of time, solution temperature and agitation in the solutions) to ensure the optimum results were obtained from the images recorded. The students had to work quickly and with confidence under these conditions. From the dried glass plate negative images, the students then made "contact" prints in yellow safelight conditions to produce the ideal contrast and image resolution for the intelligence analysts and commanders in the field. Some of these prints would need to be enlarged to illustrate more detail for briefings and some would be laid down to form a line of images (called a line overlap) or even several lines to form a composite picture map called a "mosaic". It is interesting to note that the rapid expansion of the use of aerial reconnaissance from aircraft by both sides in the earlier days of the conflict actually gave birth to the fighter aircraft whose objective was to shoot down the photo reconnaissance aircraft and subsequently enemy fighter planes engaged in similar operations.

The life expectancy of the pilot was little more than a few weeks, though some lasted considerably longer. It was always a very dangerous game and continued to be so throughout many subsequent conflicts over the years. The need for a totally dark work room created a need for specially adapted vehicles to be used in positions on airfields as mobile dark rooms and some tented accommodation and locally adapted buildings were often commandeered. The experiences of adapting and making do was to become the innovative hallmark of the photographers determination to continue production, despite the less than ideal conditions frequently encountered. The need to follow and support the squadrons demanded constant changes to their amenities and supply support. Their attitudes became synonymous with that of a circus team constantly changing and adapting to circumstances beyond their control The School trained operators to develop and print photographic plates, chemical mixing and enlarging prints. The large numbers of negatives and prints being produced required annotations to be made and printed with the pictures to identify which squadron, sortie and negative number was the source for each of the images. They also trained airmen in producing lantern slides for briefings and maintaining air cameras and preparing maps for photography. The technique of photographic interpretation also improved. In 1915, Laws commanded the RFC School of Photography at Farnborough.

In September 1916 promotion to Captain followed for Laws and he was posted to the HQ of Training Brigade. The command of the training school was taken over by Lieutenant Cyril Porri in 1917. On 1st April 1918, the Royal Flying Corps, founded by Captain Fulton, became the Royal Air Force, "fathered" by the late Lord Trenchard. By the end of the Great War, Laws was recognized as "the most experienced aerial photographic adviser in England and possibly the world."

Post WW1

As a Squadron Leader in the RAF, Laws went on to the Directorate of Scientific Research where he designed the F 8 aerial camera which used a 7" x 7" camera format and interchangeable lens units. In 1924 the F 24 aerial camera came into service (using a format of 5" x 5") proved very reliable despite the lower image resolution quality. Between the wars the RAF was reduced from 200 squadrons to just 33. In 1919 Hugh Trenchard was invited by Churchill (the secretary of state for war) to resume as Chief of the Air Staff (CAS). His mission was to re-vitalise the RAF. He held this position for 11years until his retirement in 1930. If Victor Laws was known as the "Father of Photography", Lord Trenchard was to be known as the "Father of the RAF". Trenchard recognised that aerial photography "was of extreme importance" and training continued at the School of Photography, Farnborough. The RAF gained a high reputation for its ability to provide photography for mosaics, maps and charts.

In 1924 Laws took charge of the School of Photography for 6 years and was promoted to Wing Commander in January 1927. He moved away from the Photography branch in 1930 as CO of the Aircraft Depot at Hinaidi in Iraq. Next to the purpose built School of Photography there was a hanger named after the base at Hinaidi which was eventually demolished to provide extra car parking facilities. Laws returned to the UK in 1933 as CO of Farnborough. Disappointed with the peacetime eclipse of his specialty, he retired from the RAF in 1933 to take up a lucrative position in charge of photographic survey in Western Australia. Around the same time Laws established himself as a leader in commercial air survey. He participated in aerial surveys covering many areas of the British Empire. In 1933-34, he was expedition leader of the aerial mapping of Western Australia for the H. Hemmings Company, an enormous task using two DH 84 Dragons. When Adolf Hitler became Chancellor of Germany and the flouted the League of Nations by creating the Luftwaffe, the start of the race to re-arm began. Unfortunately the RAF had no trained photographic interpreters at this time and left with little knowledge of photo reconnaissance needs in wartime.

WWII

Rejoining the RAF at the beginning of World War II, Laws was appointed Deputy Director of Photography as a Group Captain at the Air Ministry. When his American counterpart, Colonel George Goddard, met with Laws in London, Goddard described him as "short in stature, very proper in manner, - just as wary and sensitive as I might have been had he come prowling around my laboratory at Wright Field, out to prove his goods were better than mine." He retired as Group Captain in May 1946. After retirement from the RAF, Laws served in a management capacity for several air survey and cartography companies. Laws authored several articles and treatises on aerial photography.

Victor Laws was invited as a special guest to attend the opening ceremony of the new purpose built RAF School of Photography, on 3rd December 1965. It was formally opened by the late Air Marshall Sir Alfred Earle, KBE CB, a former student and Deputy Chief Instructor (during the 1930's) and colleague of Victor Laws.

Group Captain Laws OBE died in October 1975 at the age of 88, and was known by all those connected with photography as "Daddy Laws", the father of aerial photo reconnaissance

Note by the author

A Remarkable Find!!
Jane's "All the World's Aircraft – 1917"

Twenty years ago I came to live in the village of Sheriffhales, a few miles from RAF Cosford. The house had been converted from an old pub called the "Rising Sun" which was part of the Duke of Sutherlands Estate around the turn of the last century. One of the villagers I came to know had presented my wife with an old dilapidated copy of Jane's "All the World's Aircraft - 1917". It revealed some fascinating links in the history of aviation and early photo reconnaissance.

My first discovery was the list of Aviators Certificates granted by the Royal Aero Club of the UK on page 47b. Who should be listed at No 1 but a Mr. J. T. C. Moore Brabazon (Lord Brabazon of Tara), who was, together with Victor Laws, the co-founder of aerial reconnaissance in WW1. The certificate was granted on March 8th 1910.

The second surprise was entry 27, a Major Fulton; this was the man who founded the Royal Flying Corps formed from the Army balloon regiments and Royal Naval Air Service. His name lives on at RAF Cosford, where there is a large accommodation block named after him as "Fulton" block. Sadly, he was killed in action during WW1 and it was as a tribute to his memory that his mother donated the funds to build the accommodation for RAF apprentices stationed at RAF Cosford (built in 1938).

As I perused some of the other names I soon realised I was reading a roll call of "whose who" in aviation history:-

Hon C S Rolls; S F Cody; Hon Maurice Egerton; A V Roe; T Sopwith; E V Sassoon; G De Havilland; Harold Blackburn; Edward Hotchkiss and Major Trenchard.

Many familiar names were mentioned as the qualifying airfields: -

Brooklands; Hendon: Upavon; Salisbury Plain; Eastbourne; Eastchurch; Nertheravon; Shoreham: Beaulieu

All common entries up to 1915 then suddenly Farnborough appears on the 11th of March and the link of dates with the founding of the School of Photography and the famous "Cody tree" tree where S F Cody used to tie his aircraft to test the engines. During 1915 the Maurice Farman biplane was the aircraft, which most pilots seemed to qualify on. The earlier Bleriot Monoplane seemed to have been superseded.

Some of the airfields were also a surprise – In May, Werribbee (Australia). My home town of Birmingham also appears in June 1915 and becomes more used as time moves on. Toronto (Canada) in July 1915, using the Curtis Biplane, (the legendary American Mr. Curtis, also being listed among the Aviators). Then I found a real gem, the appraisal of "Aircraft in War" and the section on aerial photography, by a Captain W. E. De B. Whittaker (The Kings Regiment):-

PHOTOGRAPHY

"Photography has passed from the experimental stage and has become an integral part of the art of reconnaissance. The Germans have given some attention to this subject and would have appeared to have attained a high degree of efficiency, but it does not seem to be an essential part of aerial scouting as practiced by the enemy.

Italy, whose flying corps was engaged five years ago in the execution of a photographic survey of the country, probably does not underestimate the value of photography. France also appears to produce excellent photographs of the theatre of war as seen from above. But in system there is every reason to assume that England, if not necessarily superior, is second to none. The most elaborate maps of enemy territory are constructed daily from photographs taken during the morning reconnaissance.

By this means all movements of the enemy (in trench warfare) can be gauged in so far as the construction of new redoubts, new trenches, new emplacements, and so on are concerned. The effect of a bombardment is indicated and good or bad work on the part of the gunners can be illustrated to that arm without possibility of refutation.

The insidious growth of wire entanglements is revealed in time for counter preparations to be made. Bomb dropping becomes a precise art under the remaining influence of the revealing photograph. No longer is it simple to hit an enemy railway (in the subsequent report) from impossible heights and under adverse conditions.

No doubt photography will be as great an aid in strategic reconnaissance as it provedly is in tactical scouting. As a preliminary step in great bombing raids on towns far behind enemy lines, it can assist in the selection of objectives. Even to the most inexperienced, a photograph is simpler to read than a map.

The results of aerial photography attained at the present time are so surprising in their excellence that if the comparative infancy of the subject is taken into account the future possibilities are vast and various."

That old book is a mine of advertisements with many names of companies who struggled to meet the demands of war to become the giants of modern industry. I found many famous local names such as "GKN", the lifeblood of military industry right here in Wellington, Shropshire.

No doubt there are some of you reading this and you are wondering about that picture, document or book, tucked away somewhere. Is it important, does it really matter? It certainly does. Many records are making history from the moment they are created. The relevance or importance may not always be obvious.   So keep them safe and treasure your memories, one day they may provide a vital piece in the jigsaw of history

Dave Humphrey 2013

Colin Williamson

Designer of the "LB 1"
(Laws Brabazon camera)

Group Captain Laws signs the visitor's book,
at the opening of the new school, RAF Cosford 1964

The site of the first school at South Farnborough

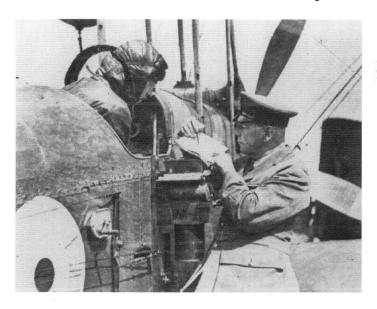

The LB 1 (Laws Brabazon) camera fitted to an aircraft of WW1

WW1 pilots de-briefing after a reconnaissance sortie

Planning the sortie flight lines

Legends and Heroes | 42

WW1 trenches –
"A" – trenches dug prior to attack
"B" - jumping off trenches in front of the main line of attack

Squadron Leader Laws (centre) as CO of the School of Photography
at South Farnborough pictured outside the Sergeants Mess

The most successful LB camera manufactured by Williamson, over
500 were sold to the US military during the 1914 -18 war

Legends and Heroes | 44

Chapter 2

Lawrence of Arabia - facts and figures

Research by Dave Humphrey

Colonel T E Lawrence from an official army photograph

T. E. Lawrence joined the RAF on 30th August 1922 under the name of John Hume Ross. He completed his basic training (square bashing!) at RAF Uxbridge and joined the RAF School of Photography at Farnborough in November 1922 to begin training as a photographer. His desire to choose the trade of photography probably stems from the influence of his father (an accomplished photographer), along with his experiences as an archaeologist in Arabia. His had a close association with the American journalist and photographer Lowell Thomas who followed his wartime campaigns in the Arab revolt against the Turks. Geoffrey Buxton served with Lawrence when he also trained as a photographer at the School of Photography. Geoffrey was promoted to the rank of Flight Sergeant in 1939 at Kalafrana in Malta. Geoffrey was eventually commissioned to become CO of the RAF School of Photography in 1953/4 in the rank of Wing Commander (*see School History – List of Post War CO's).

Despite Lawrence's desire for anonymity the press continued to hound him and he was forced to leave the RAF in January 1923. By March 1923, he still wanted to find obscurity with the military and joined the Army, choosing the Tank Corps under the name of Thomas Edward Shaw. He changed his name officially to Thomas Edward Shaw in 1927 by deed poll. It has been suggested that he chose the name of Shaw as a mark of respect and his friendship with George Bernard Shaw. He transferred back to the RAF in August 1925. He was initially given clerical duties but later became instrumental in the development of sea planes and motor launches, both at home and abroad (India). The last photograph of him in the RAF was taken at Bridlington in Yorkshire before he left the RAF at the end of his term of engagement on 25th February 1935. Just a few months later, on the 19th May 1935, he died in a tragic accident, riding his much loved Brough Superior motorcycle. His motorcycle is currently on display at the Imperial War Museum in London. On a recent Antiques Road Show programme a gentleman brought a Rolex wrist watch for valuation. Inside the box was a bill for repairs made out to "Mr T E Shaw". The surprised owner had no idea who "Mr T E Shaw" was, that is until the expert revealed the true identity of the former owner and it subsequently fetched over £35,000 at auction! Such was the provenance of an item associated with one of the most revered legends of the 20th century and a little known connection with the School of Photography – until now! A copy of his book "The Seven Pillars of Wisdom" explains a great deal of his philosophy and determination to create a united Arab world under King Feisal, sadly international politics destroyed the dream and his incredible efforts to bring the Arab Nation into reality. There are a number of historians who believe this was a fundamental error and destroyed the hard won trust by Arabic people of European and Western countries, leaving a long festering wound. Some also feel it may have been the root cause which has given birth to the current extreme militant views held by some from that region.

References: **Seven Pillars of Wisdom by T. E. Lawrence** 1st published 1926 (2nd edition for public) 1935, 3rd edition 1939 and the 5th edition published in 1976, reprinted in 1979, (which is the print of my personal copy)

The Birthplace of Lawrence of Arabia

During the summer training break one August, I was planning a short holiday to Arthog in Wales with our grandchildren and went to the Gym at RAF Cosford to borrow a compass for some hill walking. On the wall in their office I noticed a reference to "Lawrence House", now the home of the Snowdon Backpackers organization. It is located in Church Street, Tremadog just north west of Portmadog on the A487. At the end of our delightful stay at Arthog we made the 30 mile detour on our way home and I called in whilst Carole and the grandchildren went shopping in Portmadog (a delightful town which I do recommend). I spoke to the young lady in the reception office and gave her a file with copies of all our collated information on T E Lawrence to hand on to the manager Chris Hinton. In return she gave me a leaflet with the local history of our hero and I reprint it here.

T E Lawrence was born in the house on 16th August 1888, actually in the room that is now the blue toilets upstairs! His father, Sir Thomas Chapman, was a land owner in Ireland who abandoned his wife and ran away with the family governess Sarah Lawrence, to Tremadog. The subsequent army career of Colonel Lawrence during the 1st World War1 as the legendary army officer who led the Arab Revolt, driving the Turks out of Arabia, was made into a blockbuster film story directed by David lean back in 1962, which was awarded seven Oscars.

After the war, he turned down a knighthood because he felt that the British had not kept his promises to the Arabs. He was King Feisal's main advisor during the Paris Peace Conference. Despite support from Lloyd George and Woodrow Wilson, his plans for an independent Arabia were defeated, and the French subsequently moved in to Syria.

Greatly disappointed by this, he turned to writing his book "The Seven pillars of Wisdom". This was described by Winston Churchill as one of the greatest books ever written in the English Language. His life in the RAF as a student of photography has been recorded in a number of books and military magazines.

The manager of Lawrence House is Chris Hinton. Anyone who would like to visit the house will be made most welcome, especially if you have some addition details to help them with their collection on the legendary T E Lawrence.

The address is: -

Snowdon Backpackers Ltd, Lawrence House
Church Street, Tremadog, Portmadog LL49 9PS

Lawrence of Arabia

The myths and the reality
— By Dave Humphrey 2013

My personal fascination with the life of T E Lawrence covered a number of years since I learned of his association with the School of Photography at Farnborough as a student. Sir Winston Churchill described his book: "Seven Pillars of Wisdom" written in 1926 by Lawrence, as one of the greatest pieces of literature he had read. After many years of searching, I discovered a copy at my local Oxfam charity shop. I confess it was not an easy read as he used a number of English language words from an era I am unfamiliar with. Despite this I was held riveted by his detailed description of the various geological differences in the vast areas of land he roamed with the many Arab tribes he gathered around him.

His ability to effectively persuade the tribal leaders and the remarkable understanding he accrued of their intricate tribal laws, allowed him to win them over despite their instinctive reluctance join up against the Turkish invaders. It was likely that his personal endurance and ability to accommodate extreme discomfort with their life style, that won the respect of the many varied tribesmen and their leaders. He also understood the psyche of the Arab people more than anyone from the western hemisphere and more to the point he respected their values and needs. To this end he found it necessary to act as executioner when a dangerous situation threatened to break up the cohesion of the tribal alliance because of a blood feud which spilled over into a murder. His personal turmoil during the campaign came about because he understood that the British and French authorities were unlikely to honour their promises to grant the Arab nation their own autonomy, once the objectives of disrupting and finally destroying the Turkish army's ability to remain in the zone of conflict had been resolved. He frequently relates his frustration at the ignorance of the British Authorities in their lack of understanding of the needs to persuade and respect the support of the Arab tribes. He also felt great shame in being unable to influence the political outcome and the promises made to King Feisal and the Arab leaders; Auda Abu Tayi and Abdulla.

It is probably this among other factors which drove him to refuse a knighthood, coupled with his attempts to avoid publicity from the press who subsequently hounded him after the campaign. To this end he sought solace in the RAF as an airman and then as a private in the Tank Corps in efforts to escape the attentions of the virulent press, sadly to no avail and was eventually forced to leave the safe harbour of the military.

On one occasion he witnessed the drowning of a pilot in the sea whist in the RAF and applied himself to the design and introduction of the fast air sea rescue launches at Gosport where he was pictured with the designer Scott-Paine. A few years ago I read the RAF News article describing the renovation of the original launch which he is pictured handling. Lawrence was always fascinated by speed and I am sure he was also involved in the float design for the Supermarine Schneider Trophy winner aircraft built and designed by R B Mitchell. I am also aware that Lawrence was a frequent visitor to the Wolverhampton factory at Pendeford where the engine was produced. Perhaps he also met the legendary R B Mitchell during this time.

I have noticed many parts of his book described the kind of self-inflicted determination to endure extreme hardship and endurance in living off the available nourishment found in the desert environment. Among many misconceptions about the desert environment is the "Hollywood" glamorised notion of beautiful shifting sands and extreme heat. The reality of the environment, where Lawrence undertook many battles, was extremely varied. It ranged from blistering heat down to freezing temperatures at night, often accompanied by ferocious wind driven rains and snow storms. The lands he roamed with the Arab tribes varied dramatically from those desert sands to mountainous escarpment with savagely punishing flint rock strewn tracks, scrub forests and many combinations of all of these facets. He survived by living off the land and from the meat of the camels which died whilst traversing the fiercely demanding routes. All this inspired me to compare the training mantra of the SAS: to endure extremes of climate, topography and hardship as a means to survive to fight. The ability of Lawrence to speak fluent Arabic and to win the hearts and minds of those he sought to encourage against the Turkish militia was a masterful achievement. I can't help wondering if his book, "Seven Pillars of Wisdom", was a major influence in the ideas and principles held by Colonel David Stirling, founder of the SAS. If this were true, I deem it would be a most suitable epitaph to the memory of a most remarkable British legend.

Dressed as the legendary
Lawrence of Arabia

King Feisal
of the Arab nations

The last photograph of Lawrence as AC Shaw taken at RAF Bridlington in Yorkshire
25th February 1935

Lawrence astride a Brough Superior motorbike

Lawrence with boat designer Scott-Paine at Gosport

Lawrence at the helm of an early Air Sea Rescue launch.

Post script: This launch was recently discovered in a derelict condition and faithfully restored at Gosport.

Chapter 3

Wing Commander Sidney Cotton OBE

"Aviator Extraordinary"

Founder of No 1 Photo Development Unit, Heston

Observations on a remarkable and controversial officer

Sidney Cotton circa 1944

The Australian born controversial Wing Commander Sidney Cotton OBE was always outspoken and known to "call a spade a bloody shovel". He refused to suffer fools gladly, regardless of rank, which culminated in his unwarranted undoing at the height of the conflict in WW2.

As a young pilot in WW1 with the RNAS, he designed a very efficient flying suit which was so successful; he patented the design and marketed it as the "Sidcot" flying suit. There is a story that the famous Baron Von Richtoven was found to be wearing one when he was eventually shot down and his body laid to rest in it. After the First World War ("the war to end all wars"), Cotton acquired the "Dufay Colour" film manufacturing company and began marketing the photographic colour films. He was successful to the point of having his own chauffeur and like modern day successful businessmen. It was during this time when he roamed Europe with his own aircraft, that he was approached by the British military intelligence services and asked to use his business as a front for clandestine aerial espionage. He agreed and flew a Lockheed 12A twin engined aircraft all over industrial and military targets currying favour during Hitler's climb to dominance in the 1930's. Many of the German High Command actually flew with him and obligingly directed him over their prize industrial projects unwittingly pointing out useful targets. Using secret cameras installed in the aircraft, Cotton was able to provide highly valuable evidence of the German military might to British Intelligence. The day before war was declared; he escaped out of Berlin by the skin of his teeth. His aircraft was the last civilian flight out of Tempelhof, just as the Gestapo net was about to ensnare him.

His expertise in aerial photography and his revolutionary concepts were encouraged by those with the foresight of the impending air struggle. His powers of persuasion in obtaining two Spitfires to customise for aerial reconnaissance, was a tribute to his negotiating skills when Fighter Command was about to be embroiled in the Battle of Britain. The undoubted success of the PRU and its subsequent triumphs are history now, yet he had the tenacity and foresight to drive the system into being, albeit paying a savage price with his RAF career which was terminated by those who controlled "the proper channels" whom he ignored with such a cavalier attitude. He was a strange figure, even in those times, with his own chauffeur and a private car at his beckoned call. Perhaps it was jealousy of his unorthodox success that drove those with less insight and forethought to damn him so cruelly at a time when his undoubted genius was shown to be wide ranging.

© Dave Humphrey

"Sidney Cotton's Air Force"

(Article reproduced by kind permission of Roy Conyers Nesbit)

Having gained a measure of fame for inventing the Sidcot flying suit, Sidney Cotton really made his mark on British aviation history with an audacious spree of clandestine photo-recce flights over Europe in the months before World War 11.

ROY NESBIT *outlines Cotton's life and achievements:*

One of the most remarkable but maverick aviators of the 20th Century was an Australian, F. Sidney Cotton. Born on June 17th, 1894, on a cattle station at Goorganga in Queensland, he grew up in affluent circumstances when the family moved in 1900 to their new homestead, a 10,000-acre property about 40 miles from Brisbane. In 1910 his father decided to send Sidney and his two younger brothers to school in England. Louis Blériot had flown the English Channel on July 25, 1909, and Sidney was already fascinated by flying. He spent much of his time at school studying aviation and making model aeroplanes, including one of 6ft span, fitted with a single-cylinder petrol engine. In 1912 the three brothers returned to Australia, and two years later Sidney was apprenticed to a sheep station. Dissatisfied with this life, he took a ship back to England and joined the Royal Naval Air Service on November 26, 1915. His Service record in the First World War, now available at the Public Record Office, does not tally in certain respects with the personal account Cotton gave to the author Ralph Barker for the latter's biography *Aviator Extraordinary* before the official document became available. Cotton qualified as a pilot on Maurice Farman Longhorns at Chingford in Essex, and on January 24, 1916, moved on to Royal Aircraft Factory B.E.2cs at the Central Flying School at Upavon in Wiltshire.

After about 20 hours flying, he was posted on February 22, 1916, to a new Flight at Dover, equipped with B.E.2cs and Breguet de Chasse pusher biplanes. By then a flight sub-lieutenant, Cotton was engaged on sea patrols. In the following May he was posted to the 5th Wing of the RNAS, also equipped with Breguet pusher biplanes. This Wing was operational at Coudekerque near Dunkirk, and Cotton was involved in several bombing operations, primarily against Ostend docks and airfields. His service was interrupted by a lengthy period of sick leave, and by July 17 he was at home in Yarmouth, his records stating that he did not wish to fly seaplanes or at night.

Sub Lt Cotton (2nd from left) RNAS Circa 1916

He requested a transfer to the 3rd Wing, and on August 5, 1916, joined this unit at Luxeuil, near the German and Swiss borders. He flew Sopwith 1½ - Strutters and took part in a number of raids. One of these was on October 12, against the Mauser factory at Obendorf, when the Wing suffered heavy losses among the aircraft despatched. On that occasion Cotton forced-landed in friendly territory with engine failure. Other attacks took place from Ochey, near Nancy, against targets in the Saar valley. During this period Cotton devised a new flying suit made from cotton overalls, with thin linings of fur and airproof silk, Plus deep pockets below the knee. He registered this design and named it the "Sidcot". The flying suit was later adopted by both the Royal Flying Corps and the RNAS. Although it remained in general use by the RAF and Fleet Air Arm in both World Wars, Cotton never attempted to make any monetary claim for his invention Cotton left the 3rd Wing at the end of January 1917, and was on sick-leave front February 14 for a fortnight. He was then posted to Hendon, initially on ground duties which concerned the preparation of aircraft for long- distance sorties. He was pronounced fit for home flying on May 11, 1917, fitness for full active service following about ten weeks later. His next posting was to the Yarmouth Special Flight on August 9, 1917. This unit operated from Bacton in Norfolk, and consisted of no more than two Airco D.H.4s equipped for long- distance work over the North Sea.

On September 2, 1917, Cotton was posted to No 2 Wing on *HMS Ark Royal* in the Aegean, but three days later applied for termination of appointments on the grounds of defective eyesight. His resignation was accepted on September 9, 1917, and he returned home to Australia. When he tried to join the new Australian Air Force, his application was turned down. Cotton could not settle down with his father after the war, and tried to make a career in aviation. In January 1920 he attempted to fly from Hendon to Australia in Airco D.H.14A G-EAPY but the machine turned over near Naples during a forced landing and was damaged. After it had been repaired, he entered it in the 1920 Aerial Derby around London, but the engine caught fire on the last stretch and the machine was written off when he made another forced landing.

In January 1921 Cotton bought a Westland Limousine III passenger aircraft G-EARV and two Martinsyde Type A Mk II biplanes, G-EATY and an unregistered example, and shipped them to Newfoundland, where he also acquired an Airco D.H.9. He subsequently added three Westland Limousine IIs, G-EAJL, G-EAMV and G-EARG, to the fleet of his Aerial Survey Company. Several years were spent on the island, flying mail to and from the mainland seal-spotting from the air for sealing companies and carrying out air photographic surveys for various concerns. In 1923 he also acquired Avro 554 Antarctic Baby G-EBFE, which had been used by Shackleton in his last Antarctic expedition. Cotton sold these business interests in the autumn of 1923 and concentrated on promoting American inventions in Britain and vice versa. These ventures proved profitable, but in June 1927 he was engaged by Daniel Guggenheim for the sum of £5,000 to hunt for the French pilots Charles Nungesser and François Coil, who had left Le Bourget in Paris on May 8 in an attempt to fly non-stop to New York in their Pierre Levasseur PL-8 biplane *l'Oiseau Blanc* and were thought to have come down somewhere in Newfoundland. He acquired a Fokker seaplane for this purpose, but his efforts proved fruitless.

By this time Cotton had made sufficient profit to invest in the stock market from an office in London, but he was hit badly in the financial crash of 1929 and needed to rebuild his fortunes. He began to participate in the development of colour photography, but in March 1931 was commissioned by Samuel Courtauld, the chairman of fabric manufacturer Courtaulds, to hunt for his nephew, Augustine. The latter had been part of the British Arctic Air Route Expedition of the previous August, and had volunteered to stay behind in its meteorological station on the coast of Greenland when the main party headed for sanctuary. Courtauld acquired American-built Bellanca Pacemaker monoplane I-AAPI from Italy, and it was registered G-ABNW and fitted with skis. In May Cotton sailed with the aeroplane for Reykjavik in Iceland, together with a supporting crew, but, exactly when he was due to take off on May 10, a ground relief party reached Augustine Courtauld, who was close to death. In late 1932 Cotton bought rights to a method of colour photography invented by Frenchman Louis Dufay and formed a company named Dufaycolour Ltd. There followed a series of negotiations with various international photographic companies, involving financial negotiations which were not resolved to his satisfaction until 1943. Meanwhile, events were moving swiftly on the world stage, and by September 1938, the month of the Munich Agreement, it was apparent that a new European war was likely. In that month Cotton was approached in London by an old friend, Alfred J. Miranda Jr of the American Armaments Corporation, who was associated with Sqn Ldr Fred W. Winterbotham of RAF Intelligence in the Air Ministry.

The Deuxième Bureau de l'Armée de l'Air was collaborating with M16 of the British Secret Intelligence Service in developing espionage systems in the western part of Germany. Both organisations realised that aerial photography might achieve results, and a clandestine method had to be found. Miranda and Cotton flew to Paris, where they discussed the project with Paul Koster, the European representative of the American Armaments Corporation, and it was agreed that a civil aircraft should he used. On his return to London, Cotton met Winterbotham and the two men decided that a Lockheed Model 12A would be the most suitable aircraft if fitted with extra fuel tanks. One, G-AFKR, was sent from America, arriving at Southampton in January 1939. Cotton chose an RAF flight lieutenant as his co-pilot for the flights, a Canadian named Robert H. Niven. A company was formed as a cover, Aeronautical Sales & Research Corporation. and the two men flew the Lockheed to Toussus-le-Noble, south-west of Paris. A French camera with a focal length of 30cm was fitted, and on March 25, 1939, they photographed Krefeld, Hamm, Munster and the Dutch border from 15,000ft. The Black Forest was covered on April 1, and Wurttemberg six days later. Karlsruhe, Bruchsal, Heidelberg, Mannheim, Ludwigshafen and Eberhach followed on April 9. Then they flew to Tunisia, which at the time was a French Protectorate, and on April 25 covered the Italian port of Tripoli, the airfield of Castel Benito and several other military sites. The Lockheed was then handed over to the French as F-ARQA and two more were ordered, one for the French (F-ARPP) and one for the British (NC16077).

These arrived in early May and the British gave their aircraft the civil registration G-AFTL. Cotton installed extra fuel tanks behind the cockpit and three F24 cameras in the fuselage, one vertical and two oblique, enabling an area 111 miles wide to be photographed from 21 ,000ft. Holes were cut so that warm air from the interior prevented condensation in the cameras. These were concealed by small sliding panels, and the system was operated electrically from the cockpit. Cotton also -invented and installed a pear- shaped transparent blister which provided the pilot with a downward view from the cockpit. This was adopted by the RAE and more than 100,000 were manufactured during the Second World War; it became known as the "teardrop" window. He had the Lockheed painted a light duck-egg green for camouflage at high altitudes, registering the colour under the name "Camotint".

On June 14, 1939, Cotton and Niven flew from Heston to Malta, where they met Flying Officer Maurice V. "Shorty" Longbottom, an experienced reconnaissance pilot. On the following day the three flew over Sicily and took some excellent photographs of Comiso, Augusta, Catania and Syracuse. Then, on June 16, Cotton and Niven photographed the Italian-held islands of Kos and Leros in the Dodecanese and flew on to Cairo. From there they photographed Massawa in Italian Eritrea on June 19, flew on to land at the British island of Karnaran in the Red Sea, and then on to RAF Aden. On the following day they photographed a submarine base being constructed on Hafun in Italian Somaliland. On June 21 they covered Massawa once more, and then flew back to Cairo via RAF Atbara in the Sudan. They flew to Malta the next day, photographing Italian airfields at El Adem, Tobruk, Derna, Bernice and Benghazi en route. Their spy flights were rated as extremely successful when they returned to Heston on June 25. The first flight to Berlin, on July 26, 1939, was legitimate. No cameras were carried, and Cotton used the occasion to interest a German combine in his Dufaycolour film. However, the Lockheed was modified to carry two Leica cameras in the wings, concealed by sliding panels, and these were carried when Cotton and Niven flew on to the International Sports Pilots' Show at Frankfurt on July 28. The new and attractive aircraft was much admired by the manager of Tempelhof Airport, Major Bottger, who was taken up on a pleasure flight two days later. While they were in the air, Cotton secretly photographed Mannheim.

The Siegfried Line was photographed on the return trip to Heston. Cotton and Niven visited Berlin again on August 17, when targets north of the capital were photographed. The cameras were removed for a further flight to Berlin on August 22, but hand-held Leicas were used to photograph warships at Wilhelmshaven on the return flight. On August 27, during a "business trip" to Copenhagen, they photographed Sylt and airfields in the Frisian Islands. Then Niven took off on September 1 in a single-engined Beech 17 which had been painted in Camotint, and photographed Wilhelmshaven once more. On the same day, Germany invaded Poland.

When Britain and France declared war on Germany, on September 3, the RAF did not possess any units devoted wholly to photographic reconnaissance. Strategic photography was the province of the Bristol Blenheim IV, while tactical work was carried out mainly by Westland Lysander's of the army co-operation squadrons. These aircraft were extremely vulnerable to single-engined fighters and their range was limited. But the successes of Cotton and his colleagues had impressed the authorities and a new RAF unit, named the Heston Flight, was formed on September 23, 1939. It was commanded by Cotton, who was given the rank of squadron leader, acting Wing Commander. Niven and Longbottom were appointed as pilots, and specialist photographers joined the groundcrew. The first aircraft in the new unit were the Lockheed 12A and the Beech, plus two Blenheim IVs which were being modified. The idea of using Spitfires originated with Longbottom, but was seized upon by Cotton. He managed to persuade Air Chief Marshal Sir Hugh Dowding, Commander-in-Chief of Fighter Command, to relinquish two of these precious machines, N3071 and N3069, which arrived at Heston on October 30, 1939, and were stripped of all armament and unwanted weight.

Two F24 cameras were mounted in the wings, the exteriors were smoothed over and teardrop extensions added to both sides of the cockpit canopies. These first two machines were known as Spitfire PR Ia's. Extra fuel tanks were fitted in Spitfires which arrived later, as well as cameras which could be mounted in a variety of positions, depending on the nature of the sortie. Experiments were carried out with camouflage colour schemes for high- or low- level photography. Apart from duck-egg green, there were light blue and pink, although at a later stage a darker blue became standard. The Heston Flight was renamed No 2 Camouflage Unit on November 1, 1939, and four days later Longbottom flew Spitfire N3071 to Seclin in France. Other personnel arrived in the Lockheed, and this detachment was named the Special Survey Flight. Longbottom flew the first sortie over Germany on November 18, and two days later part of the unit moved to Coulommiers, east of Paris. The Flight was an informal organisation, hardworking but with minimal Service discipline. Those who remained at Heston called themselves "Sid Cotton's Air Force". On

January 17, 1940, No 2 Camouflage Unit at Heston was renamed the Photographic Development Unit (PDU), and the Special Survey Flight in France became 212 Sqn on February 10. By the end of January these two units had photographed 6,000 square miles of enemy territory without loss, while the French Air Force had photographed a similar area for the loss of 60 aircraft and Blenheims of Bomber Command had photographed 2,500 square miles for the loss of 16 aircraft. Although Cotton's remarkable results were achieved with limited resources, some RAF officers did not approve of his working methods, regarding him as "quite out of control". This distrust intensified when Cotton began, without authority, to use two civilian companies, the Aircraft Operating Company and Aerofilms, which had sophisticated equipment and facilities for interpreting photographs. But the work went on, more Spitfires arrived, and in February three Lockheed Hudsons were allocated to the unit, though one of these was shot down in error by a Hurricane pilot on March 3. One of the remaining two, N7364, was employed on a most unusual task. Fitted with extra fuel tanks and piloted by Fg Off Frederic Burton, with Sqn Ldr Hugh C. MacPhail as expedition leader, it was flown via Marseille, Malta and Egypt to Habbaniya in Iraq, arriving on March 26. The civil registration G-AGAR was then painted on the machine and it *was* flown on photo-reconnaissance missions over the Russian oil installations at Baku and Batum in the Caucasus. These flights were intended as a preliminary to a combined attack by the RAF and the French Air Force, since at the time the German-Russian non-aggression pact was in force and supplies of oil were feeding the Wehrmacht. The Hudson returned to Heston on April 13, but by then the planned bombing attacks on Baku and Batum had been cancelled owing to more important events. Six days before, Longbottom had flown a new long-distance version of the Spitfire, the PR I C, and photographed Kiel for the first time. His pictures had disclosed preparations for the anticipated invasion of Norway, which began on April 8.

The Blitzkrieg began in the west on May 10. The Allied forces reeled back in the face of the Wehrmacht advance, and on May 16 Cotton received orders to evacuate 212 Sqn to Heston. Some of the personnel were flown home by various means. Other men in the squadron were still in France after Dunkirk, and it was not until June 9 that they set off in the direction of Poitiers. while Cotton circled above in the Lockheed 12A. All managed to return home eventually, by air or sea, after various adventures, but Spitfire PR I B P9331 was left behind and captured intact by the Germans. They also captured from a railway train the French copy of the proposed attacks against Baku and Batum, achieving a propaganda coup when this was shown to Stalin. Cotton, Niven and four others flew to Jersey on June 17, stayed overnight and reached Heston on the following day. Here Cotton opened a letter from the Permanent Under Secretary of State for Air, Sir Arthur Street. This expressed appreciation of his work but informed him that the PDU was to be removed from his command and taken over by Wing Commander G.W. Tuttle, to serve under Coastal Command. In a Service which could not tolerate such unofficial and entrepreneurial behaviour, Cotton's dismissal was almost inevitable. One of the young photo-interpreters, Constance Babington Smith of the Women's Auxiliary Air Force, described him as "tall, quick, wolf-like, with horn-rimmed glasses and thick grey-white hair". He was made an Officer of the Order of the British Empire and placed on the RAF Reserve List, effectively ending his career in the Armed Services. Nevertheless, he pursued a very eventful and adventurous life until his sudden and unexpected death on February 13, 1969, at Ford Manor, Lingfield, and Surrey.

His life has now been commemorated in an Australian video entitled *The Last Plane out of Berlin*, by Jeffrey Watson Productions. It can be demonstrated from official and other records that Sidney Cotton was in the habit of exaggerating some of his achievements. Nevertheless, the legacy that he left for the RAF was of incalculable value. His little PDU was expanded into numerous photo- reconnaissance squadrons, engaged on strategic and tactical work in north-west Europe, the Mediterranean theatre and the Far East. The interpretation of their photographs became a prime source of intelligence, probably equal in importance to the breaking of the German *Enigma* codes. In 1938 Generaloberst Werner Freiherr von Fritsch of the Wehrmacht had forecast that the military organisation which had the most efficient reconnaissance units would win the war. He was proved absolutely correct.

Sidney Cotton with his Lockheed 12A
(photo presented to Dave Humphrey by Lord Wolseley)

JSPA Newsletter Article - Dated: November 2004

By Dave Humphrey

During the August training school shut down of 2004, my wife Carole came home with an invite to attend a school show at Bishton Hall, just the other side of Cannock Chase. I went along, as you do, with mixed feelings and a little trepidation (having sat through my fair share of school plays and shows!). As it turned out it was something really special – a "pilot" run of a future show to be called "The Little Mermaid". There were a number of well known TV stars and personalities including the famous composer, Charles Davies.

Also attending was Sir Charles and Lady Wolseley. After the show, which I really did enjoy, we were introduced to Sir Charles and his lovely American wife who insisted on being called Jinnie. Our conversation moved into the history of the Wolseley family and post war events in Malta. It turned out to my amazement that Sir Charles' mother was engaged to none other than the legendary Sidney Cotton in 1949! They still have the engagement ring he gave to her. Sir Charles became very interested from then on when he discovered my fascination

Lord Wolsely's mother with Sidney Cotton at the Officers Club Malta in 1949

with the life of the legendary Sidney Cotton. He very kindly gave me a copy of a photo of his mother dancing with Sidney Cotton at the Officers Club in Malta at the time of their engagement. He also gave me the original print used for the cover picture to his autobiography, "Aviator Extraordinary". I managed to reciprocate the hospitality and generosity by presenting him with a copy of the TV biography made by Australian, Jeff Watson for the Discovery TV Channel, titled "Last plane out of Berlin".

Sir Charles also related a remarkable story of Sidney Cotton's friendship with late Surgeon Rear Admiral Beach, who was in charge of the RN Hospital, Bighi, in Malta during that time. On his return to UK Sidney had a place in London and he was playing host to his friend (who was a ships doctor at the time). It seems the party went on into the early hours when his guest should have been leaving to rejoin the ship at Portsmouth, due to sail the following day. Sydney, being the perfect host, offered to fly him down in his plane later in the morning and all would be well! Like all best laid

The late Surgeon Rear Admiral Beach

plans the time went a little faster than scheduled. Sidney was trying to get to Portsmouth airport drop off his guest but he realized that time was running out and failing to join one's ship was a very serious offence for his guest. So Sidney lined up for a landing rather closer to his guests destination; the main road near the docks! They do not call Sidney Cotton "aviator extraordinary" for nothing! He was down in a trice with a perfect landing, offloaded his guest in the nick of time and was airborne without so much as a curious bobby in sight!

SIDNEY COTTON

Father of the RAF Photographic Reconnaissance Unit

By Deryk Wills

Sidney Cotton served In the Royal Naval Air Service as a fighter pilot in the First World War flying a Sopwith one-and-a-half-strutter. He was an Australian, born on 17th June 1894 on a cattle station at Goorganga, Queensland. He was brought up on his father's second cattle station and fruit farm at Jost Vale, forty miles from Brisbane, in an affectionate and financially sound family circle. He came to England and went to Cheltenham College for two years and returned borne in 1911. In 1915 the strong call of duty urged him to get into the war and yearning for a life with aeroplanes and adventure he left home refusing a generous £1000 a year paternal allowance. Returning to England he chose the Navy because of his love of the sea. He was described later as a big man weighing a hard 15 stone with a character of complete independence, with the needling self-assertiveness of a small man. He made a loyal friend, one who preferred giving to receiving. Being an Australian he was always capable of calling a spade a 'bloody shovel' no matter to who it was

The "Sidcot" flying suit

During the 1st World War he designed a flying suit which was made up by the tailors, Robinson & Cleaver and registered by the name of 'Sidcot'. A suit which was adopted and worn by airmen in both World Wars and many of the world's first long distance record breaking flyers. In fact, Baron Richthofen, the greatest fighter pilot of the war was found to be wearing one when he was at last shot down. Between the wars Cotton mixed frequently successful business activities with flying adventures. When still a young man, using his own capital, he flew the Newfoundland mails and organised an aerial survey of the island. Cotton learned about aircraft and flying the hard way. He became on expert. In 1923 he sold out his stake in Newfoundland where he had five operational aircraft, a large working yacht, shore establishments, and a very big timber business. By September 1938 he was to be found in London in business with a new type of colour film, Dufaycolour. Several of his friends had discussed the pending German menace with him and he had stated that he would be ready to take part immediately if there was a war. On a visit to Paris with one of his American associates, A.J. (Alfred) Miranda, he was introduced to a Paul Koster. He sounded Cotton out on this subject and asked if he would be willing to co-operate on certain work. The day after he returned to London the telephone rang and the caller said he was a friend of Paul and could he come round right away. Three minutes later the caller was at the door introducing himself as Major F.W. Winterbotham.

Fred Winterbotham was a shadowy figure who worked for the British Secret Intelligence Service (M16) who actually had the rank of Wing Commander in the RAF. It is worthwhile to give a brief history of him here as he was to become one of the major figures behind the scenes during the war. He was described by Cotton as "A man of about my age (then 44), dressed in a grey suit which toned with his grey eyes and greying hair. There was a look of determined discretion about him". Winterbotham told Cotton that he represented official Intelligence organisations in England and in France. Germany was expanding its forces and at the same time had clamped down the strictest peacetime security yet seen anywhere. The requirement was for a privately owned aircraft able to take clandestine aerial photographs of German and Italian fortifications, aerodromes and factories. Cotton was well-known as a flying man on the Continent, and also he had business Interests there. Would he be willing to let Winterbotham buy him a suitable aircraft, and if so, what would be best for the job?

"A Lockheed 12A" was the reply. "What remuneration would Cotton require for such work?" Winterbotham asked.

The answer was "None, as long as out of pocket expenses were met". Winterbotham then explained that Cotton need only to be the official owner of the plane, because Intelligence flights would be under the control of experts, the French Deuxième Bureau, who had the first Interest in the flights. Cotton had some reservations about this arrangement. The joint SIS/French venture had set up a commercial front in Paris called the

Aeronautical Research and Sales Corporation as a cover all these activities. The Lockheed was delivered in January 1939 which had been ordered by Miranda in New York. Cotton flew it solo and fell in love with it. He was more reluctant than ever to hand it over to the French, who produced ham-fisted pilots and photographers. The first flight was chaotic over the Rhine with a French cameraman at the back of the cabin with a very cumbersome camera. Cotton demanded to see the photographs and was very dissatisfied with what he saw. He proposed to the French that he should take over the photographic side, which he believed he understood better than anybody in Europe. Instead of the slow and massive camera he proposed to make a camera frame to take three F24 s two angled outwards and one looking straight down. He knew that the results of the F24 were disappointing, but he also knew he could Improve on them dramatically by using better films and fine-grain developer. Also condensation caused problems by freezing the air around the cameras affecting the shutters and film transport so he would pipe warm air to the cameras to overcome this. The French refused to do things his way. They would not submit flight plans and routes they wanted to fly were very haphazard to say the least, which alone were enough to attract attention. So Cotton told them to take the Lockheed. He ordered another Lockheed after explaining the situation to Winterbotham and he readily agreed. Time was running short. The second Lockheed arrived in May and Cotton prepared it with a mixture of ingenuity and thoroughness. Extra fuel tanks were fitted and 'teardrop' windows so that the pilot could see below and astern. The 'teardrop' windows were Cotton's idea, he registered the design but as they were fitted only to operational aircraft he never did put in any claim at the end of the war. Well over 100,000 were made. Airwork, a private firm at Heston made him secret emplacements for five cameras with metal slides to cover the camera ports. These, when closed were very hard to detect. Three Williamson F24 cameras were in the belly and a 250 exposure Leica camera driven by windscreen wiper motors mounted in each wing. All controls were electric and connected to the pilot's seat.

One day at Heston he watched the Maharajah of Jodhpur's private plane take off, when he looked up seconds later he could not see It. Cotton realised that the pale duck-egg green paint was a wonderful camouflage. He had the Lockheed painted just a shade paler than that, and patented the colour under the name of 'Camotint'. Winterbotham's first assignment for him was to photograph military establishments in and around Italy. His co-pilot for the trip was a young Canadian, Bob r4iven. On June 14th, Cotton recorded that he "was introduced to a young RAF pilot in Malta by the name of 'Shorty' Longbottom - height five foot four - and a very good pilot who was very interested in my views on aerial photography". Shorty' joined the team for a brief flight while he was on leave and his knowledge of cameras and flight impressed Cotton.

Sidney Cotton (right) with "Shorty Longbottom in WW2

The whole trip lasted for eleven days, staying only in the best hotels making photographic cover of the Eastern Mediterranean, North Africa and Ethiopia. Some reports talk of Cotton being given a cover by Winterbotham as a Film Director looking for locations for films. Most conveniently, the Germans were genuinely interested in his colour film. The Dufaycolour agent In Berlin, a man called Schoene, had flown in the Richthofen circus with Goering, and knew all the senior Nazis. When Cotton first arrived at Tempelhof Aerodrome, on July 2, 1939, there was a jackbooted guard of honour. On demonstration flights .he took many clandestine photographs of military installations sometimes even when high ranking Nazi officials were passengers. On 19th August he made a hurried return to England. He had to report that Goering had offered to fly to England in the Lockheed to meet Lord Halifax, the then Foreign Secretary. It appears that Goering was convinced that Great Britain would declare war on Germany if the invasion of Poland went ahead, and he wanted to sound out the Cabinet's intent ions for himself. Hitler was being advised otherwise by Ribbentrop that war would not be declared over Poland.

Chamberlain approved of the plan and told Cotton "to bring his friend over". By the time Cotton had got back to Berlin the situation had changed. Ribbentrop was in Moscow and on the 23rd August the Russo-German pact had been signed. Goering's flight to England was cancelled. Winterbotham had arranged that if war looked near he would send a telegram. 'Mother Is ill, Mary'. The telegram was delivered to Cotton at the Adlon Hotel, Berlin on August 24th. A further telegram arrived saying 'Mother very low and asking for you, Mary'. In the end, after several delays, Cotton and Niven were allowed to take off in the Lockheed. They had to follow a narrow prescribed route out of Germany, but 'While over the Dutch border, East of Groningen, Cotton saw the German battle fleet anchored in the Schilling Roads outside Wilhelmshaven, and photographed it was the last private aircraft to leave Berlin before war was declared. With war declared Cotton's association with Winterbotham continued. Naval Intelligence was the first to get in touch. Ian Fleming, the creator of James Bond, visited Cotton's flat with an urgent job for him. There was a chance that the west coast of Ireland was being used as a refuelling post for U-Boats operating In the Atlantic. So on the 12th September the Lockheed took off, refuelling at Speke to photograph the whole of the coastline. "The RAF are having camera trouble", Winterbotham reported one day. "The First Sea Lord wants some photographs of foreign ports and the RAF can't get them, and everybody is raising merry hell". He asked Cotton to go next morning to talk with the Director General of Operations, Air Vice-Marshal Richard Peck. Cotton was apprehensive about this interview as he already suffered hostility when landing at RAF stations due to his inability to disclose destination and purpose.

There's no doubt that he enjoyed being secretive and being able to give the RAF some hassle. While Peck was extremely good mannered and diplomatic, Cotton sensed hostility. Bad feeling existed between the Admiralty and the Air Staff on the subject of photo-reconnaissance. Cotton had made a name for himself on that subject with the Navy and this had upset the top brass of the RAF. Peck asked if there was any special equipment needed to get pictures from aircraft when the cameras were freezing up all the time. Cotton explained that it was not the cameras freezing but the condensation around them that was. Peck was very surprised that the RAF's own cameras, the P24, were being used by Cotton. How then did he explain the excellence of his pictures when the RAF was having all this trouble?

Another meeting was arranged with an even higher ranking officer, Vice-Chief of the Air Staff, Air Marshal Sir Richard Peirse. Peirse told

Cotton that aerial cover was urgently needed of Flushing and Ymuiden. RAF crews had tried repeatedly to get this cover and foiled. Could Cotton make any suggestions? "Lend me a Blenheim and I'll get you the pictures right away". The RAF could not let that happen. How could a civilian fly a military plane? What would happen if he got shot down? All sorts of problems were brought up. Cotton's argument was that he would take the risk. If they wonted a photographic specialist, he was the man. But all that the meeting decided was to have another meeting next morning were there would be some Blenheim pilots and experts from RAE Farnborough present. He was sure that they did not believe his condensation theory. Cotton was depressed and went back to his office. The morning mist had cleared and it had turned into a lovely warm day. He had an idea! He rang Bob Niven at Heston and asked him to get a weather report for Holland. It was good with big woolpack clouds for Ideal cover. He Instructed Bob to get the Lockheed out and warm her up.

The next job was to ring Winterbotham to check on reports of German fighter patrols. He also asked him to arrange film processing at Farnborough as there were no facilities at Heston, and warning that they might have to work through the night. Kelson, his personal servant, and chauffeur, drove Cotton to Heston, the Lockheed had warmed up, and they took off less than an hour after the unsatisfactory meeting in Air Vice-Marshal Peck's office. Immediately after take off Cotton asked Heston control to tell Fighter Command that 'White Flight', his normal protective code for the Lockheed, was going out to sea of the Kent coast on a test flight and returning to land at Farnborough. Because of the low altitude of the protective clouds, he few at eleven hundred feet, crossing the coast at Ramsgate. He set course for the Scheldt estuary. They found the clouds were ideal cover and over the target perfect photographic weather. All five cameras were running as the made a run across Flushing and Ymuiden. They landed at Farnborough where the Photographic Section worked into the early ours. Next morning there was just time for Cotton to get two hours sleep before the meeting. Peck opened it promptly at ten o'clock with a repeat performance of the day before with a lot of senior officers ready to put, this civilian, Cotton in his place.

After about half an hour Cotton opened his briefcase and took out the album of photographs, and asked, "Is this the kind of thing you want?"

Peck examined each print and praised them all. "These are first class Cotton", he said, "But we wouldn't expect this quality in wartime". The album went round the table and then somebody asked when the pictures had been taken.

"At three fifteen yesterday", Cotton said. For a few seconds there was silence and then the room exploded as the truth dawned.

"You had no right to do such a thing....flouting authority....what would happen if everyone behaved like that?" Somebody even suggested that he should be arrested. Cotton could stand this nonsense no longer.

He got to his feet and said F*** the lot of you", and walked slowly to the door and slammed it as he went out.

Next morning a conciliatory Air Vice-Marshal Peck telephoned Cotton at his office. He wanted to know when it would be convenient for Sir Cyril Newall, Chief of Air Staff, to call on Cotton. Cotton replied that he could not put Newall to all that trouble he would call and see him, as well as calling on Peck. In fact Newall took him out to lunch at the United Services Club where he asked him,

"Would you be prepared to help?"

"Of course I would" he replied.

"Then take charge of the RAF's Photographic Section".

Cotton said that it would not work because the regular officers would resent his intrusion, as they already did. The best solution would be to form a special unit, give him the necessary aircraft and the processing facilities. He would like to start at Heston with his present nucleus of picked men.

"But Heston is a civil airport", said Newall.

"Exactly, sir, nobody would suspect that secret work would be done from there". Cotton was commissioned as a Squadron Leader with an acting rank of Wing Commander.

The new unit consisted of Cotton, five officers and seventeen other ranks. The hangers at Heston were requisitioned plus the offices at Airwork, the flying club and part of the Airport Hotel. 'Shorty'

Longbottom, home from Malta joined the team. At the beginning all processing had to be done at Farnborough but Newall agreed that a photographic section should be built at Heston. Cotton would still liaise with everybody through Winterbotham. The new unit would be known as the Photographic Development Unit. The next problem was aircraft. Cotton was determined to have Spitfires. Stripped, polished, tuned and unarmed so that nothing aloft could catch them. The experts told him that the Spitfires were not suitable and in any event were unobtainable for that purpose. In the end he had to have two very slow Blenheims. He flew the two aircraft to Farnborough where the Chief Superintendant, Mr. A.H. Hall, was most interested in his ideas. Cotton's modifications increased the Blenheim's top speed by eighteen knots, but they were still for too slow. However the "Cottonising" of the Blenheims got to the notice of Sir Hugh Dowding, now C-in-C, Fighter Command. He had to use Blenheims as long range fighters. Dowding turned up at Heston to satisfy himself that Cotton really could make these slow aircraft go much faster.

When the Air Ministry told him they had no facilities for 'Cottonising' his Blenheim fighters, Cotton promised that if the Air Marshall would requisition another hanger at Heston he would do them at a rate of eight per week. Cotton kept his promise. When they were finished they were painted the some pale green as the Lockheed, and this became the standard camouflage for RAF fighters. The grateful Dowding invited Cotton to tea with him at Bentley Priory. Cotton left the tea table with a promise that two Spitfires would be delivered to Heston the next morning. Two black marks now appeared against Cotton and Dowding. The senior officers would not forget this.

A PR Spitfire in "camotint" at RAF Cosford, June 2000

Dowding was later to lose his command after winning the greatest battle In English history. As for Cotton, he was told that he had no authority to get new aircraft, particularly Spitfires. "How ore you going to service them?" they asked. "They need trained Rolls-Royce staff. Did he intend getting those as well?" (Yes, he did.) His official reply was that his unit was attached to Fighter Command and that the reallocation of Spitfires was a domestic matter inside the Command.

While the row continued they were already being converted. They were disarmed and the external surfaces were polished into a hard gloss. By doing this their maximum speed increased from 360 to just less than 400mph. He next intended fitting a 30 gallon tank under the pilot's seat to increase the range to 1,250 miles at 30,000 feet. The RAE experts said that this would shift the centre of gravity too far to the rear. He also intended fitting cameras weighing 64 lbs immediately astern of the new tank. The some centre of gravity argument was produced. But Cotton knew too much about aircraft to be argued with. He called for a screwdriver and opened an inspection panel towards the tail plane and showed the inspectors lead weights amounting to 32 lbs. These had been put there by the manufacturers to counterbalance the extra weight of the new three-bladed steel propellers. At last he was ready to start taking pictures.

Legends and Heroes | 74

One Spitfire was to be held back and used as a training aircraft for a unit, destined for expansion. Shorty Longbottom started work from French airfields. The Belgians would not allow Anglo-French aerial reconnaissance over their territory because they were afraid of upsetting the Germans. Because their maps were considered inadequate by the BEF Cotton was asked to do it unofficially. There were quite a number of incidences of compasses going wrong and wandering into Belgium airspace after that. He was soon on excellent terms with Air Marshal Sir Arthur Barrett, who commanded the RAF in France.

The first ever photographic sortie of any kind In a Spitfire was flown by Shorty on the 18th November 1939; he took off at 1pm bound for the German border. Clouds prevented him from getting to his target but he did get some good pictures of the country just west of the frontier from 33,000 feet. The second sortie two days later was successful over Germany. The unit in France was known as 212 Squadron, RAF. As exposed film poured in, Cotton had a problem of getting it processed and interpreted. By the end of the war the Allied Central Interpretation Unit employed 550 officers and 2,000 other ranks, providing 80 per cent of our intelligence on the enemy. At the outbreak of the war our interpretation capacity consisted of two RAF officers at the Air Ministry, two Army officers, and a small unit at the Admiralty. Aerial reconnaissance from 10,000 feet was suicidal, so Cotton insisted that the task must be done from 30,000 feet. To get the Interpretation done, Cotton went to an old friend, 'Lemnos' Hemming who was running an aerial survey business at Wembley called the Aircraft Operating Company.

He had trained interpreters who worked with stereoscopic Instruments and used a large sophisticated Swiss calibrating and measuring machine known as the Wild. Hemming also produced a camera with a 20 inch focal length lens which gave a scale of 1/18,000 at 30,000 feet, as against 1/72,000 for the standard 5 inch lens of the F24. Cotton's unit successfully used both cameras until the Air Ministry produced the F.52, with a 36 inch lens, which gave a scale of 1/10,000 from 30,000 feet and became the standard air camera of the war. Then Spitfires were fitted with two F.52 cameras slightly offset so they produced a double picture with a 30% overlap. The lens aperture was f6.3 and the unusual feature was the gloss register plate was coloured yellow to act as a filter. This cut down the light loss within the camera. The negative size was 9 x 7 Inches and the magazines held 500 exposures. General Vuillemin, French Chief of Air Staff in return for certain photographic favours, gave Cotton access to his airfields. Cotton found these more favourable to his needs than the RAF fields where station commanders resented the duck-egg green Spitfire, the Lockheed and the manservant driving a large private car with an Illuminated Union Jack on the back. The manservant was Cyril Kelson. His father was a Leicestershire publican. Vuillemin had a special hanger built for Cotton at his own field, Coulommiers. It could house the Lockheed and two Spitfires and was roofed in straw thatch to resemble a haystack. It escaped the German attacks on French airfields in May 1940. Both the RAF and the French had been trying for weeks to photograph the Ruhr and suffered heavy losses. Bob Niven, on December 29th, was able to cover the whole of the southern half in less than 30 minutes. During the next few clear days was able to photograph the cities of Cologne, Dusseldorf and much of the Siegfried Line.

Losses of aircraft on photo-reconnaissance for the RAF were 40 in three months, and the French, 60 in the same period. The total of square miles covered was very low. Cotton was dismayed and annoyed of the futile loss of crews and aircraft and made his views known. The RAF didn't like Cotton but the RAF at the present time needed him and his expertise. Nine days after he presented the figures of losses to Peirse the first of his new Spitfire aircraft touched down at Heston. Cotton put forward a proposal that Herrrnlrg's Aircraft Operating Company with all his trained interpreters should now merge with his unit. It was refused, so Cotton used the facilities privately as he had been doing for several weeks. Peck was unconvinced of their value. Air Marshal Barratt himself selected one of his own officers to join the Photographic Development Unit as an administrative officer to take some of the load off Cotton's shoulders. He was Geoffrey Tuttle and was able to take over the day to day running of the unit now that more aircraft and pilots joined them. He reported to Heston on the 9th February 1940. Cotton never regretted the day Tuttle came; he had the flair that Cotton needed. Tuttle did indeed have flair; he later became Air Marshal Sir Geoffrey Tuttle. Early In February the Admiralty, dependent on the RAF for photographic reconnaissance, urgently needed to find out the whereabouts of the battleship Tirpitz. They wanted confirmation whether she was still at Wilhelmshaven. The Admiralty by passed the Air Staff because of the delays and came straight to Cotton. On the 10th February Longbottom produced photographs from more than 5 miles up and Hemming's staff declared that the ship was still in her dock.

The first set of prints went to the Air Ministry where they sat for 36 hours. The Admiralty was desperate for Information and had not yet been shown the photographs. By now Cotton was forbidden to deal direct with the Admiralty, but he was now so fed up with these Inter-Service jealousies he delivered a set of prints to the Director of Naval Intelligence, Rear-Admiral J.H. Godfrey. Cotton was wheeled in to see Sir Dudley Pound, the First Sea Lord. Pound insisted that Cotton attend a meeting In the War Room that evening with the Air Staff.

"Would that be wise?" asked Cotton. The answer he got was that Churchill wanted him there.

The outcome of that meeting, a very stormy meeting, between the two services was another black mark against Cotton. The Admiralty wanted to know why the RAF had not requisitioned the Hemming Company. In fact they were told that if the RAF did not do it then the Admiralty would. Cotton did not let on that the RAF had already been offered the company and had turned it down. Sir Dudley Pound feared that the Germans would make a sudden air strike against his naval bases in the south of England. The Air Staff gave assurances that their early warning for enemy aircraft was adequate. Pound wanted to know if Cotton had the secret device fitted to his Lockheed which gave a radio signal of friend or foe (1FF). This device had not been fitted because nobody had suggested it. The idea was that Cotton should fly over Portsmouth and the Portland area without giving his 'White Flight' code to Fighter Control. With a Naval Observer, Cotton took off without submitting flight plans and climbed to 14,000 feet. Circling over the target area to give plenty of time for the early warning system to pick them up, it was a nice clear spring day, ideal for- the job in hand. There was no evidence that they were seen or noticed. With cameras running a run was made along the coastline. When Pound look at the resulting pictures he groaned, "You have got all my secret asdic stations!" A memorandum was sent to the Air Staff saying "we have today received Information that unidentified aircraft were flying In the vicinity of Portsmouth and Portland yesterday. What can you tell us about it? The reply from the Air Staff was short and to the point, saying that there was no aircraft in that area at that time, British or German. Later, at a conference in the War Room when Peirse saw the photographic evidence he exploded with a single word, "Cotton!" But when tempers cooled down the Air Staff had to admit that the system wasn't working as it should. Cotton was severely criticised for being disloyal to the RAF, but he believed it was all part of the muddled thinking of a very few senior officers and their inter-service rivalry. It was another black mark against Cotton. Things started to happen in France. On the 7th May a photograph taken by a Spitfire showed that a large number of German tanks were hiding in the Ardennes forest. A number of low level sorties were carried out as requested by Air Marshal Arthur Barratt, C-in-C. British Air Forces, France, and It confirmed the evidence. The interpreters estimating that there were 400 tanks visible in the area. Barratt had no authority to call in the heavy bombers so he enlisted Cotton to be a kind of emissary to ginger Bomber Command along. Air Marshal Sir Charles Portal told Cotton at an interview that the RAF had no plans to bomb the Ardennes. Plans for raids had to be made weeks ahead by the Air Staff after approval by the War Cabinet. It was impossible to just lay one on for that afternoon. Anyway Portal was not convinced by the photographic evidence and clearly regarded him as a nuisance.

On the morning of 10th May the Panzer divisions began to roar out of their forest hiding place to begin their main thrust against Western Europe. The French wanted to award decorations to Cotton and five members 4 his Unit. Cotton was to get the Commander Legion of Honour and Croix de Guerre with Palm but the Air Ministry refused them. They were offered again at the end of the war and were again refused by the Air Council. He was eventually awarded the OBE. Both Shorty Longbottom and Robert Niven were awarded the Distinguished Flying Cross. The Air Ministry press release announcing the awards stated that these two officers had been decorated for their part in developing a new system of photographic intelligence. Strange publicity for a secret unit! The Germans attacked Holland, Belgium, Luxemburg and France and photographic reconnaissance became very important. At a meeting In London on 10th May with the pressure of events Cotton was naive enough to believe that at last he was getting the support he required. During the next few weeks he was constantly flying backwards and forwards across the Channel. Rumours were being heard of that the Air Ministry was at last realising the value of the Unit. So much so that they were planning to take it over and put it on a true service footing, replacing Cotton when they did so. He went to see the Director of Intelligence, Archie Boyle, who ridiculed the idea, which was reassuring.

On or about the 18th May, Winterbotham ordered Cotton to fly the Lockheed to Paris escorted by Spitfires from Fighter Command. There he was to pick up Commander Wilfred Dunderdale, the MI6's resident officer and two passengers. They were Richard Lewinski and his wife and various pieces of luggage. Lewinski was a Pole who once worked as a mechanic on the German code machine, Enigma, at the AVA Telecommunications factory. It is not certain that this was his real name. Later reports show that it could have been Palluth (code-named Lenoir). He had been spirited out of Warsaw by the Polish and French Secret Service under the German's noses. Cotton was not in on the Ultra secret so he did not realise the importance of his passengers and also the drawings and the wooden model of the Enigma machine which they were carrying. At Orly Airport the passenger lounge was crowded with rich Frenchmen willing to pay a small fortune for a passage to England. Cotton, it appears, was reluctant to turn down hard cash for his spare seats and had to be threatened with a courts martial to get him to take off. It must have broken his heart to turn down all those attractive offers. There was no problem evacuating the Squadron from France. They made it by plane and boat from La Rochelle. Cotton and Niven got away in the Lockheed carrying four passengers. One was a girl secretary who had been left behind because she had refused to leave without her Collie dog, a defiance that Cotton thoroughly approved of and reported that the dog seemed to enjoy the flight. As they approached the English coast they ran into heavy fog, and with the safety of the passengers in mind they returned to Jersey and spent the night there. After making a long detour over the Atlantic because of German air activity he landed his Lockheed back at Heston on the 18th. June. There was a letter waiting for him. Here is the text in full:

Air Ministry, Dept.OA, London, S.W.1
16h June 1940.
SECRET
S.58864/S.6.
Sir,
I am commanded by the Air Council to inform you that they have recently
had under review the question of the future status and organisation of the
Photographic Development Unit and that, after careful consideration, they
have reached the conclusion that this Unit which you have done so much to
foster, should now be regarded as having passed beyond the stage of
experiment and should now take its place as part of the ordinary
organisation of the Royal Air Force.

2. It has accordingly been decided that it should be constituted as a unit of
the Royal Air Force under the orders of the Commander-in-Chief, Coastal
Command, and should be commanded by a regular serving officer. Wing
Commander G.W. Tuttle, D.F.C. has been appointed.

3. I am to add that the Council wishes to record how much they are
indebted to you for the work you have done and for the great gifts of
imagination and inventive thought which you have brought to bear on the
development of the technique of photography in the Royal Air Force.

I am, Sir,
Your obedient Servant,
Arthur Street.
Wing Commander H.L. Cotton, A.F.C.
Royal Air Force Station,
Heston, Middlesex.

It should be noted that they got his initials wrong and added a decoration
to which he was not entitled. Sir Arthur Street was the Permanent Under-
Secretary to the Air Minister.

It was on astonishing time to dispense with his services. He had carried
the Unit on his shoulders and no one, not even Tuttle, had his insight of the
many problems still to be solved. He had hardly expected this form of
dismissal, but it was the way of the Air Council resolve to get rid of him as
soon as they could. The Admiralty which had been responsible for some of
his unpopularity was too lazy or too discreet to stand up for him. Later
when Cotton offered his services to the Admiralty they were told that it

would be considered a hostile act by the Air Council if they employed him. The Air Ministry knew his brilliance had made them look foolish and they never forgave him. His efforts to get himself reinstated with the Photographic Development Unit proved hopeless. Cotton was posted to the pool depot at Uxbridge, though he was told that had no need to live there. When pressed, Peck told the RAF he had other plans for his considerable abilities. He was left to his own devices, although he was still being paid as a Wing Commander. On 3rd October he obtained a release in order to be free to go to other interested parties. Authority was given to retain his rank as acting unpaid but to wear his uniform when duties made it necessary. Fed up with this inactivity Cotton thought of an idea which might help night fighters now that the night Blitz had started. He teamed up with Wing Commander W. Helmore, a Ph.D. of Cambridge University, to produce a very strong searchlight of about 30 seconds in duration mounted on an aircraft equipped with airborne radar, so that attendant night fighters would be able to shoot down the bomber.

They called their plan "Aerial Target Illumination" and patents were applied for in their joint names. On the18th October they took the plan to Lord Beaverbrook, Minister for Aircraft Production, who said that if Dowding thought well of it then he would provide facilities for a series of trials. All went well and the work went ahead, but there was opposition from the Air Council. On the 24th January he was told that he was discharged from the A.T.I. project. In face of such persecution he decided that it would be best if he and Helmore went their separate ways. Helmore remaining to progress the job while Cotton tried to push it through from behind the scenes.

On 3rd March the Air Ministry wrote him the following letter:

Sir,
I am commanded by the Air Council to inform you that as it is no longer necessary for you to retain the acting unpaid rank of Wing Commander, or to wear Royal Air Force uniform, the authority granted by the Department's letter of the 3rd October 1940, numbered as above, is hereby withdrawn with effect from the date of this letter.

You will, therefore, remain on the Unemployed List of Officers of the Royal Air Force Volunteer Reserve In your substantive rank of Squadron Leader, but as it seems unlikely that your services will again be required on the active list of the Royal Air Force, the Council would be prepared to give favourable consideration to an application by to resign your commission, in order that you may feel entirely free to follow civilian employment.

I am, Sir,
Your obedient Servant,
Arthur Street.

Cotton resigned his commission. Meanwhile the concept of searchlights was being developed on a parallel course by Wing Commander H. de V. Leigh for anti-submarine work. Unable to join the Navy because of the pressure put on the Admiralty by the Air Council, It was clear that they were determined to obstruct Cotton In anything he might attempt to help the war effort. He decided to work behind the scenes as a civilian, helping the Admiralty, without remuneration. On Monday, 25th August 1941 he was summoned to meet Air Commodore D.L. Blackford, Director of Intelligence (Security). In his office were two other officers and a secretary to take verbatim notes. Cotton was offered a seat. "I hope you are not going to take this as anything personal." said Blackford, "but the fact is that I've got orders to investigate certain matters concerning you on the highest authority". In fact several charges were laid against him. They were, 'Visiting an R.A.F. station where secret work on the A.T.I. was being developed, passing restricted Information to a foreign power - allowing Americans to visit a secret establishment'. Cotton pointed out that the A.T.I. project was his idea and he held patents to prove it.

This took the Security Director by surprise. "This is not the Information we have", he exclaimed.

After a morning of questions he was allowed to go but to return for another session the next day. He returned to his flat very troubled at the sequence of events. At that time his flat was an open house to many people. That night two friends dropped in for dinner. One was an American, one of Roosevelt's special envoys in the U.K. He listened to Cotton's story of that day and came up with the information that the Air Ministry had recently invited some U.S. trainee cadets to Heston to see some new equipment, namely the Helmore Turbine Light. He promised to send round a copy of the invitation and the names in the morning. Next morning, completely out of the blue, came a letter from the Ministry of Aircraft Production. "Referring to your application for patents for a searchlight on aircraft", it said, "this is to be put on the Top Secret list and the patent applications are to be impounded for the duration of the war". Soon after breakfast the information from the Americans arrived. At the subsequent meeting the case against Cotton collapsed when he produced his evidence and he heard no more of these accusations. Towards the end of 1943, Desmond Moreton of the Ministry of Economic Warfare, one of Churchill's personal assistants, heard something of Cotton's story from a mutual friend and expressed a desire to meet him. Moreton came to the flat and spent many hours going through the various documents.

Next day Moreton telephoned. "I mentioned your case to the Prime Minister", he said, "and he remembers you well. He has told me to make an immediate investigation from the Prime Minister's office".

It appears that Sir Arthur Street was given fifteen minutes to produce Cotton's file. The results proved that there was a plan to shut Cotton up and oppose everything he did. Such was Churchill's anger that the Air Ministry had to back down.

It is interesting to note that in Fred Winterbotham's book, 'The Ultra Secret', published in 1974, he records at length about the secret spy plane photographing Germany in 1939, but he never mentions Cotton by name. The RAF had a long memory and never forgave Sidney Cotton. After the war, Cotton's enterprise still flourished. In 1948 he came to the aid of the people of Hyderabad blockaded by the new state of India with an airlift of supplies. Pakistan said they would pay all the costs but it took Cotton fourteen years to get the money. Oil concessions in the Middle East attracted his attention 'and were negotiated over a period of time with Saudi Arabia. After 1956 he was involved in trying to repair the damage between the British and Arab governments after the Suez Invasion. As historian Ralph Barker explained, his talents and enthusiasms took him all over the world, and gave him a day-to-day existence as full of incident and excitement as of variety, in the course of which he had more dealings with people in high places than many Cabinet Ministers. Author, Nigel West, reports in his history of M16 "although Cotton's enterprise produced a wealth of information for interpretation, his unorthodox approach was not well received by the RAF".

Sidney Cotton died in 1969 but is still not forgotten. George Millar who wrote a book on the Bruneval Raid met a retired Air Marshal about a year after Cotton had died. The Air Marshal is not named, unfortunately, but this was his summing up of the man: "A born pilot with a marvellous pair of hands, but an adventurer, an out and out adventurer. Cotton was impossible; he was his own worst enemy, always narking at authority. I had a good deal to do with him, for my sins, in 1940. His own fellows would do anything for him. But one could never get hold of him, because he was always flying here or flying there. When you command a unit, you've got to be chair borne some of the time. I always felt he was enjoying the war at the taxpayer's expense". Geoffrey Tuttle made a remarkable success of the Photographic Reconnaissance Unit after Cotton had gone. As Constance Babington Smith, a fully-fledged member of the 'Cotton Circus' reports "There could have been a disastrous drop in morale after Cotton left. But Tuttle had the good sense to accept the flying club atmosphere. He was quite prepared to overlook a pilot's blue suede shoes if that pilot was getting good photographs". It is interesting to note that when, in later years, Tuttle and Cotton met, it was always Tuttle, an Air Marshal, who addressed Cotton as 'Sir'.

Post script Background to Wing Commander Winterbotham:

In the First World War he joined the Army at seventeen and later transferred to the Royal Flying Corps. He became a fighter pilot with 29 Squadron in France in April 1917. In a 'dog-fight' over Belgium on 13th July he was shot down and taken prisoner and spent the next 18 months in a POW camp. He made full use of his time by learning German, being already fluent in French. On his return, Winterbotham went to Oxford where he took a law degree. Then came a period when he travelled seeing the world and in 1929 decided to return to England and find himself a job. The RAF beckoned again and he joined Its Intelligence Branch with the brief to find out from secret sources what foreign air forces were up to. He became Head of Section 1V, the air section and had an office on the sixth floor of the SIS Broadway Buildings in Victoria. He was described as a 'swashbuckling character' by his colleagues. By 1934 he was making regular visits to Germany where he was welcomed as a 'sympathiser' by Hitler and his top advisers and Generals. In 1938 his cover was blown and was warned not to return to Germany. During the Second World War he organised the whole of the Ultra information distribution making sure that only the selected few received it through his Special Liaison Units (high level code signals units) throughout all theatres of operations. Churchill entrusted Winterbotham with this top secret assignment and to report to Churchill direct on any important matters. There was never a breach of security. After the war he retired as a Group Captain and was awarded a CBE for his services.

© Author - Deryk Wills

JSPA Newsletter - published July 1999

Sidney Cotton's life story immortalised on TV –
"Last Plane Out of Berlin"

After more than fifty years, the name of the controversial Wing Commander Sidney Cotton OBE is given the recognition he so richly deserved.

Jeff Watson, originally from Birmingham UK, is a well-known Australian documentary producer. He first approached JSOP* as the result of information given to Dave Humphrey from this very newsletter. Earlier this year, Jeff was invited to visit the JSOP Photo Museum and meet Jack Eggelston, one of the few remaining original members of Sidney Cotton's No 1 Photo Reconnaissance Unit.

Jeff was so impressed with the amount of equipment and information available, that he made arrangements to return with a film crew. On October the 6th Jeff came back and spent the day interviewing and filming Jack's recollections. There was also a full working set up of the F24 camera prepared along with other exhibits in the new Museum's location. Jeff has sent a copy of the final production, which we will place among the other documentary's produced. This has been a truly remarkable end to the century for military photography and a well deserved tribute to all those who made it possible.

Post script: The documentary was subsequently transmitted by the Discovery channel on Australian TV entitled "Last plane out of Berlin".

Dave Humphrey

Sidney Cotton at the controls of his Lockheed 12A

Cotton's Lockheed 12A at Heston May 1939
(a rare picture)

The F 24 camera fitted to the Lockheed 12A

The final resting place of
Sidney Cotton

Chapter 4

Jack Eggleston

Reminiscences of the start of photographic reconnaissance units

By Jack Eggleston

Introduction

Fifty years is a long time to remember and the old grey cells aren't what they used to be, however, I've been asked to pen a few thoughts and some reminiscences of wartime PRUs and particularly about the beginning and early days of the original photo recce unit. This, and subsequent photographic units were of inestimable value in helping the Allies to win the Second World War and many hundreds of RAF photographers served in them. I write from the point of view of an ex-boy airman photographer who was involved from the start of the wartime photo reconnaissance units (PRUs) in 1939.

Photo by Ian Dunning

Between the wars

Large volume air photo recce started during the First World War when many thousands of prints were produced for intelligence purposes. During the time between this and the next World War, aerial photography in the RAF was of course carried out and aircraft and cameras improved. However when the next war was imminent and particularly during the early days, it was found that photography from relatively slow bomber aircraft was not giving the quality of strategic information required, despite the bravery and determination of the aircrews, some of whom were airmen photographers. Many pre-war RAF photographers were employed on aircrew duties. In those days, it was part of their job when pin-points, line or feature overlaps, or mosaic photo flying was required. Some were classed as photographer/air gunner, and entitled to wear the "flying bullet" badge, for which they were awarded an extra 6d (2.5p) per day when on flying duties. It was realised that to obtain high quality aerial photography and intelligence under wartime conditions, special aircraft flying reliable detail — producing cameras and aircrew trained in the techniques of modem aerial photography would be required.

The aircraft would need to have the capabilities of high speed, high altitude, good sky camouflage and long range. Cameras were needed that were reliable, with a film capacity to cover large areas of terrain, did not freeze-up at high altitudes or suffer condensation and most of all, could produce images containing as much detail and information as possible. This state could not of course be obtained immediately but help was at hand in the shape of a venturesome Australian, Sidney Cotton; a civilian entrepreneur who had been a Royal Navy pilot in the First World War. Sidney Cotton in co-operation with British and French Intelligence Services, had flown over Italian possessions and Germany several times in his own long-range airliner, a specially modified two-engined Lockheed 12A, and had taken many photographs using hidden cameras. He arranged these flights under various business guises, often with high- ranking Nazi guests flying with him. As they with pride and arrogance, pointed- out their "wunderbar' factories and facilities, he was able to photograph these installations using automatically operated cameras hidden in the belly of the aircraft. When it seemed that war was imminent, British Intelligence, who helped Sidney Cotton's exploits, got more interested in the act and a collection of photographs recording German war preparations was built up. Before the war broke out it was decided to form a photographic development unit at Heston, then a civilian airport just west of London. Its function would be to investigate Cotton's and others' ideas for improved aerial photography and intelligence collection. This came to fruition in late 1939 when a few RAF types were posted in to form an RAF unit.

The pilots were all hand-picked and the photo-interpreters, who came later, were specialists in their particular subjects. The NCOs and airmen were a small and specially selected servicing crew of about twenty men. Some engine fitters and airframe riggers, an electrician, an instrument maker, an armourer and four photographers. We photographers were chosen by Flt Lt Bill Dunton of the School of Photography, Farnborough and Sgt Wally Walton, who was the first photographic NCO of this new unit. They chose lads who had passed out first, second and third, from the fifth entry of boys at the School of Photography, LACs Whin Rawlinson, Ron Mutton and Jack Eggleston. Paul Lamboit a civilian who worked with

Sidney Cotton on one of his enterprises; the "Dufaycolour' method of colour photography, was commissioned as a Plt Off and joined us a little later as our photographic officer Within a month or so he was promoted to Sqn Ldr. Paul Lamboit was of course a complete photographer and an expert on colour photography but not versed in RAF methods. He had to be coached in the techniques of RAF cameras and photo systems. At that time there were no processing facilities at Heston, and we LACs looked after the cameras and camera fits and also carried out aircrew duties as photographers. Films were processed at the Royal Aircraft Establishment at Farnborough. A few weeks later when it was realised that more photogs were needed, several more airmen were 'posted in and processing facilities also created. I remember Arthur Johnson, Jim Muncie, Jimmy Purvis, Joe Wyley, Sid Mills and Cpls Jock MacDonald and Donaldson among others.

Wing Commander Sidney Cotton

The first Commanding Officer was Sidney Cotton who was immediately re-commissioned as a Wing Commander and with him came his co-pilot Flt Lt Bob Niven. As I remember we also had as pilots, Eg Offs "Shorty" Longbottom, MacPhail and Slocum, and later Flt Lts LeMesurier and Milne. The aircraft we started out with were Wg Cdr Cotton's own Lockheed 12A with its concealed cameras and pale green fuselage, and I think also, a twin-engined Beechcraft. A little later two long-nosed Blenheims (lV's) and two Hudsons arrived. For liaison trips etc., we had a singlet engined Beechcraft which had belonged to the King of Iraq and still sported his Royal crest. Some time later Wg Cdr Cotton obtained two Spitfires which were delivered in Oct 39 (tail numbers) N3069 and N3071, Mk PR IAs, which the units modified in order to obtain the required capabilities for photo reconnaissance.

The Spitfires were modified to become long range aircraft which could fly high and fast. They were suitably sky-camouflaged and fitted with automatic control operated cameras and film magazines, which could obtain the necessary detailed images of large areas of terrain. These aircraft were flown by pilots trained in photographic flying techniques and became the backbone of photo recce. It was some time before this improved state of aerial photographic intelligence collection could be obtained, so modification of other various aircraft and experimental and operational flights were also carried out until more suitable aircraft came into use later in the war. The aircraft were first stripped of their armament and then modified as much as possible in order to increase air speed.

I remember flying in a long-nosed Blenheim with Fg Off Slocum. It had a long focal length camera pointing forward and mounted on the navigators table in the long nose of the aircraft. We also had hand-held cameras that could be slung on a wire and pivoted through the opening of the forward facing lower hatch. The idea was to obtain forward facing obliques as the aircraft dived on its target. On this particular flight we did not use the cameras for some reason, and were returning to base. We flew through a cloud and on emerging, there, slap in front of us was a huge barrage balloon and others glinting in the. sunlight at various distances. The pilot slammed the throttles open, pulled the stick back and banked steeply to port and we managed to avoid the obstacle. At a lower height we could have hit the hanging cables. Then still keeping a safe height and a good look-out, we managed to get back home.

The modification of aircraft for wartime photography involved experimenting with different cameras, having focal lengths from 36 to 48 inches, and various camera fits. This was done in liaison with Wg Cdr Cotton's collaborator, Mr Harry Stringer, together with the aircraft and photographic experts of the Royal Aircraft Establishment at Farnborough about twenty miles south-west. F24 cameras were fitted in vertical positions, as split pairs, forward facing and as side facing obliques. Cameras could be mounted in the wings, housed in small pods, or positioned in the fuselage. They were protected from condensation and the effects of cold by electrically heated muffs or by warm air ducted from the engine. Particular attention was also paid to obtaining vibration free mountings for the fixed cameras. All experiments aimed for a camera fit which would be best for the particular conditions of air photo recce anticipated. Modification also consisted of stripping the aircraft of all armament facilities and unwanted weight. An extra twenty to forty knots was obtained by minimising airflow spoiling protuberances and by creating a smooth, polished skin surface; even rivet heads were smoothed over. This task was carried out with a will by airmen of the unit regardless of rank or trade. The Spitfires in particular were treated this way and were experimentally sky-camouflaged for high or low level recce photography with variations of pale pink, light blue, duck-egg green and later, a darker blue which was generally adopted. The pilot's cockpit was modified with tear-drop extensions each side for visual navigation, and with marks to aid oblique target sighting. Extra fuel tanks were fitted and on later Spitfires the wing units were converted to hold many more gallons of fuel. It was said that the PR Spitfire was like a flying petrol bowser with cameras attached. This aircraft modification for wartime air photo recce was called "Cottonising". Late in 1941, 36" focal length F52 cameras were introduced and fitted to Spitfires. These gave a larger image format than the F24 and for the most, became standard for vertical and split pair fits with F24 cameras as obliques, all fitted in the fuselage. A few modified F8 survey cameras (these were mostly updated versions of the old F8 survey camera) with their large image format were also used.

The Original unit had various names which seemed to change week by week, to confuse the enemy I suppose! "Heston Flight" became "No 2 Camouflage Unit" then the "Photographic Development Unit" and again "212 Squadron" for the detachments in France, before it was designated later as the "Photographic Reconnaissance Unit" (PRU) with about twenty Spitfires some Hudsons and Blenheims, and forty or so pilots and crews.

In the early days the unit was very informal, not at all like the regular Air Force we were used to. Some pilots particularly the ex bush-pilot types often wore suede desert boots, spotted neck scarves, and wore their caps at jaunty angles with tunic top buttons undone. We young airmen delighted in this informality. There was no sign of a SWO (Station Warrant Officer) to harass us, no working parades, no kit inspections and minimum saluting. We were "Sid Cotton's Air Force", working on and with the aircraft, all mucking in together and the end product was good quality intelligence - producing photography. This routine, I understood, happens to some extent on todays operations and exercises but of course without the casual dress. The airmen in France found the local beer was too weak, so Wg Cdr Cotton flew barrels of British beer across to France in his own Lockheed aircraft. I was told that he once flew too high and that on landing it was seen that the wooden barrels had broached and the aircraft was awash with beer froth. This unconventional life as Sid Cotton's Air Force was not to last. After a few months the necessary degree of discipline was gradually introduced. It seems also that Wg Cdr Cotton's informalities and his unconventional approach to getting things done had not met with Air Ministry approval. He was eased over and replaced by a regular officer, Wg Cdr G Tuttle DFC, in mid 1940. Our new Commanding Officer was an enthusiast for Sid Cotton's ideas and had been his deputy on the unit. He was gentle in leading us back into the ways of the RAF. Sidney Cotton, the father of the PRU, was awarded an OBE in 1941. All who knew him and those who recognised the extent of his contributions to the art and science of air photo intelligence collection and to victory in the war surely think he deserved a lot more than this.

At first our films were processed at the Royal Aircraft Establishment at Farnborough. Later, dark room and photographic interpretation facilities were constructed in various buildings on the unit near Heston, and at Wembley, not too far away. There were no RAF processing or printing machines then; just roly-poly spool tanks, hand contact printers and enlargers. Developing and fixing solutions were mixed by hand from dry chemicals. The exposed magazines for processing at Farnborough were often flown there in the Beechcraft. This trip was only a few miles away and considered a "jolly" for the pilot as the single-engined Beechcraft was a sports-type plane. I remember flying with a Canadian, an ex bush-pilot I think. After take-off he told me to fly the aeroplane and he leaned back in his seat, took out his pipe and baccy pouch and leisurely lit up. We flew on with smoke and sparks puffing from his pipe encouraged me to make turns until he took over for the landing. In the early days of the war and during the eight month "phoney war" before the Battle of Britain, the pre-war aircraft and cameras still in use sometimes failed to obtain satisfactory pictures, because of technical and flying difficulties, despite the heroic attempts of the aircrews. At this time the photographs and intelligence obtained by Wg Cdr Cotton's aircrew was by comparison, superb, and his aircraft could penetrate further into Nazi Germany. The enormous value of using photo interpreters who specialised in particular subjects was also realised.

During the winter of 1939-40 the unit expanded and detachments were established in France as Flights of 212 Squadron in liaison with the British Expeditionary Force and of course, the authorities at home. The first Flight was stationed at Seclin near Lille on the Belgian frontier and the other at Essey, an airfield near Nancy, behind the French Maginot defence line. These Flights could thus more easily obtain photo cover of strategic areas of territory from west to east. At that time there were no suitable processing facilities in France and films had to be flown back to Heston. However, a short time later a processing unit was set up just east of Paris at the village of Tigeaux. A chateau and other buildings were commandeered for technical use and the accommodation of photo section and Flight personnel. The squadron's films were processed in mobile photo vehicles. Some aircraft moved to Meaux/Villency and Coulommiers airfields nearby, not far from the Army and RAF headquarters.

At Coulommiers our Spitfires were housed in a well-camouflaged hanger across the main public road and away from the airfield buildings. We had to hold up the traffic whilst they taxied precariously along the narrow road with the airmen holding the wing tips taking gigantic strides across the roadside gullies. Those who were in the squadron cafe at Tigeaux one afternoon might remember the six inch deep, yard wide cake that arrives from Paris in a chauffeur driven limousine. It was iced in light and dark blue with "Good luck to the Royal Air Force" piped across the top and with an RAE roundel below. When we cut and ate the cake it was

Legends and Heroes | 93

found to be well laced with cognac and confiseries. I can see it now, and I remember why.

The "Phoney War"

The period from the start of war to May 1940 was known as the "phoney war' when Hitler hoped to end the conflict with Britain before he invaded Russia. During this time there were many belligerent operations, particularly at sea, but relatively few enemy sorties over Britain and no ground fighting in France. Our aircraft flew and fought over Germany but for the most part dropped only propaganda leaflets. Recce photo acquisition continued from Heston and from the Flights in France. In the spring of 1940 Wg Cdr Cotton organised with the British Intelligence Services, photo recce flights over the Russian oil fields in the Caucasus, and the Black and Caspian Sea ports. At the time Germany and the Soviet Union were ostensibly friendly, having agreed a non- aggression pact in 1939 and it was thought that Russian oil was being sent to help the Nazis.

The Wing Commander decided to use a modified Lockheed aircraft because of its long range. The crew was Flt Lt MacPhail, Fg Off Burton and two airmen, LAC Allan Dixon and LAC Bissett as crew and photographers, with a battery of cameras including two for hand-held obliques. They made successive and successful flights from Habbaniya in Iraq, and although shot at, managed to avoid fighter aircraft and anti-aircraft fire. Later Sqn Ldr MacPhail became the Commanding Officer of No 2 PRU in the Middle East The PRU unit had its mishaps, forced landings and fatalities, although we usually did not know of these until personally involved due to the wartime need for the concealment of such incidents. In France Sgt Walton and Whin Rawlinson were the photographers on the Flight at Essey near Nancy and I was at Seclin near Lille. Ron Mutton continued on photo aircrew duties from Heston until he was killed in an unfortunate accident when returning from an operational sortie. The photo recce Hudson was shot down over the Thames estuary by our own aircraft on the 3 Mar 1940. The pilot Fg Off Dennis Slocum, Ron and all the crew except the co-pilot — Sgt Read were killed. It seems that the fighter pilots mistook the unarmed Hudson in its greenish blue sky camouflage for an enemy bomber. Reflections from the perspex blister which replaced the original upper gun turret may have been misinterpreted as gun flashes. The other PR Hudson and crew, with I think LAC Dixon as photographer, were shot down sometime later over enemy territory. This crew luckily survived and was taken as prisoners of war. Whilst we were in France one of our Spitfires made a forced landing at an unused flying field near Laval, not far from Le Mans, 150 miles south west of Paris. This was where Wilbur Wright demonstrated his flying machine in 1905. The aircraft had tipped onto its nose and the propeller was damaged (N3117). We had a long road journey down to fit a new prop and to retrieve the cameras and film magazines. The aircraft was deep in a muddy area at the edge of the field, but using elementary French and various gestures, we managed to muster about fifty French soldiers to lift it out. Fifteen or so crouched with bent backs under each wing and a few near the tail, and on a shouted order they all straightened up and literally walked the Spitfire onto safer ground. It was at this remote field that we found an old hanger full of ancient aeroplanes and fascinating flying machines in various states of disrepair. Some dated from well before the First World War. The hanger was guarded by an ancient Poilu who himself looked older than the aeroplanes. It seems that he had been detailed for guard duty during the First World War and then forgotten by the authorities.

In April 1940 the German Army and Luftwaffe invaded and occupied Denmark and Norway. In May they attacked France and the Low Countries and made a rapid advance. In June, 212 Squadron's photo unit at Tigeaux and Flights on nearby airfields were forced to retreat, mostly to the Orleans area about eighty miles south of Paris. After the Dunkirk evacuation and the French surrender in June, we were told to make our way home. Most of the personnel got back to Heston by one means or another. I was one of the lucky ones who flew back from Orleans in a Hudson aircraft. Although we were tracked by a Messerchmitt 109 over the French coast, we saw him turn tail and disappear rapidly when a Spitfire arrived to challenge him. There was a surge of relief in the heart and swell of patriotism as we saw the familiar roundels of our rescuer. Some of the other personnel of 212 Squadron went further south before they were forced to destroy their vehicles and equipment. Some came back home weeks later after taking the long way round through Southwest France or Spain, some managed to get a lift in a coal boat, and many a tale was told when they got back to Heston. A rather dramatic escape was made by one of our pilots, Flt Lt Wilson together with Sgt Walton, Jim Muncie and two other airmen of 212 Squadron. They managed to patch up a badly damaged Fairey Battle aircraft which they found abandoned. Parachutes and all unnecessary items were removed to lighten the load and all five crammed into the aircraft. Then after a hair-raising take-off, Flt Lt Wilson and his intrepid crew made a circuitous flight back home to Heston. There was a story going round that they had first jettisoned the bombs by putting an old mattress under the Fairey Baffle and then pulling the bomb release. After the French debacle it was expected that the Germans would invade

England. Photo recce was intensified and hundreds of PR sorties were flown, mainly to cover the probable invasion ports and preparations.

The PRU is formed (Photo Reconnaissance Unit)

Wg Cdr Tuttle was now our Commanding Officer and we became the "Photographic Reconnaissance Unit". "A" Flight was stationed at Wick near the tip of Northern Scotland, to cover the Norwegian ports and strategic areas via Sumborough in the Shetlands, and B Flight at St Eval in Cornwall to cover the shipping, harbours and areas of West and North West France. In later months the Flights would swap locations. C and D Flights at Heston concentrated on cover of the enemy Channel ports and coastal regions. The coastal areas of the Nazi "Festung Europa" could thus be photographed from Bergen to Bordeaux and beyond. During this period an unusual incident occurred. The airfield at Heston was grass, with hard standing near flying control and the hangars but no solid runways. To prevent blown up mud and dirt fouling the lens windows of downward facing cameras as the aircraft taxied out for take-off, "mud flaps" were fitted. A Spitfire would taxi out with a photographer sitting on one side of the tail-plane and a rigger on the opposite side. After the lining up and engine checking they would jump off and the photog would remove the mud flaps, give the pilot a thumbs up sign, and off he would go. On this particular occasion the pilot was a Polish officer, Fg Off Richard Drygalla. The photog removed the mud flaps and gave the sign but the rigger, AC Rhodes, was still sitting on the tail-plane with his arm round the rudder fin. As the throttle was opened for take-off, the slip-stream held him back and he remained sitting on the tail as the aircraft managed to become airborne. The pilot did his-best to trim and fly the tail-heavy Spitfire but only managed to bank around for a skilful landing and the aircraft ended up crumpled on the airfield. Luckily both pilot and passenger were not seriously hurt if somewhat shocked, and after a check up and a night in sick quarters the airman was back at work. It seems that the Polish pilot did not realise he had a passenger until he landed, and as he struggled in broken English to explain his tail-heavy flying. However, other than a messed up Spitfire, all was well. The photographic angle of this incident is somewhat ironic. Our cameras were kept in the flying control building, some with magazines on, ready for fitting into aircraft. If I had been alert to what was happening I could have picked up a loaded twenty inch F24 and taken a few shots of the Spitfire and its unwitting passenger in full flight. After this incident, mud flap clips were fitted with a cable release operated by the pilot as soon as he was airborne. The released flaps tended to fly off like "Frisbees" so they were fitted with coloured ribbon tapes to help them flutter down vertically and also be more easily found by the photog. This whole procedure could of course be abandoned when we moved to an airfield with solid runways.

It was during the Battle of Britain, when London in particular was being regularly bombed, that a PR Spitfire made a forced landing at RAF Homchurch just east of London. It seems that there was vital photo intelligence in its camera magazines and these had to be collected for processing, with all haste. It was evening and the quickest way to Homchurch airfield from Heston in the west, was straight through the centre of London. The swiftest transport was Wg Cdr Cotton's sports car which was still at Heston, and his civilian chauffeur Sid Kelson I think it was, knew London well. So off we went at a rate of knots along the great west road and straight through the centre of London. There was hardly any traffic because of the bombing and we went non-stop, touching over 60 mph through London. I can't remember any traffic lights, I suppose they were switched off, and I think we had a police car somewhere ahead. There was smoke and fire, firemen and rescue teams at work, and I remember seeing huge flames flaring from broken gas mains. We got to Hornchurch airfield, collected the film magazines, did an about turn, and a reversed repeat of our initial journey. Heston was bombed several times in September 1940 and on the last raid of that month a parachute mine completely destroyed the main hangar.

Several PR aircraft were destroyed and others badly damaged. The unit was then moved to RAF Benson near Oxford, a larger and more suitable airfield with a solid runway. The photographic interpretation organisation moved from Wembley to Medmenham, about twelve miles from Benson. Processing and printing machines were introduced into the photo section at Ewelme next to Benson airfield, to cope with the many thousands of photo images which were produced each week. Mosquito aircraft were also modified and used for photo recce along with the famous PR Spitfire. It was 1941 when PR Mosquitos came on the scene. These handsome twin-engined aircraft with their exceptional long range and high speed were excellent for the photography of areas beyond the reach of a PR Spitfire. They also carried more navigation aids and a navigator who could concentrate on obtaining accurate photo cover. The first PR Mosquitos were flown from Wick and from the airfield at Leuchars in Scotland. Later in the war they were used to cover Japanese held territories in the Far East. In general the PR Mosquito had a similar camera fit to the Spitfire, an F52 thirty six inch split pair and an F24 fourteen inch oblique. The aircraft had of course, more space for cameras than the Spitfire, so later and in addition as required, F24 forward facing cameras or an F24 split pair, or a vertical camera might be filled. For a brief period they were also used on night-time photo recce, using photoflash bombs for target illumination and American K 19 night cameras.

The detached Flights at St Eval and Wick continued and there were other units and training Flights on airfields around the country. The one I was familiar with was Mount Farm, a satellite of Benson. Here our Spitfire pilots were later reinforced by American pilots of the 7th Photo Recce Group USAAF. They flew twin-engined F4-F5 Lightnings and Spitfires with American star markings on photographic missions. One memory I have of Benson is of a bitter winter's day when flying operations were particularly imperative, and all ranks were out clearing snow and ice off the runway with picks, shovels and spades. Spitfires on sorties continued to take-off on the part already cleared, and we had to run or duck down to avoid them as they hurtled overhead at full throttle. In mid-morning the NAAFI wagon arrived and we crowded round for a welcome cuppa. The SWO had stuck his spade in a snow pile and because he was the SWO, was standing a little aloof from the herd when a Spit began its take-off. The SWO flung himself to the ground and the propeller tip neatly sliced the handle off his spade. I remember in early 1942 our Flight was detached at our favourite location, St Eval in Cornwall. We covered the coastal areas of West and Northwest France.

The chief target was the harbour at Brest where the German battleships Scharnhorst, Gniesenau and Prinz Eugen were safely bottled up and subjected to regular bombing and torpedo raids. They were expected to attempt a breakout at any time so visual and photographic sorties were flown almost every day by our Spitfires and Hudson aircraft, 9 PR Spitfires were lost during this surveillance. On one of the early sorties it seems that when the aircraft came out of a cloud it was almost over the battleships at Brest. The Germans, not sure of its identity, challenged, using a signal lamp and the Hudson navigator replied by using his Aldis lamp and flashing F * * * Hitler, before they disappeared into cloud again having quickly photographed and counted the correct number of ships. Seconds later all hell broke loose as the Nazi guns opened up in a fury. At that time I had a short local course on using the Vickers K guns which were now fitted to the Hudsons, but was taken off part-time photo flying duties on promotion to Sgt; I confess, much to my relief. Full-time aircrew on PR units and in particular, air gunners, were being trained in the simple techniques of using hand-held cameras and changing film magazines, so trained photographers were no longer needed for normal flying duties.   At St Eval we were not far from the sea and most of the Flight was billeted at Watergate Bay, now the site of RAE St Mawgan which was then called Trebelzue. We lived in a requisitioned hotel, only yards from a magnificent beach. There were happy days of swimming and surfing when we were off duty and plenty of girls on holidays in near-by Newquay, much better than our winter sojourns at windy Wick.

The processing section and photo interpreters were also at Watergate Bay. Films were processed, put through a meths bath, chamoised off then dried by winding them onto a drying drum. This was a large cylindrical drum with horizontal slats of wood to hold the film in place. On a rush sortie when every minute counted, the photo interpreter used to attempt his first-phase interpretation by crouching and viewing the damp negatives as they were wound onto the drum. I can't vouch for the truth of this as I wasn't there at the time. However it seems that on one film, an image, probably caused by a water mark or blob on the camera register glass, was found on one negative of a sea area and identified as a possible enemy ship. Perhaps the PI had been briefed to look for a ship or submarine, who knows. Remember it was at the time of Schamhorst and Gniesenau. Luckily, before a flash signal could be sent to the Navy at Plymouth to get the destroyers into action, one of the airmen noticed that the same image mark could just be seen amongst the detail on the next few negatives which showed land areas. The image then faded, presumably as the original water blob or whatever, evaporated.

Whilst at St Eval we were bombed and machine gunned a few times usually without any warning. I remember jumping into a slit-trench near our dispersal area and seeing the perspex nose of a Heinkel bomber flying straight towards our dispersed aircraft. It was very low, a height of fifty feet or so, and I could see the bombs tumbling out. As I dropped face down to the bottom of the trench there was a dull thud and a huge weight crushed me down, then all went dark. I thought it was the end. However it was only an eighteen stone Irish painter who had been spraying camouflage paint on a dispersal track. He ran for his life, flung himself into the slit-trench and landed on top of me. The enemy bombers seemed to favour a very low level attack, to avoid detection I suppose. Perhaps because of this, many of their bombs failed to explode and some were in a horizontal position when they hit. One made a neat hole in the side of the hangar and came to rest on the hangar floor. After the raid, some brave souls lifted this and other unexploded bombs and carried them out onto a grass area where they could be dealt with by the bomb disposal team.

Despite our recce efforts and those of other RAF and Navy units on blockade, Schamhorst, Gniesenau and Prinz Eugen managed to escape through the English Channel and North Sea. The ships and crews, escorted by a massive Nazi naval and air force escort, had luck and poor weather on their side. It seems that the escape was also made possible by a series of mistakes involving an unserviceable recce Hudson, French agents who were not on the ball, a British blockading submarine which was forced to dive just before the break-out and the German jamming of our detection Radar A PR flight on the morning after the ships left Brest, brought back poor quality pictures also obscured by smoke and by screen laid by the Germans as they departed. After some delay, valiant attempts were made to find and then sink the battleships and many lives were lost, but with some damage, they eventually made port. Although it was a hollow victory and did not in fact help the Germans, Hitler made the most of it in his home propaganda.

North Africa Invasion

Benson with its satellites and its film processing unit at Ewelme continued to be the main base for photo recce operations from the UK. Together with the detached Flights at Wick and St Eval and several other units, the PRU produced thousands of prints daily of enemy territory, of both strategic and tactical importance. Later, several more PRUs were formed together with photo interpretation staff. These were for the most part used for operations overseas in the Near, Middle and Far East theatres of war, and after the Normandy invasion, in Europe. In late 1942 the Allied invasion of Northwest Africa was launched, mainly at Oran and Algiers. This was the time of El Alamein and Rommel's retreat to Libya with his Afrika Korps. The PRU unit involved was No 4 PRU (Sqn Ldr 'Freddie' Ball DFC) which was later to become 682 Squadron and its associated mobile field photographic sections.

Together with the American photo units and Allied Squadrons from the Libyan area, these were to form the Mediterranean Allied Photographic Reconnaissance Wing, ready for the invasion of Sicily and Italy. The task of 682 Squadron along with the American photo units was to cover the Mediterranean area and to reinforce the photographic efforts of squadrons with the W Army in Libya and those of the very small unit in Malta. Fg Off Adrian Warburton DFC, later a much decorated Wg Cdr, and his photographers, Cpl Shirley DFM and LAC Hadden DFM were then carrying out daring photographic sorties from the besieged island flying in 'Maryland' aircraft. No 4 PRU personnel landed at Algiers and we marched the ten or so miles to Maison Blanche airfield with full webbing equipment, packs, tin hats, full ammunition pouches, extra blankets and Sten guns slung. Wally Walton was our photo officer and soon to become a Sqn Ldr. He had selected his small gang of photogs from the many at Benson and a good bunch they were. After a night's sleep on the concrete floor of a hangar, we set to work building a photo section and collecting our J Type photo trailer and processing equipment from the docks at Algiers. A couple of nights later we were bombed. Our Spitfires were hit with incendiary bullets and burned furiously, lighting up the whole area. We could hear the enemy aircraft circling above in the dark and having a field day. Several men tried to put out the flames to no avail, and were machine gunned for their pains. The photo section was destroyed and one photographer killed. Most of the five injured including Wally Walton, were patched up and soon back at work.

There were several lucky escapes as found in the light of day. Some of the penetrating bombs did not explode, the fins of one could be seen down a hole in the side of the section and antipersonnel "butterfly" bombs lay around in the debris ready for anyone to step on. The end of the photo trailer I was in when the first bombs fell was riddled with shrapnel holes. Replacement Spitfires soon arrived via Gibraltar, the processing unit was moved, and we built a section and squadron accommodation at La Dersa, a chateau and farm just up the road. Most of the processing and printing equipment had been destroyed or damaged but we patched up as much as possible and also made some out of what material we could lay hands on. The squadron was back in business. Some time later we also received and installed some processing machines which the American truck driver delivered in style. He drove under the low arched entrance to the farm and scraped the machine crates off the back of his truck to land with a crash on the ground! I remember one night at La Dersa, six of us slept on mattresses on the floor of a small room in the chateau. Sgt Samson, a pilot awoke to find two red eyes staring at him on his pillow. He shot out of bed, grabbed his revolver and started firing at the startled rat much to our consternation. After Maison Blanche was bombed and before La Dersa was completed we used another J Type photo trailer for processing some vital American PR films. The American photo processing unit set up in Algiers was having their first experience of wartime operations and was not yet fully prepared. However, a USAAF PR Flying Fortress had landed with several important films which needed quick action. There were six film magazines as I recall. The squadron did not have the suitable equipment for processing these large format films so we improvised a make-do procedure using the photo trailer. This was moved to an empty technical training school at Maison Carre near Algiers which had a good water supply and plenty of indoor space for drying the films. Many buckets of developer and fixer were prepared and LAC North and I went into the trailer and filled the long sink with developer. We had half broom sticks and some film clips.

The first magazine was unloaded and whilst LAC North held the spool I clipped the film onto the broom stick and we wound the film into the developer. Then he clipped the other end to his stick and so we turned, back and forth through the developer for the calculated time. The sink was emptied and a quick water- rinse given followed by the fixer and then a quick wash. We repeated this five more times and our wrists ached for hours afterwards. Other photogs then wiped off the films and hung them in loops to dry using the overhead shafts that drove the lathes in the school workshop. The films were stained to hell but the information was there and the American P1 Major was "dee—lighted" and the news was passed to his headquarters and on to General Eisenhower in Gibraltar. After the enemy attack at Maison Blanche when our Spitfires were set alight and the photo section destroyed, the Squadron was more fortunate.

We had a few mishaps but as far as I recall, almost all the PR sorties over enemy territory were successful and the pilots returned safely home. Pilot casualties were relatively few; although there was one which I remember with sadness. Perhaps the most disturbing casualties in war4ime are those that just disappear without trace. Roy Taylor a young Australian Sgt pilot was one who did not come home. Roy was returning from a photographic sortie over Italy. We presume that he made an error in navigation and it was thought that he had force landed in the Atlas Mountains. We did not see Roy again. He was a brave gentle and unassuming man, too young to die so far from home. We bade farewell to No 4 PRU and although looking very much the same, became 682 Squadron. Then in early 1943 after the British and American armies advanced along the length of Algeria and into Tunisia, we moved by road to the salt-flat airfield at La Marsa. This was about fifteen miles from the city of Tunis and close to the magnificent Punic ruins of ancient Carthage.

The last German and Italian force had surrendered in May 1943 and our aircraft were now much nearer to the main targets in Sicily and Italy. La Marsa became the headquarters of the North West Africa Photographic Reconnaissance Wing, later to be renamed the Mediterranean Allied Photographic Reconnaissance Wing (MAPRW) an amalgamation of all the photo recce units, mobile section and squadrons in North Africa; American, British and South African. Our Commanding Officer was Lt Col Elliot Roosevelt, the son of the President. We had the honour of being inspected by the President who had already conferred his official citation on the Wing. This was our first formal parade in years, as he in his jeep rode slowly past our ranks lined up on the airfield. Soon after this, Lt Col Roosevelt was posted away to take up other duties and the unit was taken over by Lt Col Karl Polifka of the USAAF. Both officers were renowned photo flyers.

At La Marsa we had a captured German army motor cycle with a sidecar and used it to collect film magazines for processing. When it first arrived, one of our Sgt pilots wanted to have "first go" on it so we gathered round to watch and cheer him on. He got quite a shock when he revved up and let in the clutch as instead of going forward he went back. The bike was fitted with a reverse gear. An interesting thing happened when our squadron personnel were inoculated for something or other. The batch of vaccine that the photogs got was contaminated. Consequently, a small group of men all came up with a huge scabby blister on their arms at the same time, and these had to be removed with the victim under an anaesthetic. For the medical officer this presented an opportunity not to be missed, a batch of similar and fairly fit young men, all with the same affliction.

The 'truth drug', sodium pentothal I think was just coming into use as an anaesthetic and the doctors wanted to find out for themselves how useful it was and how it affected people. This was all explained to our little group and we volunteered to take part in an experiment. As the FS I got the first jab, the smallest dose. I was on a stretcher whilst the doctors, nursing sisters and volunteer photographers gathered round to watch. I counted up to eighty before the numbers became slurred, and soon I was as drunk as the proverbial newt, but not unconscious. All inhibitions went, and as the doctor started to cut I encouraged him by shouting "Go on Doc, cut it out". I also made verbal advances to the nursing sisters. I remember slurring "Come here you lovely thing" to one of the prettiest nurses. The spectators could not control their laughter but I didn't care, and after a rest was soon back to normal with a bandaged arm but no hangover. The next victim had a slightly larger shot of the drug and only counted to forty or so before his speech slurred. I could now see why they laughed at me. They took out his false teeth and he too, though normally a staid and very sedate character, was grabbing at the nursing sisters and mouthing endearments. The other lad's performances were not interesting at all, as with larger doses they went quickly off into the land of Nod.

Invasion of Sicily & Italy

When Sicily was invaded in mid 1943 it was decided that a film processing detachment would be established on the island and preparations were put in hand. We sailed from Bizerta in a large flat- bottomed tank-landing craft, through a rough sea and were very thankful when we could unload at the Sicilian port of Syracuse and step onto firm dry land. A small section was set up near Lentini just south of Catania and with a distant view of the Mount Etna volcano. The section consisted of a Type J photo vehicle and a darkroom tent, which was a small marquee, plus a fifteen hundred-weight truck and a couple of power generators. It was set up above the sloping bank of a large stream so that we had a water supply for technical and domestic use and a drainage system. We processed and printed the sortie films of No 60 PR Squadron of the South African Air Force who were flying PR Mosquitos from an airfield a half mile away. Most of the detachment were photogs, and we all mucked in together and did our cooking and all the other domestic things of camp life, and all went well. The Luftwaffe raided the airfield and our site but we managed to carry on without fatalities.

I remember when Catania fell to the B Army commandos, we nipped into the town and "liberated" a petrol pump which we then rigged to pump water up from the stream to the darkroom tent. In daylight it was safe to wash films and prints, and bathe ourselves in the stream, but at night when a lot of our work was done no lights could be shown. Whilst the unit was at Lentini I had a great experience. Our mail was not arriving so I got a lift to Malta in a Dakota aircraft to find it. On the way we saw a heart-warming spectacle. The Italian Navy had surrendered and we flew alongside the fleet as the giant battleships steamed in line astern to anchor in the Grand Harbour at Valetta in Malta this was 10 Sep 1943. I can't remember whether or not I found the mail, or why I didn't have my camera with me. Sicily was occupied and landings were made on the toe of Italy and at Salerno just south of Naples. Italy then capitulated and switched sides by declaring war on Germany. Early in 1944 the Allies landed at Anzio south of Rome, and after fierce battles, particularly at Monte Cassino, Rome was occupied. This was the time of the massive Allied invasion of Normandy. The battles to defeat Germany were now being waged on land, from the south and the west, whilst the armies of our Russian Allies pressed forward from the east. All these operations were prepared and executed with knowledge of enemy dispositions, provided by the photo reconnaissance organisations of the Allies.

The Russians had their own system but were assisted by our PR operations. There was a Squadron of PR Spitfires complete with processing facilities, operating from Russian airfields and frozen lakes. Aerial photography and its interpretation was thus a major factor in the battle for final victory. As Rome was freed I managed to visit the City. I knew of an elderly lady who had taken refuge in a nunnery there when the Germans came. She and the mother superior, and the Irish nuns were overjoyed with their liberation and I was made extremely welcome. This visit and the walk around Rome and the Vatican City, escorted by two charming young Irish nuns in their distinctive dress was an unforgettable experience. It also brought stares from the passing soldiery   In Italy the PR squadrons, processing section and interpretation organisation of MAPRW was now established and later became 336 Wing. The main unit was at San Severo near the airfield there and not far from the airfield complex at Foggia on the eastern side of Italy. Our aircraft were Spitfires, Mosquitos and American F4 - F5 Lightnings and covered areas of Northern Italy, Southeast France, Austria and the Balkans, and even as far as Germany, Czechoslovakia and Poland. Flights also operated from the Mediterranean islands of Corsica and Sardinia. The processing unit at San Severo was in a large converted school building. It contained banks of film processing machines and multi-printers, plus all the other PR facilities such as hand processing equipment, mosaicing section, film duplicating facilities and a storage library. Two mobile field processing sections operated in conjunction with PR flying squadrons. In general one of these followed the forces advancing up the east side of Italy and the other undertook a similar procedure on the west side. Each MFPS carrying out a leapfrogging procedure as the aircraft and Armies advanced on the retreating enemy. Whilst working with the western No 2 MFPS I made a liaison visit to the island of Corsica which had previously been taken over from the Germans by irregulars of the French Resistance arid then by the Free French Forces. It was an interesting flight as on the way to Ajaccio airfield we passed over Elba the island of Napoleon's incarceration, and close to the island of Monte Cristo, the former penal colony of literary fame in the Tyrrhenian Sea. We had a good relationship with our American Allies in San Severo. In many sections and on the Squadrons and Flights,

Brits and Yanks worked together in harmony. We had a small detachment of photogs at an airfield near Alghero in Sardinia with the F4 - F5 Lightning's of the 23rd Photo Recce Squadron USAAF. The Yanks with the Brits and some Free French photographers worked well together and our detachment received an American commendation for initiative and hard work. I well remember that the "chow" was excellent. White bread which we had not seen for ages, waffles and maple syrup with eggs and bacon for breakfast, lashings of coffee, and ice cream when we wanted it. The odd bottle of Scotch which we could get but they couldn't was worth its weight in gold to the American tipplers. San Severo and Foggia were the domain of the USAAF, and we worked in close liaison with their PR squadrons. One of the trials carried out by the USAAF was in night photography over German occupied Yugoslavia, using the newly invented Edgerton Flash. This was a gigantic electronic flash fitted to the belly of the aircraft and fed by a large generator. The idea was to fly over the territory and obtain overlapping pictures by using the flash with an open shutter camera. However it seems that after a few flashes on a straight run, the enemy anti-aircraft batteries were able to predict with some accuracy the height and position of the next flash, and take the necessary action. The large concentration of USAAF personnel in the San Severo, Foggia area, meant that we were able to indulge in some of the   that we had not really missed until then.

Not only coffee and doughnuts dished out freely by smiling Red Cross ladies, but shows given by the American entertainers of those days. I remember when Joe Louis the Brown Bomber, then heavyweight champion of the world visited the area. After the show and his exhibition bout, some of us crowded into the ring. Joe shadow boxed a little and then made a few jabs in our direction. Thus it could be truthfully boasted later, "I've been in the ring with Joe Louis".   One of our F52 thirty-six inch cameras was put to use in an unorthodox way. Most of the river valleys in Italy run in an east-west direction and as the army advanced in a northerly direction they were often held up at a river crossing by enemy defences and artillery, well hidden on the opposite side. The camera, also well concealed and camouflaged, was positioned on the approach to a crossing to record the terrain and any detected enemy preparations. This was often a tricky situation for the photographer. The camera support had to be rock steady and a deep lens-hood was needed in order to prevent any surface reflection which could have revealed the position to the enemy. After photography, the recorded images would then be used when the plan of attack was made. In 1944 for a reason which I can't recall, I was detached for a time to a film processing unit which was sited near Naples and close to the foothills of Mount Vesuvius. It was an interesting situation as the volcano was having one of its rare but periodic eruptions and I remember seeing American vehicles well dusted and tents weighed down with volcanic ash, like dark grey snow. 336 Wing had a leave centre at Sorrento not far from Naples and good use was made of this by the photogs and personnel of San Severo. It was an interesting experience to visit Naples and the wins of Pompeii, Amalfi, and the isle of Capri, where we visited the famous Blue Grotto, the site of the villa of Tiberius the notorious Roman Emperor and the cliff top home of Gracie Fields, a songstress of those days.

In the spring of 1945 the German forces in Italy surrendered and a short time later there was a complete surrender in Europe. Our photographic units in Italy were then gradually dispersed to various areas. Eventually fifty or so photographers went into Austria and set up a photo section in a requisitioned hotel in Velden on the Worthersee, a lake not far from Klangenfurt and close to the Yugoslavian border. Our chief task was to make a photographic record of the bridges, river crossings and military features over and along the Austrian part of the Drau River. This runs almost parallel with the national borders of Austria, Hungary and Yugoslavia and eventually joins the Danube in Northern Yugoslavia. The operation was of course precautionary on account of the nearness of the Russian armies in Northern Austria and Marshal Tito's communists just over the hills. We enjoyed our stay in Austria which lasted until mid 1946. The task did not need more than a few photogs so we had plenty of time to spare and after the rigours of wartime service we made the most of the amenities. We had a beautiful lake, our own speedboat, and skiing weekends in the mountains, a captured German staff car and a Kubel Wagen, and even the joys of tree felling to fuel our wood burning stoves. Later we delighted in wild rides on captured Cossack horses. It was for us an enjoyable life, but it was even better to know that we would soon be going home.

So much for reminiscences of the early days of photographic reconnaissance units. It can be said that the great leap forward in the acquisition and interpretation of aerial photography which was started and achieved during World War II, was one of the major factors which led to the Allied   victory. The memorial to the wartime PRUs at RAF Benson is a replica of a Spitfire PR 11. This replaces the original, a Spitfire 19 which is now on display at the RAF Museum, Hendon. The memorial plaque presents a tribute to the Officers and Airmen who served with the PRUs and squadrons and particularly to those who failed to return.

© John ("Jack") Eggleston (circa 2000)

Dave Jenkins, Jack Eggleston, Lord Lichfield, Dave Humphrey – at the Military Photography Museum opening June 2000

WO Jack Eggleston – former RAF Boy Entrant, 1936

The spitfire camera fit (cockpit controls)

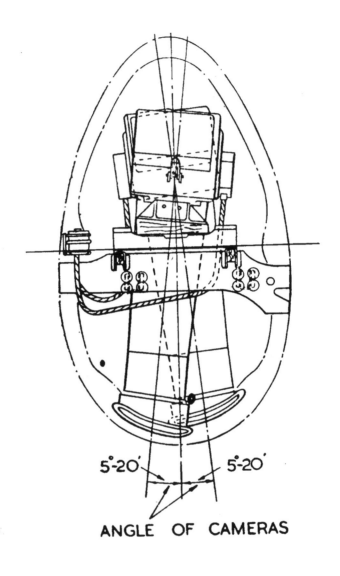

5°-20'   5°-20'

ANGLE OF CAMERAS

The Spitfire F52 camera installation option.
Two cameras fitted in tandem behind the pilot

Chapter 5

THE DARK ROOM
BOYS

The story of
No 3 Mobile Field Photographic
Section (3 MFPS)

by
Leading Aircraftsman C. L. TAYLOR
(Northern Italy, March 1945)

* Original typesetting by:-

TIPOGRAFIA. EDI.TRICE TREVIGIANA S. a R. L. TREVISÔ.(Italia) . 1945

The story of the RAF wartime photographer has never been fully detailed. Their training was unique, their trade was unique. Their characteristics were diligence, endurance, innovation and determination to produce the highest quality images possible under extreme conditions. Their equipment and tools were designed to be used under ideal conditions. Their mobile darkroom articulated vehicles were designed for use on normal tarmac surfaces with reliable and adequate support of mobile power and water services. Their materials and chemicals needed to be hauled with them and re-supplied (not always) frequently to produce millions of photographic prints, vital to the intelligence feeding the front line military commanders.

This is the factual record of a mobile photographic support unit following the allied advance from North Africa in July 1943 across to Sicily and up through Italy until victory on May 8th 1945. It demonstrates the spirit of endurance and determination of these (extra) ordinary men who created solutions to the seemingly impossible, when things went badly wrong. No. 3 M.F.P.S. produced a total of 3.35 million pictures in 1944 alone, using a crew of just 40 men which included a few drivers, support electricians and maintenance men. At the height of one hectic occasion the CO and his crew managed just 5½ hours sleep in 64 hours. At best they endured extremes of heat and humidity, at worst floods, gales and snow. Most of the vehicle "drivers" were the photographers, with little previous experience of the huge articulated vehicles which they affectionately called the "elephants". Yet they kept their "circus" and the show on the road with many enforced detours over dangerous mountain routes, through drifts of sand and muddy quagmires. This reproduction of their wartime record is dedicated to the memory and achievements of these remarkable wartime photographers.

Dave Humphrey - January 2011

* *Editors Note on the original document –*

The Italian printer's errors appeared on the original document (produced in 1945), in spite of repeated proof readings by the author Leading Aircraftsman C. L. Taylor – "So difficult does our Italian compositor find the task. His quixotic splitting of words has been retained, to avoid adding to the already formidable number of corrections". All photographs have been scanned from the original document.

This copy produced by Dave Humphrey, has been amended and revised for clarity and ease of reading to a current format and typestyle. No words have been altered from the author's original document, only the format and pagination has been compressed to accommodate current publication methods.

The original photo composite cover produced by 3 MFPS photographers

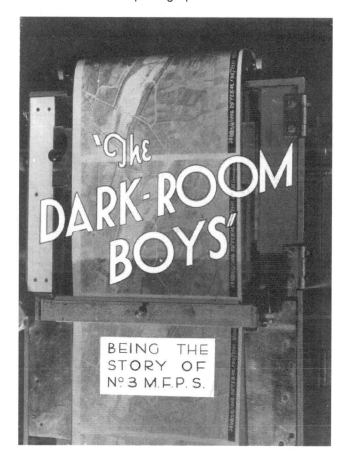

"The Dark-Room Boys" – being the story of No 3 MFPS.
The back ground picture shows a line of aerial photos rolling off the Multiprinter.
Some 3.5 million prints were produced by No 3 MFPS alone.

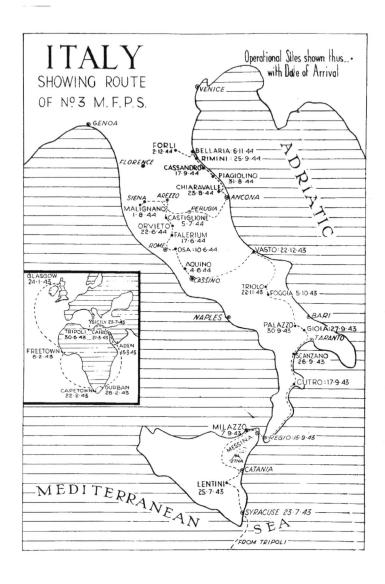

ITALY

SHOWING ROUTE

OF N° 3 M.F.P.S.

Operational Sites shown thus... •
with Date of Arrival

INTRODUCTION

This book is primarily a souvenir for the men of the Unit. But it will reach other people interested in our work, and it is also in part intended as a documentary. Unfortunately, it cannot successfully be all these things at one and the same time. As a souvenir for ourselves it is too prosaic and omits much of the lighter and brighter side of life: no personalities shine through the story and there is no more than a hint of the hundred and one delectable incidents over which we will chuckle to our dying day. On the other hand I have felt it necessary to include a chapter describing the work of the Unit; though as a documentary the book deals very inadequately with technical details of many aspects of the operations. But there it is: I can do no other. I have held the balance between contending requirements, and if in trying to cater for all parties I have succeeded in catering for none, it is just too bad, or, as someone connected with the Unit would say, "Just one of those things". Again, I was reluctant to write this story now. I am still in the Service and the Unit is still operational. That means I am not free to say all I want to say, for instance, I cannot patronise those responsible for the good show put up by No. 3 M.F.P.S. The bald facts, so far as I am able to give them, must speak for themselves. And when I say "bald facts" I mean it: I have no use here for false modesty or masterly understatement.

We have done a useful job and have done it well. We have produced the aerial photographs supporting the Italian campaign of the Eighth Army; we have turned tout more than half a million prints in a month; and our total for 1944 was 3,350,000. It is a small unit too, never more than 100 strong. And at the peak production we had barely 40 on the photographic strength "The fewer men..." Not that we view our work out of perspective with that of many a score of other specialist units. We appreciate that we are just one cog in the modern war machine - just one unit among many, each of which has its reward in the knowledge of a good job well done. Nor can we pretend to have been in great danger. The Wing to which we are attached has generally occupied the most forward aerodrome and that has occasionally brought us, uncomfortably near the line. But we are under no illusion, and when it comes to talk of danger we pay all homage to the men who "die daily" - the men who fly, the men in the tanks, and the men who slog it out face to face with the enemy in no man's-land. Indeed, we rate our discomforts and difficulties far higher - the discomforts and difficulties inevitable when living and working in the field. Scorching summer and freezing winter; clouds of dust and seas of mud; long stretches of work at high pressure and under hard conditions. It is what we have managed to do in these circumstances that we are proud of.

Finally, let me discharge some debts. I have had access to official documents belonging to 285 Wing and No. 3 M.F.P.S. In addition, various people have furnished facts, figures and dates that were beyond my ken. Not a man on the Unit but has willingly allowed me to sift his collection of photographs. The ones I have chosen are not the best pictures, but the ones that best illustrate the story). Corporal Evans has spent many hours at the typewriter, and Corporal White is responsible or the map and for the caption lettering. Above all, LAC Ward has given of his typically sound workmanship in preparing the photographic plates, which, I feel, constitute a feature that will commend itself to all who read "The Dark-Room Boys". March, 1945.

C.L.Taylor

What we are and what we do

What is No. 3 M.F.P.S. and what does it do? If the story that follows is to be read in its proper perspective, an answer is necessary to these two questions. This unit, then, is No. 3 Mobile Field Photographic Section, and its job is to do the "D and P" (developing and printing) in the aerial photography of enemy territory on which the modem army sets great store. I know what Napoleon said, but an army has always needed something more than its stomach to march on. One of the many things a modern army marches on is aerial reconnaissance. Indeed, it has been claimed that 80 per cent of our intelligence about the enemy is gained thereby. What happens on the reconnaissance sorties, with which No. 3 M.F.P.S. deals, is that a reconnaissance aircraft, or "recce kite" (generally a Spitfire), flies something like five miles high while a pair of electrically controlled cameras (one pointing slightly to port and other to starboard) take a series of photographs at time intervals calculated so that each exposure overlaps part of the area covered by the next. The most common negative size is 9 inches by 7 inches and up to 500 negatives may be exposed on the film with which each camera is fitted. That means there may be as many as 1000 different photographs on one sortie. On the other hand, a sortie specially flown to "pinpoint" a specific object (a ship, a bombed bridge, and a factory) may yield only a dozen pictures. We do not service the cameras: that is done by the photographic staff (the camera bashers), belonging to the reconnaissance squadron.

We step in when the 'plane returns to its landing ground. Our "jeep" awaits it. The magazines containing the films are taken from the Spitfire and rushed (together with the "recce" report containing technical data) to our Unit, where they are delivered to the articulated vehicle housing the continuous processing machine. The body of this vehicle is divided into two compartments. The first is a dark-room., where the film is mounted at the end of the machine an4 fed into a tank of developer and then into a first fixing bath. The operator here has the responsibility of deciding the time required for correct development. The film rid on a series of rollers, some fixed to the top of the machine and others attached to rods that can he lowered or raised to vary the time that the film remains in the developer. The film being panchromatic, the only light is very subdued green. So, in addition to the responsibility of deciding the correct development, the operator, has to endure the rigours of solitary confinement in the dark. The fact that processing is continuous also means that he is required to join (still virtually in darkness) the end of one film on to the beginning of another.

A Spitfire lands, the film magazines are removed and passed to a waiting Jeep. The pilot completes his reconnaissance report.

The magazines are rushed to the articulated vehicle where the film is processed by the CPU (continuous processing machine) and wound up onto a spool.

A second vehicle houses the office where the film is numbered on the titling bench before being passed to the printers

A third vehicle houses the multi printer which produces prints (from the films) seen on the drying drum before being cut from the print run by a hand trimmer.

Another vehicle ("J" type) is used for films which need to be processed by hand. These processed on a spool unit dipped into a series of tanks and

dried individually

Hand printing is completed in yet another vehicle (a "J" type) using either a contact printer or an enlarger.

The prints are despatched by Jeep to the Army Interpretation Unit working with 3 MFPU

Legends and Heroes |

The unit has occupied many varied sites from farm yards to railway stations. Here the Unit is set up at a wrecked hanger in Rimini Airport.

Films processed from each sortie are kept in labelled tins and stored in the "Film Library" (a trailer) for future needs.

Sortie films are put in labelled tins and stored in a trailer for future use. (Photo WARD)

Corporals Cutting and Barrow starting up the generator.

If the adhesive tape used for this purpose fails to hold and the join breaks, or looks like breaking, the crew are on their toes nursing the film, safely through the machine. Prints can be done again if they are unsatisfactory: if anything goes wrong with a film "you've had it". From the first fixing bath the film passes through a light-tight letter box in the partition separating the two compartments, and the rest of the processing takes place in normal lighting. Continuing its tortuous career, or, rather, its long series of ups and downs, the film passes through a further set of tanks - second fix, first wash, second wash and methylated spirit. From this last tank it rides on to an endless belt running round a slowly revolving drum and comes under a series of strip lights, the heat from which, together with the blast of air induced by rapidly rotating fans, dries it before it is mechanically spooled at the end of the machine. At normal speed the machine passes film through at the rate of four feet a minute. When a complete film has been wound on to the spool it is cut from the following film and is rushed into the artic (as I shall hereafter call the articulated vehicles) used, as an office. Here it is wound rapidly across a glass titling bench so that a number may be stamped on each exposure. Supplied also with a titling strip giving the necessary "gen" (information) about the sortie, the film is now ready for printing.

The bulk of the printing is done in one of the two multiprinters with which No. 3 M.F.P.S. is equipped, each housed in an artic. The general target for each is 10,000 prints a day. The maximum is far higher, the production rate being about one thousand prints an hour. When, however, the servicing and cleaning and the replenishing of solutions are taken into account the production of 10,000 prints is a useful day's work for one crew. Although the multiprinter looks very different from the continuous; processing machine the operations are similar in a general way. The machine occupies almost the full length of its vehicle and the crew of four work by yellow "safelight" illumination. The film is mounted at one end and is led to the printer-head, through which it passes in contact with the paper, fed from a roll long enough to print 1,000 exposures (prints). The responsibility resting on the man at the printer head is considerable. He has already had to decide the grade of paper best suited to the contrast of the processed film. He now, as each frame appears, has to decide the length of exposure necessary to provide the best print. There can be no correction during print development: it all depends on the exposure he sees fit to give. From the printer-head the band of paper passes into the main body of the machine, where it undergoes much the same treatment as the firm in the processing machine, riding on rollers through tanks containing developer, fixer and water. From the wash the paper passes round a drying drum (the sizzling that sometimes occurs at this stage has given the "Multiprinter" its name of "fish-frier") and the roll emerges from the machine carrying a seemingly unending string of prints, which are chopped off one by one. The pile thus accumulated is sorted in batches as required and the prints go to the office to await collection by the Army or R.A.F. Units for which they have been produced. A big sortie, from which many prints are required (for instance, a demand for four prints off a sortie containing 8oo exposures produces over 3,000 photographs) may take several hours; but an urgent job can be rushed through at great speed. On occasion, the prints from a "panic sortie", flown to show the result of the bombing of .a bridge, have been ready for the interpreters within 45 'minutes of the sortie reaching the Unit. I am content to remark baldly that this is good going. In 'describing how the Unit deals with sorties I have confined myself to the more or less mechanical methods made possible by the introduction of the continuous processing machine (CPU) and the Multiprinter. And it is true that these machines do the bulk of the work. But it would be unfair to ignore the part played by the "hand basher" (hand printer operators), between them and the machine minders there is friendly rivalry. During the first eight months of its operations the Unit had to rely on hand: processing of films and this method is still retained for occasional use on heavy days and as a reserve setup to the C.P.U. In printing, however, "hand bashing" plays a regular part in the daily production. Some film's are more suitable for hand printing; and some orders, such as a demand for an odd print off a few negatives occurring here and there on a film, are essentially a job for the hand printers.

Throughout the tour these teams (two men - a printer or exposer and a developer - work together) have made a substantial contribution to the output: in the early days, indeed, when the Multiprinter was an uncertain factor, the bulk of the work was done by hand. Fortunately the Unit has always had several brilliant teams and they have frequently put up an impressive performance. With the despatch of the prints to the appropriate interpretation unit the responsibilty of No. 3 M.F.P.S. ends. But I must mention the use to which the prints are put. Briefly, the experts to whom the pints are submitted view them "stereoscopically" (without having done this it is impossible for anyone to appreciate the extent to which the photographs are in this way "brought to life". It is as though the viewer were looking down on an actual model in high relief); and they are able to glean an amazing amount of information from them, this despite the most ingenious attempts at Camouflage. Indeed, the interpreters claim that directly or indirectly they can break down any known camouflage. The net result is that the photographs provide targets for our shells and bombs, and enable the interpreters to prepare annotated maps of enemy defences for our tanks and infantry when attacking. Deprived of such knowledge, an attack against modern defences would be almost impossible: at best, very costly. A small example will suffice. When our Unit reached one area we found among many other grim features of the vast battlefield 30 wrecked British tanks - and the graves of their crews. The tanks were lost and the men died because a group of anti-tank posts had not been detected and consequently were not marked on a map that was otherwise a miracle of detailed information about the German defences. The Interpretation of aerial photographs will make one of the most fascinating stories of the War when it comes to be told. The production of ordinary sortie prints by no means completes the work of No. 3 M.F.P.S. It has supplied the Army with many mosaics (photographic maps made by fitting together a number of aerial prints and then photographing the composite picture). Thousands of photographs of Service men have been taken for identification cards. Subjects such as enemy equipment, captured enemy defence positions showing novel features, modifications to Service aircraft, and so on, also mean occasional demands on the Unit, which runs a special section to deal with such activities.

Just one word about equipment and personnel. The photographic vehicles comprise four articulated vehicles (office, processing machine, two multiprinters); two "J types" – (darkroom vehicles that formed the basis of R.A.F. mobile photographic units before the evolution of the artics); and a variety of trailers for print drying, film files, stores, etc. Then there are several trucks (three-ton and 15-cwt), a range of generators, and a "jeep". Altogether, there are just over 20 prime moving vehicles, many of which draw a trailer when in convoy. The Unit is now (March 1945) about 8o strong. There is one officer (F/Lt T. J. Mathews, officer commanding since March 1944), one Warrant Officer, three Sergeants, and about 50 photographer Corporals and Airmen; the rest being motor transport, drivers and mechanics, electricians, instrument repairers, cooks, stores keeper, clerk, dispatch rider. That, briefly, is the "setup". But I cannot close this account of the work No. 3 M.F.P.S. without a further reference to the units with which it co-operates. No. 3 M.F.P.S. is a detachment of 336 Wing, which, from its base at San Severo, controls most of the Allied photographic work in the Central Mediterranean. But the Unit is under the operational control of 285 Wing, which also ministers to various needs, such as non photographic stores, medical attention, accounts, oversight of motor transport, and so on.

285 Wing, being responsible for tactical reconnaissance in support of the Eighth Army, has control of various squadrons that fly the sorties with which No.3 M.F.P.S. deals. For the greater part of its tour the Unit has handled sorties flown by the pilots of 683 Squadron, though in some of the earlier months it was 682 Squadron that delivered the goods. Other units

whose sorties have been processed include 40 S. A. A. F. (which made a speciality of oblique shots), 225 Squadron, A.O.P. Squadron, and 318 Polish Squadron. The consistent good work of the pilots of these squadrons is something of which the men of No. 3 M.F.P.S. are very conscious. The interpretation units with which No. 3 M.F.P.S. co-operates are (for the Army) M.A.I.U. West (Mediterranean Allied interpretation Unit, West) and (for the Royal Air Force) Ph. I. S. (Photographic Interpretation Section). The Army sorties mainly cover the battle area and strategic areas beyond and the R.A.F. sorties are generally concerned with locating targets for bombing and also assessing damage after a raid. The Unit also does work for C.B.O. (Counter Battery Officer), whose interest is enemy artillery. For a long time a panic early morning sortie has been flown when ever weather permits, to furnish C.E.O. with the latest photographs, on which to base counter-battery shoots. This is a rush job: the prints are generally available an hour or an hour-and-half from the receipt of the sorties. And I must find space of speak of the excellent relations that exist between No. 3 M.F.P.S. on the one hand and M.A.I.U., West, Ph. I. S., and C.B.O. on the other. By far the greatest bulk of orders comes from M.A.I.U., West. They will ask for anything up to 50,000 prints on one order. We think they appreciate that we try to achieve the impossible to deliver the goods: and we, in our turn, appreciate the accommodating attitude they invariably adopt, a good example of co-operation between the two Services. Talking of co-operation, I might mention in passing that it is the insistence by Main Army on 285 Wing being close to their H. Q. that has so regularly brought us on to the most forward aerodrome or landing strip - and consequently all too often all too near the front line. And, having said so much, the way is cleared for the story of the career of No. 3 M. F. P. S.

The circus sets out

Miscalled "The Blue Train", No. 3 M.F.P.S. should really be known as "The Circus" particularly as its big articulated vehicles are affectionately referred to as "The Elephants". Affectionately, that is, by the men of the Unit. To the rest of the world they are a menace: they have left a trail of wreckage from Cairo to the Plains of Lombardy, more than 13 feet high (the bigger type), over 33 feet long, and weighing more than 12 tons, these unwieldy vehicles are as so many Gulliver's in Lilliput. They have torn down power cables and telephone lines, smashed overhead lamps in many a street squeezed through narrow Italian towns (taking odd corners and balconies away with them), smashed great gaps in olive groves and such-like, created consternation among traffic controllers by requiring routes to be held specially open for them or specially large landing craft to be provided for them, and they have put hundreds of miles on to their journey by having to go circuitously about to avoid certain Bailey bridges or narrow mountain villages. While all the world wondered - wondered what they could be. They were accused of being everything from travelling brothels to Black Marias for prisoners of war.

And, of course the story of No. 3 M.F.P.S properly begins where the men and their machines got together and set out on their grand tour. But that was in Egypt so we had first better look at what came before. It was on Christmas Eve, 1942, that F/Lt May was posted Officer Commanding No. 3 M.F.P.S., a photographic train planned to go to the Middle East. He had earlier been in charge of a similar train operating in St. James's Square with G.H.Q. Home Forces, and he now invited the crew to join him under his new command. It says something for the spirit that had pervaded the unit when he was in charge that practically every man volunteered, even though it meant an overseas posting. Most of them are still with No.3 M.F.P.S. - the "old originals", Sgt Marsden, Cpl Mervill, LACs White (now corporal), Ward, Reynolds, Robertson, Greenwood, MacMillan, Baldwin, Dodd and Hewett - the foregoing being photographers; Cpl Miller, LACs Clay, Helliwell and Mc Diarmid, motor transport; Cpl Cutting, electrician; LAC Joiner, instrument repairer; and LAC (now Cpl) Evans, clerk. At Cairo, by the way, the Unit was brought up to strength by the addition of LACs Gilles, now, corporal, and Baker, (both photographers). Things happened quickly. In less than a month the men were on the high seas, bound for Egypt via the Cape. They sailed on January 17, 1943; disembarked at Cape Town, where, no ship offering, they were treated as an urgent draft and sent by train to Durban (a luxurious two day trip reminiscent of prewar travel). There they boarded a troop-ship that got them to Tewfik on March 21st.

The convoy traversing the desert.   One of the articulated vehicles at Sollum.

It was easy to become mobbed by youngsters, some wanting to sell, some asking for "baksheesh". Here the CO goes through the ordeal.

Flt Lt May, the first CO of the unit who led the convoy through the "Blue".

The ancient site of a Roman amphitheatre at Sabratha sets the stage for an ENSA concert to entertain the troops.

Legends and Heroes

They were held up in Egypt, however, for three months, during which time the vehicles arrived in penny numbers. The first came early in April and the last - well nobody quite knows because, when the movement order came in June the Multiprinter s still missing and No. 3 M.F.P.S. annexed the Multiprinter that had arrived for another photographic train then also assembling in Egypt. Altogether there were 10 vehicles - three artics and seven others. And it goes without saying that the attics were not on shore long before they mad their presence felt. When one of them was being driven from Port Tewfik to Motor Transport Base Pool, Heiwan, it decided, with characteristic flair for publicity, to break down in front of the main railway station in Cairo at peak traffic hour. Recourse was had to a tow-rope and it was while being towed that it caused an Arab tram driver to panic and leap from his moving and very crowded tram when he thought a collision inevitable. There was no collision - but what happened to the driverless tram no-one on No. 3 M.F.P.S. ever heard. The time spent in waiting for the vehicles was not entirely wasted, for every member of the Unit was given a driver's course, and some of these auxiliary drivers have continued to serve throughout the tour. LAC Dodd, for instance, has driven an artic over practically the whole of the three thousand miles that have carried the Unit from Cairo to Northern Italy. The part played by auxiliary drivers as a whole cannot he too strongly stressed. It was on June i8th that the great trek across the Western Desert began. The destination was Tripoli, where 285 Wing, which had supported the Eighth Army during the campaign now brought to a victorious conclusion, was waiting to continue the partnership in the invasion of Sicily.

No. 3 M.F.P.S. was to replace the photographic section of the Wing and so make possible an expansion of the air photographic cover on which increasing Em1portance was being laid by the Army. All sorts of trouble was cheerfully prophesied by people at M.T.B.P. The artics would never make Sollum; Derna would beat them and so on. But, in fact, the run ranks as one of the least eventful of the tour, this despite the many diversions where bridges had been blown. There were no Baileys, and a diversion across the desert and over a wadi was no joke. Fortunately, the worst that happened was that a vehicle occasionally stuck in soft sand. The much vaunted Sollum pass proved no obstacle, and the descent at Derna was safely made. The traffic controllers took no chances here: they closed the road and ordered the drivers of the artics to engage bottom gear. But if the trek was without untoward incident (if we omit the losing of a generator on the second day out, when the towing attachment broke), it teemed with interest. The route was marked by places whose names had recently rung round the world. El Alamein, Mersa Matruh, Tobruk, Barce, Benghasi,

Misurata. Each day brought new reminders of the savage campaigns of the Western Desert, campaigns that had in the previous year culminated in the triumph of "Monty" and his Eighth Army over Rommel and his Afrika Korps. Even without all this, of course, such a trip would have been memorable. Fifteen hundred miles through "The Blue": 1,500 miles of blazing midsummer sun, glaring sky and weary waste of sand but also of blue Mediterranean (in which to bathe as opportunity offered); 1,500 miles clocked in less than 13 days, including 180 miles one day, which is possibly a record for a convoy including artics. It was a good show. But at the same time the C.O. was not at all happy about the low power (27h.p.) of the artic prime movers. His fears were justified when the Unit moved through Sicily and Italy. As his successor once commented, "That a 15-cwt truck should have a higher horsepower rating than a prime mover which has to tow a 12-ton trailer is tragic". To return to "The Blue", Sormon, the headquarters of 285 Wing, was reached on June 30th. Sicily was invaded on July 10th; and on July 16th the Unit moved with Wing to Sabratha (setting of famous Roman amphitheatre: portent of the day when the train would pass through Rome itself), ready to embark at Tripoli on July 20th. It was while running to Sabratha that the Sussex J Type overturned and LAC, MacMillan hurt his leg, the injury later necessitating his removal to hospital from Sicily. The artics of course, made themselves a nuisance to the embarkation authorities. No ordinary landing craft could carry them: it was necessary to send to Sicily for tank landing craft. Meanwhile, the advance party got their vehicles on hoard (not without an up and down with the Navy whether a vehicle should make its way to the landing craft or a landing craft to the vehicle) and then some of the men indulged in high diving from the landing craft while in the harbour. The crossing of the Mediterranean was uneventful - in melancholy contrast to what awaited the party in Sicily. The troubles of No. 3 M.F.P.S. were beginning.

Double, double toil and trouble

The troubles to which I now have to refer can be quite simply explained. In the first place, the train was required to develop films as well as print them, and it just was not equipped for the work. (Indeed, the only film spool units available were F 24 type, for 5" film, modified to take F 8 size, 9" wide). Secondly, even for printing (for which the Unit was primarily designed) it was not properly equipped, because for a long time there was no water-proof paper, and without it the Multiprinter was a doubtful asset. Thirdly, the generators were quite inadequate. Fourthly, the train was absurdly understaffed. Only eleven photographers: And of these, one or more always in sick quarter's with malaria 'or some other of the ills to which flesh is heir in the Sicilian summer. Fifthly, the demands made on the Unit far exceeded what it was designed to meet. Instead of the expected maximum of 3,000 prints a day, it found itself trying to turn out several times that number - in addition to processing the sorties. Add to all this, that as a unit in the Field a e Blue Train was an experiment and had to proceed on a basis' of trial and error. To begin at the beginning, things went wrong from the moment of landing at Syracuse on July 23rd.

The traffic controllers were worried because German planes were strafing the town. They refused to allow the various drivers to wait one for the other but hustled them from the dock area and away out of the town. The result was that the various elements of the Unit found themselves scattered far and wide in odd collections of two or three vehicles. They spent the rest of the day looking for one another, but it was not until next morning that they became a united party again. Meanwhile, they "lived rough)" and more or less "on the country". The C.O. for instance, breakfasted off prickly pear. It was on July 25th that the party reached Lentini West and prepared to operate, within a few miles of where the fighting for Catania was raging. Next day brought the first sortie, the long-remembered "S 1". It was an F 8 camera and it had 400 exposures port and 400 starboard. The inadequacy of the processing equipment has already been mentioned, and there is no need to go into further details. All that need be said is that this inadequacy, together with the humidity, did their best or worst to wreck the sortie. It had to be washed in a stream, which alone speaks for the conditions under which the job was tackled. But if washing was difficult, drying was almost impossible. That evening the strange spectacle presented itself of a dozen airmen - photographers, electrician, instrument repairer, transport drivers - strung out across a Sicilian field holding a long sticky film and waving it gently in the breeze. Mosquitoes stuck to it as flies to a fly-paper; moths settled affectionately on it; wisps of vegetation draped themselves around it... The rest of the sortie went through more happily, but the work of processing and printing kept everybody hard at it all through the night - including the C.O., who put in three or four hours washing and drying prints. Orders for reprints off the first part of the sortie came in at about breakfast time, while the men were still wrestling with the initial set off the second half... The nightmare over, there came a brief respite from operations. The arties joined up on July 3oth, and the Unit moved a short distance to Lentini Francesco airfield. The rear party, in the charge of Sgt Marsden, had embarked at Tripoli on July 28th; a fortuitous call at Malta enabled them to have a quick one at Valetta; and they duly landed at Syracuse without a clue to the whereabouts of the advance party. All they could gather was that the Unit was "somewhere in the Lentini area: try D.A.F. H. Q." The artics signalised their arrival in the island first by tearing down scores of Service telephone lines around the docks and then by holding up traffic while they travelled the wrong way along a one-way road because they could not manage the right route. To round off the day, a dispatch rider who was supposed to be their guide left the party, but not before he had misdirected them. They were stopped just a mile or so short of the enemy's lines thus more or less repeating what had happened to some of the advance party. The Unit welcomed during the next few days about 10 photographers from 285 Wing. Even so, the work expected of the Unit was more than it could deal with, and a detachment of North Africa Photographic Reconnaissance Wing established itself in a neighbouring field to share the work. improvisation also helped. For instance, when one generator blew up, the Unit managed to secure a captured German generator; while a bath "borrowed" from an Italian house solved the problem of washing large numbers of prints.

That August was a hard month and a hot month, and life was rough and ready. There were no tents at first: we worked fantastic hours and slept when and where we could (I can now say we because I was among the reinforcements sent from 285 Wing). If we were unlucky and had worked all night, we snatched an hour of rest before the summer sun made sleep impossible. In the early days, too, there was no cook, though we did not grumble on that score, for Corporal Miller (in charge of motor transport) dispensed compo rations to everybody's satisfaction. While we struggled with the work, so closely linked with the bloody business that was going on around Catania, we were presented with the contrasting peacefulness of the Sicilian scene. Harvesters, wearing high-crowned broad-brimmed straw hats reminiscent of film versions of Mexico and driving teams of oxen drawing lofty cage-like carts, carried away the barley - and ably seconded by a host of gleaners, men, women, and children some of whose un-shod feet were wrapped in rags to protect them from the sharp stubble. All around were groves of oranges and lemons, leaf and fruit a rich green in contrast to the pale gloom of the olive trees. Tomatoes and melons abounded, and could be had for the asking - or the taking. Eggs and vino were ours for a trifle in the way of cigarettes - very different from the terms exacted later when the people had grown more sophisticated. Then there was the stability and splendour of the weather. Each day dawned bright and clear and the 'sun was hot within the hour. Uncomfortably hot until 10-30 or when a never failing, breeze sprang up and blew hard until sunset. Mount Etna visited us night and morning. When the sun, rose, there she stood, in bulky majesty far across the plain. In an hour she had faded, merged with the hazy heavens, and remained so until she reappeared for a short space before dying with the day. But the 'scene was not always peaceful. The camp field caught fire and all hands were needed to prevent the flames from reaching the vehicles. Then one of the photographers (modesty, forbids me to name him) revealed a penchant for arson. While burning rubbish he set fire to a hedge; the outbreak spread to the field beyond and several "bivvies" and some kit were destroyed. Meanwhile the hard battles for Sicily were being fought and won, with No. 3 M.F.P.S. getting an occasional 'backlash in the shade of air raids in the near neighbourhood.

The principal defence bastion at Catania fell on August 5th, while on August l7th the Allies entered. Messina and resistance in the island virtually came to an end. The way was paved for the invasion of Italy. As a preliminary No. 3 M.F.P.S., was ordered to move across the island to Milazzo, near Messina. But before telling the story of how we crossed Sicily, let me quote figures to show that the achievements at Lentini were by no means negligible. The Multiprinter repeatedly broke down, and when it was running, trouble generally arose through the lack of waterproof paper. During the month of August it turned out only 12,000 prints (it subsequently did more in a single day). But the hand printers had a total of 63,000, in addition to over 500 enlargements. Over 8,000 air negatives were developed, 21 ground negatives and 68 copy negatives. The sorties had covered a wide range of subjects - the battle area and the roads in the rear; almost daily cover of the Messina straits; and a complete survey of the Toe of Italy for the impending invasion. The strain on the men had been heavy. In the early days they were working for 36 hours at a stretch and on one occasion for 42 hours with only two hours sleep. During one spell the C. O. had 5½ hours sleep in 64 hours. No-one was sorry when the time came to move.

The "elephants" performing acrobatics at Cassandra – one to the right...

... and one to the left.

And then an encore at Cariati.

Frequent acrobatics have been performed by the "elephants", but we were not amused. These are just three of the predicaments in which they landed themselves

They got there in the end:
One of the strangest diversions that befell the articulated vehicles - they could not make the diversion near Scylla, so were driven through a damaged railway tunnel.

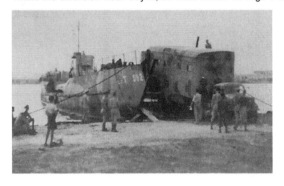

Tricky places: en route to Italy at Messina – negotiating a diversion which involved being loaded tail first onto a landing craft

This vehicle became stranded on a flooded diversion near Cerignola.

Mount Etna and Milazzo

"In theory", said the C.O. before the convoy moved off. "In theory, the second party will catch up with the first when they halt for "tiffin".

It was just another of those theories that are exploded in practice. Some of the second party got lost, somehow got ahead, spent a miserable night marooned in a misty mountain pass and were themselves caught up by the first party next day. It was September 5th and we were saying "Goodbye" to Lentini. We were scheduled to cross the broad flank of Mount Etna and set up shop on a new site near the Milazzo Peninsula in the north-east corner of the island. The Unit survived the move pretty well whole. Apart from a section of the convoy losing its way, the only misadventures were that a generator (useless as such, but serviceable in its secondary capacity as a water bowser) broke down and had to he taken in tow; that the elephant's only just squeezed through some of the narrow old towns (one of them carried away a balcony); and that a long pull and a strong pull by a bulldozer was needed before several of the heavier vehicles could be persuaded up a precipitous slope on a diversion across a dry river bed.

But if the excitement was comparatively mild, the journey was crowded with interest, the route providing an odd mixture of superb scenery and the sombre relics of recent war. Across the fertile Plain of Catania, were fields recently harvested of corn. Signs too of a grimmer harvest: hasty mounds with a rough wooden cross and a steel helmet; burnt-out vehicles; shell holes and bomb craters; shattered houses and trees. Catania airport, pockmarked, its buildings blasted flat, and the wrecks of Axis aircraft forlorn alongside perky aircraft bearing Allied markings, on towards Mount Etna. The road is bumpy and it bristles with Service vehicles joining in the great trek. A haze of white dust, through which we glimpse enclosures thick with olive trees, fig trees and vines, intermingled with little patches of corn in every nook and cranny in. the disrupted surface that speak of Etna's less tolerant days; the ubiquitous mule, always heavily laden; diversions because of broken bridges. Traffic blocks. Long delays make an average of 10 miles an hour good going. Sorry, shattered towns, to which miserable families are returning with their impoverished possessions, piled on a crazy cart; women and children waving from balconies or running alongside, calling for "biscotti" and "sigaretti". And so to a late halt for a night at the roadside - a night spent uncomfortably enough by the major part of the convoy and in misery by the nine lost souls (including four who were sick) stranded high on the flank of Etna, with little food and poor protection against the rain that poured all night. The convoy got together next day and jogged slowly on. Soon, in contrast to the black, tortured lava-covered slopes of Mount Etna appeared the broad flank of an opposing mountain, a light patchwork made of little fields of stubble - fawn, gold and brown. Between the two - Randazzo, grey and very battered. A remarkable Bailey bridge very a deep ravine below the town; and then a ten mile climb up a much hair-pinned road to the pass 4,000 feet above. We conquered and descended into a land of rare beauty, bright green valleys flowing happily between the mountains and the sea. Here and there a hill crowned with a little grey town. And through some of them we passed - though how, the drivers of our artics do not know. That night we made camp a couple of fields from the sea. Next morning the road presented us with a magnificent panorama of the coastal plain, bounded by the sea and backed by a great pile of peaks dreaming in blue haze.

And so to the new site with 285 Wing, a site so difficult for the elephants to reach that branches had to be cut away and one tree had to be chopped down. And when we reached our allotted position the ground was so soft and sandy that the vehicles sank ominously. We stayed only one night (but long enough for us to get our first sight of grapes being trodden for wine under the dusty dirty feet of laughing youngsters), and then the C.O. moved us laboriously back to the road and. along to the railway station of S. Fillppo and S. Lucia. It was an odd choice. We packed our stores in the goods shed; we converted rooms on the platform into operational quarters; and we commandeered the only rolling stock, a tanker, and used it as a water bowser (how we sweated to get it moving and how we wrestled with points to switch it to various parts of our novel section!). The station master, a solid figure of official dignity, generally wearing a pyjama jacket, used to strut about the platform seemingly oblivious of the wrecked state of the line and apparently expecting the 2-30 from Messina to arrive any time at all. Most of us camped in an adjoining vineyard-cum-olive grove - a pleasant spot affording shade and an endless supply of grapes. Not that our stay here was particularly pleasant, even with the sea near at hand for bathing, the climate was humid and there was much sickness. The work too, involved long hot hours in a stifling dark-room. There was one bright spot, however. Our arrival coincided with great good news - the surrender of Italy. Forgotten was the repugnance we had felt on seeing the grape-treading! We bought demon vino for half-a-crown a bucket and had what was really the first of many distinctive celebrations that marked our Italian tour. One man has never been allowed to forget the ardour with which he urged on his fellows another drink "because it isn't every day that Italy surrenders un-con-di-tion-ally". A polysyllabic triumph of which he was inordinately proud. On September 10th we took our first sortie on the new site and we continued busy until the day quickly came for us to join in the recently initiated invasion of Italy. We were feeling the benefit of the recruits that continued to drift in following the C.O.'s appeal for "bods". We coped with all demands, which, in the first 12 days of September (which included three days on the road) amounted to 24,000 prints. But any illusion that we were settling down to steady operations was rudely shattered by the catastrophic way in which we began our particular invasion of Italy.

Convoy hazards: "The Scharnhorst", as we called the captured water bowser, tries to emulate its namesake.

Breakdown during a dusty journey.

The enemy blew up even the smallest bridge.

The convoy crosses a big Baily bridge bear Carunchio.

Legends and Heroes | 138

The convoy leaves Vasto beach

Roadside cha or known as tea to civvies!

After a night at Venafro – note the mosquito nets over the beds.

Stranded party have a snack breakfast at Isernia.

Legends and Heroes | 139

Our far - flung train

"Branches all over Southern Italy". That became our ironical motto during the month that followed our crossing from Sicily into Italy. The original plan was simple. An advance party was to proceed to Cotrone, 150 miles east of Reggio in the underside of the Toe of Italy, and the remainder of the Unit was to stay behind until the first party was operational. But the enemy upset these arrangements. Following the surrender of Italy, the Germans pulled out rapidly from the South; the Eighth Army chased them and we chased the Eighth Army. The rear party was ordered out only two days after the first, and No. 3 M.F.P.S. (or, rather, elements of it) found themselves chasing from one aerodrome to another, trying to catch up with itself and with events. I say elements, because it was not only the rapidity with which the campaign developed that disorganised operations, but the impossibility of keeping together so heterogeneous a collection of vehicles in the conditions we found in Southern Italy. The execrable roads, the fantastic diversions where bridges had been blown, the stiff gradients and the antique structure of some of the towns caused delay upon delay, breakdown after breakdown, and even caused the artics to retrace their steps and travel hundreds of miles out of their way.

The melancholy result of all this was that the Unit was virtually off operations from the time it left Sicily until the advance party reached Foggia nearly a month later. It was a considerable time even after this before the whole Unit was got together and full scale operations could be resumed. Hence "Branches all over Southern Italy". There were times in that hectic month when one could have taken a map and pointed to a dozen spots where one or other of our vehicles could be found. To those who took part in it, the move left a nightmare memory of painful miles of buffeting, bumping and banging over bad roads and worse tracks; blistering heat and glaring sun; of discomforts, dislocations and delays; of dust, dense clouds of dust that hung over the convoy, covered vehicles and men with a grey veil and settled thickly on the trees and shrubs of an unwashed land; of poor towns and poorer people; of barefooted youngsters begging for biscuits and offering eggs and peaches; of olive groves innumerable and corn-strips interminable; of wrecked railways and bridges and mined roads; of hair raising diversions over dry river beds and mountain tracks; of meals cooked and eaten in the dark and rough beds laid down under hedge or lorry; of dejected Italian soldiers plodding wearily home from the wars. To the men of No. 3 M.F.P.S. there was the added confusion of uncertainty about what was happening. A drome would be reached, stores would be unloaded and vehicles prepared for operations, - and then off again to yet another site, another futile site. And so it continued until something like stability was reached on the Plain of Foggia. There were, of course, a score of lighter moments to lend relief to the troubles and trials of the trip. There was, for instance, the good story of young McDiarmid's faux pas. A jeep ran into the back of the lorry he was driving. He jumped down in a great rage, rushed up to the jeep and cried, "That was a blank stupid thing to do, wasn't it?" And then, noticing that the driver was an officer, he lamely added, "Sir". It is hardly possible to fit together all the jig-saw pieces of this confusing period, but here is a rough outline of what befell. The Allies invaded Italy on September 3rd, and when No.3 M.F.P.S. advance party of six vehicles (in the charge of F/LT Topsfleld, of P.H.I.S.) left Milazzo on September 14th the Eighth Army had already occupied Taranto, Brindisi and Ban. The little convoy made the best of an exceedingly bumpy journey to Messina. There F/Lt Topsfield was told that the party could not cross until the morrow. Accordingly, an attempt was made to settle for the night in a bomb-battered side street; but now came an urgent order to move to the beach. The party hastily complied, only to learn after a long wait and when it was already dark 'that the move was off once again.

Before it was light next day (12 days after the invasion) the men were attempting to snatch a breakfast when they were ordered to embark. Two vehicles were reluctant to start and were left behind. The others were reversed on to landing craft and were carried swiftly to a beach near Reggio. Here two of them followed the leader on a wrong turn, while the fourth took the right road and was not seen again by the rest until they reached the airport. Meanwhile, the others extricated themselves, eventually nosed their way through Reggio and waited for the two that had been left behind. These arrived late in the afternoon: indeed there was scarcely an hour of daylight on the road before a halt was called. Next day was dominated by diversions. The road itself was tolerable, but the fine modern bridges by which the frequent wide river beds were 'spanned were invariably blown. And the Canadians, under whose command this route came, had not been fussy in their plans for the necessary diversions. A break in the hedge, a plunge down the bank a casual passage across the stony river bed, and a precipitous climb back to the road was the routine, varied only by the differing degrees of roughness, steepness and length. One vehicle fell out during the day: the other four pulled into a station yard for the night. The following day brought the famous Montauro diversion. The Germans had blown a couple of tunnels through which the road passed and so compelled a diversion of several miles over a steep mountain road crowned by an almost it passable little town. The gradients and the hair-pin bends were bad enough, and, indeed, beat one of the vehicles, which had to be pulled off the road; but were nothing to the twists and turns and steep banks in the narrow streets of Montauro. An unending succession of war vehicles of all sorts from tanks to jeeps tore through: walls were reduced to rubble and balconies were ripped away. Our trucks contributed their fair share. And when they descended film the mountain to regain the main road the drivers discovered that they had made only about one mile of net progress. Late that night (September i7th) a final plunge in the dark over several miles of rough track brought them to their site on Cotrone airport at Cutro. The party more or less collected itself together here, and was joined by some vehicles of the rear party, though the artics had been unable to make the grade. It was at Cotrone that the tragic death occurred of Group Captain Butler, Officer Commanding 285 Wing, in an accident on the airfield. It was at Cotrone, too, that the Unit was joined by F/O Briggs, photographic officer of 285 Wing, who took charge of the party in the absence (looking after the artics) of F/Lt May. Before seeing what had happened to the artics the progress of the Unit to Foggia must be briefly outlined, without mention of the hundred and one incidents and accidents, similar to previous experiences, which befell them. The Unit left Cutro on September 24th and set up at Scanzana on September 26th. Sickness continued to take toil, and F/Lt Topsfield and Corporal Evans went into hospital from here. Gioia del Col next day (where a couple of F 24 sorties were dealt with) and Palazzo on the 30th. A little work was done here, and then, on October 5th the Unit moved to the great air base at Foggia, which had fallen on September 27th.

And now back to the artics. They were of the rear party, and the first snag was when the landing craft at Messina proved too small and the elephants had to be left behind. They crossed next day, passed the prime mover "J" type left at the roadside by the advance party, and caught up with the main body of the rear party, despite the trouble one of the antics was experiencing with its engine. This vehicle fell by the wayside next day and the other two broke down during the climb over the mountain diversion. At this juncture, a motor-cyclist with flowing moustaches descended on them: it was Corporal Rumbold, riding a machine borrowed from an Italian officer and bringing a message from F/Lt May that the elephants would never get through Montauro. The two artics were accordingly extricated, with great difficulty (there were precipitous drops waiting for the unwary) and were driven to where the other was nursing its wounds in an olive grove. A day or so later all three returned to Reggio, and the C.O. unsuccessfully scoured the area for a new engine for the one vehicle. Eventually, this artic was left behind with two men (one of whom, LAC

Reynolds, promptly had to go into hospital), and the rest of the party tried an alternative route via the north coast of the Toe and through Catanzaro to regain the south coast road only seven miles beyond the diversion that had baffled them a fortnight earlier. In other words, to cover that seven, miles, the vehicles had travelled hundreds of miles and lost two valuable weeks.

It was while on this journey that the artics made their famous run through a railway tunnel. They were unable to manage the diversion constructed at one point, and the only way open to them was through a tunnel several hundred yards long. A "J" type trailer behind one lorry was overturned during the seemingly unending pursuit of the rest of the Unit. It was not until October 7th that they caught up with the rest at Foggia. How the Unit completed its get-together is soon told. The donkey, or prime mover, of one of the artics was taken on a lorry to Reggio and harnessed to the artic waiting there. When the small party left at Milazzo in charge of stores came over, the little convoy moved off; made a long trip up the northern coast of the Toe; returned when the alleged cross-country route proved impassable; and followed the Catonzaro route, to reach Foggia some time in November. So ended a disastrous move, which brought an accumulation of accidents the like of which we fortunately never again experienced.

Through dust and ruins – many of the men travelled hundreds of hot duty miles perched on top of a lorry.

No 3 MFPS passing through battered Ancona – note the direction signs which spring up like mushrooms wherever the Army goes.

The bridge on the left has been blown and the vehicles follow a winding diversion over a dry river bed.

Legends and Heroes |

Mud and marble halls

When we exchanged Palazzo for Foggia we moved from mud into marble halls - and a month later, when we had begun to think the marble halls were ours for the winter, we were suddenly slung "back to the land". The weather broke while we were at Palazzo, and it was good news that a handsome new building awaited us at Foggia. It was the government palace, stiff with Fascist symbols, and was little damaged by the heavy bombing to which the unfortunate town had been subjected. A considerable quantity of furniture and fittings were intact too. So when we had time to get organised (work awaited us when we arrived and 'there was little leisure in the first few days or nights) we made ourselves as comfortable as service men can expect to be. Foggia is the centre of an impressive group of airfields and it seemed that the Unit might remain in the Palazzo del Governo for a long time, especially as the advance was now slowing down. The reconnaissance squadrons with which we were working took advantage of the frequent suitable days that the Italian Autumn provided, and gave us a good deal of work. The photographic section was ranged round the square at the rear of the building, and the use that was made of the facilities enabled the Unit to cope satisfactorily.

F/Lt May still had the assistance of F/O Briggs, who had a passion for improvising gadgets designed to speed production. Sometimes he struck a winner and sometimes he was not so successful. What also helped to ease the situation was the regular arrival at Foggia of reinforcements. A curious feature, incidentally, was the remarkable proportion of corporals among these recruits to No. 3 M.F.P.S. They grew until the number was 16 - nearly as many Corporals as "erks". A Flight-Sergeant also arrived; while Sergeant Marsden rejoined the Unit upon his discharge from hospital in North Africa, whither he had been sent from Sicily. On the other hand, LAC Clay, a motor transport fitter, who had done yeoman work with the vehicles, was posted home owing to ill health. It was at Fogglia that the Multiprinter began to prove its usefulness. Supplies of waterproof paper at last arrived and the figures tell their own story of increased production and the share the Multiprinter had in it. During October, 71 sorties were developed, yielding 18,026 negatives. The prints numbered 105,450 and 72 enlargements were made. November brought 86 sorties, with 19,863 negatives. Of the 100,211 prints, 38,444 were done on the Multiprinter and 62,067 by hand. The enlargements numbered 685. The sorties covered a wide range. Some dealt with the tactical battle area, others embraced strategical areas beyond the development of defences on the Sangro line was closely watched; counter-battery operations were based on photographs of artillery movements; the engineers were able to learn whit gaps they would have to span in blown bridges: shipping and ports were regularly covered; and so were aerodromes on both sides of the Adriatic. The Unit was not allowed to settle down, however. The palazzo was required by our American allies, and the new Officer Commanding 285 Wing (Wing Commander, later Group Captain E. G.L. Millington. D.F.C. broke the news that the Wing and its attachments were to move into the open. He expressed the hope that it would not be long before all were back in billets: but, as things turned out, the winter had to be spent under canvas. On November 22nd we moved 10 miles north, to a field at Triola, the site being reached only after much floundering in the mud. It was good to have fine weather for the move, but not so good when that weather brought with it six sorties, the earlier of which were processed in a completely dark trailer because no generator was available. It was a violent change from the comfort of Foggia, especially as there were few tents in the early days: some of the vehicles were used for work by day and sleep by night. But we quickly got organised, and the time passed pleasantly and busily enough until the next mile-stone was reached with the move to Vasto.

This occurred towards the end of December, so this is perhaps the point at which to record the figures for that month: 59 sorties, 1,637 negatives, 101,442 prints, and 704 enlargements. The grand totals from the time operations started in Sicily until the end of 1943 were: 290 sorties, giving 62,032 negatives; 417,949 prints, and 2,199 enlargements. It was while at Triola that the Officer Commanding 285 Wing received the following letter from a general staff intelligence officer at Eighth Army H Q:-"The recent captured document which says 'the enemy takes good pictures' prompts me to let you know that it is not by any means only tie enemy who appreciates the work of 285 Wing. The high standard and regularity of the air photographs, the persistence and skill of the pilots go a long way to provide the plan on which Eighth Army fights its battles and the defence overprints used by the gunners, the infantry and the tank commanders as well as for selecting the targets so brilliantly pulverised by the bombers and fighter-bombers in the last few days. We are very grateful. 285 Wing is doing an important job and is doing it as well as ever, which is saying a lot. We have grown used to having the best and we can rely on you always to supply it". Meanwhile, following the rapid advance that had carried them as far as Termoli by the beginning of October, the Eighth Army were now fighting hard for small gains. Late in November they forced the Sangro and by the end of the year they had taken Ortona, on the coast about 40 miles beyond

Termoli. Vasto lies between the two, and it was to Vasto that No. 3 M.F.P.S. was now ordered — Vasto, where the Unit was destined to spend six memorable months and experience strange changes of fortune.

An exhibition of captured equipment was staged at one town where the unit was stationed. A notice drew attention to the proximity of the front line.

A lorry strikes a mine near No 3 MFPS site near Rimini and an ambulance is quickly on the scene.

Some of the men reached Lanciano just after a raid and this is the sort of thing they found. What was left of railways and rolling stock would interest only a scrap metal merchant.

Vasto

If you believe in omens, the move to Vasto was ominous enough... The advance party set off one gloomy morning (gone were the dusty, blazing days on which the Unit moved during the summer) and skidded its way along roads that were greasy at best and inches deep in mud at worst. The site allotted to he Unit was a field running sharply down from the Termoli-Vasto road. A worse could hardly be imagined. The drivers had difficulty in getting on to it: to get off it was almost impossible. And there was not a level square yard. Water was many hours away, too, and if there is one thing above all others essential to a photographic unit it is a good supply of water. So, after a dismal day or two, the party was ordered to beat a retreat to Triola, where the men were accorded a full share of derision by the rear party, which had meanwhile been keeping the photographic flag flying. It was not long, however, before a fresh start was made, for a new site, on the beach below Vasto. The conditions were bad enough for the advance party, and it was dark when they found themselves plunging down the slippery slope leading from the town to the sea. But when the rear party tried to join them the conditions were still worse. This party left Triola on December 23rd and some drivers managed to get through that night - or in the early hours of the next day. Others were held up, the traffic control refusing to allow the big vehicles to proceed owing to the state of the road. The result was a couple of unpleasant nights on the road. Christmas Eve found about eight men with only a tin of bully beef between them and hunger. At Vasto arrangements had j1st been made o send a Christmas dinner to those wino were stranded when they at long last arrived, late on Christmas morning.

The Unit was complete, despite several slight accidents en route, and no praise can be too high for the way in which the auxiliary drivers had again helped the convoy to win through. Christmas Day passed as Christmas Days do in the Service - with plenty of eating and drinking. But No. 3 M.F.P.S. typically made the occasion different by shaving off moustaches. There were some strange new faces at the dinner table that day. There was no need for the men to try to make the New Year memorable: the weather did it for them. The section was quite near high-water mark, and some uneasiness had been expressed about the risk of being swamped. These forebodings proved justified when, at about three o'clock on the morning of New Year's Day, 1944, a northeasterly gale of rain and wind drove the sea at high tide far across the sands, swamping the tents and vehicles not only of No. 3 M.F.P.S., but of scores of other units that were strung for two or three miles along the beach. The sea swirled deep into the tents and there was a general panic. Scantily clad figures floundered in the dark, knee deep in icy water rescuing what they could and piling themselves and their belongings into vehicles whose floor was above the level likely to be reached by the rising flood. There is no need to dwell on the details of that melancholy night of cold and wind and rain and flood - except, perhaps, to recall that every now and then the men kept their sense of humour. Above the noise of the gale, they could be heard calling "Happy New Year!" When daylight came it revealed a sorry picture of widespread desolation. Tents were down; vehicles were axle deep in sand; others were awash; one or two had been overturned; several planes were on their back; odds and ends of Service and personal property were scattered far and wide. Salvage work proceeded apace, spade and shovel being used to dig out tents welded into the sand, while Scammells towed out the bogged vehicles. A site some little distance up the hillside was found for No. 3 M.F.P.S. But, almost before the Unit was assembled there, heavy storms swamped some of the tents and turned the site into a quagmire that caused it to be known always as "The Mud Patch". During the first few days there the Unit reached a new low in misery. We were messing with Wing, which meant that we were carried in a violently bumping truck to the beach, where, the mess tent having gone down with the rest, we ate a meal standing in the open, exposed to the full fury of apparently everlasting gale. Things gradually got better, of course, but there was always the mud, mud at least ankle deep all over the site - and stinking to high heaven. It added, in ways too numerous to mention, to the difficulties under which the work was done. And there was plenty to do.

There were many bright days as well as days of storm, and the Unit had an impressive record for January: 70 sorties, comprising 24,656 negatives; 161,549 prints (of which the Multiprinter, at last coming into its own, did 110,151, while the hand printers did 51,398); and 100 enlargements. It will be noted that the total of prints in January was 50% higher than the figure for any previous month. There were more good flying days in January than in February, for which latter month the production was: 35 sorties, with 7,757 negatives; 65,770 prints (42, I35 by Multiprinter and 23,635 by hand); and 685 enlargements. The sorties covered the now almost static battle area; road and rail communications higher up the coast; enemy defences in the Pescaro area; rail targets for R.AF. bombers; the gun line for counter-battery purposes; coastal activities on both sides of the Adriatic; and bombed targets for an assessment of the damage. So far I have said little about our contact with the Italians. But I must find space just to mention that the long stay at Vasto gave those who were so inclined an opportunity of making close acquaintance with the life and work of the peasant (very much a brother to the ox) and of the people in the little to town above the beach, a town with a literary link with England through its statue to the patriot father of the poet Rosetti. And so the winter wore away - a winter much harder than the men had expected of Sunny Italy. There was occasional frost and snow but that was a trifle compared with the wind and the rain. Great storms beat in from the Adriatic for days on end. In between, there were days of splendid sunshine, and once February was over these became more frequent and began to lengthen, while the cultivated hillsides took on a softness of form and colour prophesying that spring could nor be far behind. But before March was many days old a real change was wrought in the Unit - a change that marked a turning point in its history.

After that storm –

Vasto beach when New Years day 1944 dawned. During the night the sea (driven by a north-east gale) swamped the many units strewn along the sands.
Not a very Happy new Year!

Leaving the mud patch –

Vasto "mud patch" was reluctant to lose 3 MFPU. Most of the vehicles had to be towed, (sometimes by two lorries in tandem) and pushed before they could get through the thick mud.

In comparison the new site at Vasto beach (here seen from the air) soon wore the appearance of a holiday camp. Note the game of deck tennis in progress

Legends and Heroes | 152

Changes

For a long time the Mud Patch had been rife with rumours, rumours of change in many directions. I won't attempt to enumerate them (a Service Unit leaves a Dorca sewing meeting far behind when it comes to gossip), but deal only with these that materialised. The List great change was in the higher-up direction of the Unit. From small beginnings in North Africa, N.A.P.R.W. (the unit which, it will he remembered, worked alongside No. 3 M.F. P.S. at Lentini had expanded until it had become M.A.P.R.W. (Mediterranean Allied Photographic Reconnaissance Wing), dominating much of the Central Mediterranean aerial photography from its base at San Severo. As its name suggests, it was a combination of British and American forces, and a prime mover in its development was Colonel Elliott Roosevelt, a son of the U. S. President. It gradually assumed control over photographic personnel in Italy and elsewhere, and in due course the men of No. 3 M.F.P.S. were transferred from 285 Wing to M.A.P.R.W. But the Unit continued to operate under 285 Wing, which still provided non-photographic stores, medical service, pay, and so on.

Following this development came rumour of a change in the command of the Unit, and of the transfer to San Severo of some of the men. This rumour was borne out to the extent that F/Lt May was posted to base and was succeeded by Flight/Lieutenant T. J. Mathews, Officer Commanding No. 2 MF.P.S., which had been operating with Fifth Army on the other side of Italy. F/Lt May subsequently served in North Africa, and later in the year the men learned with regret of his death there. F/Lt Mathews brought with him Warrant Officer Cox, Sergeants Thornhill and Selby, Corporal Mason and ten men Flight Sergeant Evans returned to San Severo and a number of others from, No. 3 M.F.P.S. were also posted: for the most part they were the surplus corporals to whom reference has already been made. At the same time the Unit had important additions to its equipment, including a continuous processing machine for developing sorties, a replacement Multiprinter, a Buda generator (which gave the Unit a margin of power for the first time - but not for long), and various other items designed to increase the efficiency and productive capacity of the Unit. What, in a nutshell had happened is that the authorities, realising the importance of the work and, what is more, the still greater use that it was intended to make of aerial reconnaissance in 'the next phase of the campaign, had decided to equip the Unit accordingly. One other change contingent on all this was that the Unit moved back to Vasto beach. Not however, in quite the same circumstances as on the first occasion. A site had been carefully prepared, with hard standings for the vehicles and a sea-wall of sand to guard against a recurrence of the flood of New Year's Day. F/Lt Mathews, together with the new men and vehicles, arrived on the beach on March 6th, and the main body of No. 3 M.F. P.S. joined them on March 11th. Not without difficulty, for the track leading from the Mud Patch was almost impassable, and the vehicles were extricated only by dint of much towing and shoving. To complicate the position, seven sorties were flown that day and the result was an all day and all night session for many of the men. A spate of spring-cleaning followed. As work and weather permitted, vehicles were cleaned, overhauled and painted; and a cook-house, a showers and other facilities were built (and were known as "Cox's erections"). All this, together with the precisian with which the vehicles were arranged on the site, brought the C.O. the office of Minister of Town Planning in a mock Cabinet in 25 Wing officers' mess. Friction between the newcomers and the old hands might have been expected. In fact, there was little. With great good sense, the two parties settled lawn together and it was not long before the new men were absorbed into the general body. Circumstances helped. The weather grew more and more stable, and, having endured the rigours of an Adriatic Winter, we now enjoyed the balm of an Adriatic Spring, with its glorious sunshine, its cool breezes and its warm sea. That last month on the beach was lush - a veritable merrie month of May. The hills behind came into vivid green life for their brief season, and he vetch made bright patches of deep pink.

A stiff climb to the top brought a wide view of mountains; some with snowcapped peaks; while along the beach were rocky promontories and the place where the fishing boats were hauled. At night the fire-flies flashed mysteriously and the bull frogs were noisy (too noisy) in the reeds. Operational demands were well within the capacity of the re-equipped Unit, and we played as many of us had not played since schooldays, a light-hearted round of recreations; baseball; deck tennis; bathing and even a potted sports meeting. Hung on the traditional peg of Whit Monday, this more or less impromptu sports meeting was taken up with great enthusiasm and was a great success. The 10 events drew 150 entries - this from a unit with a strength of under 80. Great days, happy days! It was like life on a holiday camp. A visitor might even have seen a scantily clad and bare-footed airman nip out of a trailer and dash into the sea for a quick bathe between spells of work. Not that it was all play. The last months at Vasto brought a steady volume of work despite the holiday camp atmosphere. March (which had 10 days on which weather was unsuitable for flying) yielded sorties, with 18,619 negatives. Prints numbered 88,114. During April there were 68 sorties, carrying 29,537 negatives. The Multiprinter did

119,302 prints and the hand printers 33,358, a total of 152,660; and there were 1517 enlargements. The 65 May sorties contained 31,253 negatives.

The prints totaled 139,789 (multiprinters 95,282 and hand printers 44,507). Enlargements numbered '588 and ground negatives 52. The work of these three months embraced the usual wide range of aerial photographic reconnaissance - battle area; bombing and bombed targets; rear areas to detect new defences; port and shipping activities; aerodromes, etc. The preparation of mosaics, for the forthcoming offensive also made heavy demands on the pilots and the photographers. A highlight of the period was the photographing of the Pescara d, after it had been breached. The sortie was mentioned in the B.B.C. news and the photographs appeared in the Press. Novel aspects of the work included photographs of an area for anti-malarial purposes and the covering of beaches for possible landings behind the enemy lines. For the 1944 offensive lay ahead. The Eighth Army had crossed Italy to join the Fifth, west of the Appenines (while in Western Europe the "Second Front" was imminent). The time had come for No. 3 M.F.P.S. to share in the increased activities attendant of the re-opening of the campaign. During the next three or bur month's we were to be called upon to make strenuous moves and endure long bouts of hard work, during which we achieved a peak of production none of us had previously dreamed on.

Achievement

This is the proudest chapter in the story of No. 3 MF.P.S. It tells of the achievement of the Unit during the summer campaign of 1944, from the time it left Vasto at the beginning of June until it reached Rimini near the end of September, when conditions were once again approaching the static. In those four months (during which time 285 Wing generally occupied the most forward aerodrome in order to keep close to Main Army) we twice crossed the Appenines, travelled over 8oo miles (the longest run was 270 miles and the shortest 10), and were not off operations for a single day. We processed 375 sorties, yielding 170,418 negatives, and made 1,850,109 prints. During the busiest spell - July, when 550,000 prints were turned out - the number of photographers was 40, and it was only later that reinforcements arrived to relieve the situation.

But the credit for the season's achievement does not rest solely with the photographers. The frequent moves (there were 10 altogether and five in the first 30 days) laid a severe strain on the still small transport staff - four drivers and four mechanics this for more than 20 vehicles (the photographers and other trades provided the auxiliary drivers). Breakdowns were inevitable, but that the Unit was never off operations is a remarkable tribute to this small team, even when allowance is made for the general provision of Bailey bridges instead of the disastrous diversions of the previous summer. It must be remembered too, that when the Unit was established on a site it did not mean that all the vehicles were off the road. When there was no water on the site it had to be fetched and the Unit sometimes used 6,000 gallons a day. There was a ration run every two days, there were stores and supplies to haul on various occasions; there was a weekly run for N.A.A.F.I. goods (and the committee responsible for this service never let the men down); and there were a hundred and one other journeys to make.

Similarly with just two electricians; Corporal Cutting (one of the old originals) and Corporal Barrow. With five or six generators on the Unit, but never enough to provide a safe working margin, their load of anxiety (and that of the motor transport mechanics responsible for maintenance) was unending. The solitary instrument repairer, LAC Joiner (another of the original team) did not have an assistant until part way through the season, and he would be the first to agree that he could not have coped, had not the photographers included a number with an ingenious turn of mind, who were always ready to help him make repairs or to improvise (Oh, blessed word!).

So with the rest of the team. The word came automatically to my pen: but it is the right word, for if the Unit had not worked as a team No. 3 M.F.P.S. would never have stayed so long a course at so hot a pace. The figures already quoted tell something of that course and of that pace, but cannot tell the whole story. They cannot tell of the slow hot unending hours that the men worked - oftentimes only to snatch a brief rest before helping to load 20 tons of stores for a move and then perhaps taking the wheel (maybe of an arctic) for a toiling day in convoy. All the photographers worked hard, but the rest would probably agree that the greatest strain fell on the Multiprinter crews. A second Multiprinter, with four photographers, joined the train in June (without it the Unit could not have reached the figures that it did), and throughout the rest of the tour both vehicles were in constant use. The C.O. put a 20,000 ceiling on the daily production of prints, but it was frequently exceeded. There were not enough "bods" to make three shifts possible; so the men had to work in two shifts, 24 hours on and 24 hours off. No shift had to work its full 24 hours, but it was near at times; and the small hours had invariably been reached before the work, started at nine o'clock the previous morning was finished.

At the height of the summer the day temperature in the Multiprinters was a steady 100 degrees F, and for many hours on end the crew, stripped to the waist, sweated in the confined atmosphere of what to them must have seemed an infernal machine - if not a second Black Hole of Calcutta. The reek of chemicals and the heat sent many a visitor post-haste out of the half light of a multi- printer. Not one of them could understand how the men kept at it, nor could anyone else, least of all the men themselves, particularly at Castiglione of unhappy memory. It was Italian July, and the sun blazed without mercy. Work was at its most hectic: sorties, prints, reprints; sorties, prints, reprints. Sorties flown with monotonous regularity (how we all prayed for a cloud in the sky bigger than a man's hand) and in the end we (and particularly the Multiprinter crews) were almost on our knees. We kept going, and sickness was remarkably light - but the margin was narrow. And, of course, though we never stopped to think of it, the recce squadrons on the one hand and the interpretation units on the other were wearing themselves out equally with the photographers.

I need not describe in detail the tour of the Unit that summer. For one thing it ran too smoothly - and it is accidents that make news! True, there was many a breakdown, but there were none of the disasters that so drastically upset the Unit in the previous summer. So I will make it as concise as possible. Those four months were big with events. The Eighth Army had switched to the west of the Appenines. The great offensive opened on the night of May 11/12; Cassino had fallen by the 19th, after the Gustav Line, the Hitler Line; the breakthrough from the Anzio bridgehead and the fall of Rome (June 4th). Then, in August, the Eighth Army again crossed the Appenines, in their second great switch and so eventually through the Gothic Line to Rimini and the Lombardy Plain. For No. 3 M.F.P.S. the first stage was the move from Vasto to Aquino, a journey of 155 miles. A party left the 'beach on June 1st and B party remained operational until "A" party was ready to take over, was the arrangement throughout the tour. The route lay through the mountains and was studded by a series of more or less ruined towns - Cupello, Furcu, Agnone, Isernia. Venafro girded by grey mountains, was the stage for the first night, and "A" party had to spend a second night there, too, for the drome at Aquino was not ready. The journey from Venafro to Aquino next day was memorable because it took the convoy along Highway Six and through Cassino. And about Cassino there is nothing that need be said that the world does not already know.

The Unit was now close on the heels of the Army. At Aquino the German dead were still being buried and the drome was being swept for mines. There were booby traps, too. No-one from No. 3 M.F.P.S. was hurt, but others were not so lucky. One man picked a bunch of cherries and was blown to pieces. Three others lost their lives when they incautiously inspected a derelict tank. With "A" party operational on June 4th, "B" party left Vasto beach at dawn or June 5th. The convoy included all the articulated vehicles; the Unit had been virtually static for more than five months: trouble was almost inevitable. It came early. The multiprinters broke down before it was two miles beyond Vasto town, and eventually the office vehicle was pulled off the road and its "donkey" taken back to draw the Multiprinter. Other vehicles were having mechanical trouble too, while some of the Bailey bridges provided, a nice problem. One caused the artics to make as many as 17 forward and reverse movements before they could cross it. The upshot was that only a few of the vehicles made Venafro that night: two a.m. (21 hours after the start) found the last of the others pulling in at Isernia for the night.

However, they all reached Aquino by the afternoon of the next day, June 7th. And on June 10th, "A" party moved again, the shift that had just worked 21 hours (nine o'clock one morning until six o'clock the next) being required to load stores at 11 o'clock, after only a five hour break. "Just one of those things..." Most of "A" party (two vehicles fell by the wayside) reached Osa, 72 miles from Aquino, just before midnight. "B" party followed on June 12th, and on June 15th a second Multiprinter and crew arrived in response to an urgent signal about the amount of work the Unit was being expected to do. Osa had brought the Unit as near to Rome as it was likely to be, so, despite the amount of work that was being done, arrangements were made for the men to make at least time visit to the recently fallen capital. It was a case of taking time by the forelock, because on June 17th "A" party was on the road again, bound for Falerium. The 60 miles were covered in five hours; and "B" party made just as good time next day. Easily the best and most trouble-free run the Unit had enjoyed. (It also afforded a last glimpse of Rome, through which the route lay). There were plenty of other troubles however, for instance, the Unit depended on Base at San Severo more than 300 miles away, for its photographic supplies, and the rate of production repeatedly created a precarious position. At Falerium the Unit was so short of Multiprinter paper that a signal was sent for a supply by air. Before the summer was over, all sorts of supplies were being rushed to the Unit by plane - even methylated spirit. Often it was touch and go - but the Unit always just managed to cope. Water was a problem, too, for a photographic unit is a thirsty outfit - particularly its elephant. During the early part of the tour it was impossible to find a site near water, the result being that during June every gallon - 50,000 of them! - had to be carried to the Unit by water bowser from more or less distant sources. Sometimes that source was 10 miles away. The rapidity with which the campaign was developing gave No 3M.F.P.S. no peace. On June 22nd (four days after the arrival at Falerium of "B" party) "A" party moved off for Orvieto, a difficult run of nearly 70 miles. "A" party had little trouble, but "B" party was not so lucky.

The artics again! One had to be left at repair unit and another had a blow-out. The move to Orvieto nearly, involved one section of the Unit in far worse trouble. Warrants Officer Cox went ahead of "A" party to occupy the Unit site, and it was with something of a shock that he later learned that sappers found 40 mines when they swept a track over which his three vehicles had passed. The puzzled R.E. could only suppose that a timely shower of rain had caused the mines to sink a little too deep to be set off by the passage of the vehicles. At the next site (Castiglione), by the way, the C.O. had an unpleasant experience. He was driving along a track when an ox plough struck a mine in an adjoining field. The two oxen were blown to pieces. The ploughman was covered with entrails, but, was riot seriously injured. One of the disadvantages of being too close upon the heels of the enemy: when the Unit reached Castiglione the Germans were reported to be four miles ahead. Orvieto brought a breather in the sense that the convoy was left in peace until July 5th. But of work there was more than enough: every other day saw the print total top the 20.000 mark. The totals for June were: 81 sorties 35,497 negatives and 362,627 prints. There was sight-seeing to be done too, for no matter how hard they worked, the men insisted on going places when there were places to go. Orvieto was a dozen miles away, but it rewarded those who bumped through the dust to visit it. Its splendid situation (it grows out of a precipitous hill in a green valley), its narrow, clean streets, its good buildings, and its magnificent cathedral combined to afford an impressive introduction to the hill towns of this part of Italy. It was on July 5th that "A" party moved to Castiglione. It was readied without serious mishap (though "B" party again had to leave one of the artics temporarily at the roadside) and the Unit set up on what looked an attractive site - in a tree shaded enclosure quite near the lake. But Castiglione flattered to deceive; for its humidity intensified the trying nature of the Italian summer heat. Then there were the flies, mosquitoes and wasps. The flies were an all-day irritant; the mosquitoes "dive bombed" all night; and the wasps gathered in clouds wherever there was food. There was no move before the end of the month, and every day brought its busy round. The heaviest day was July 24th, when there were seven sorties, giving 4,500 negatives, and the prints totalled 28,828. The totals for the month were: - 110 sorties; 54,261 air negatives; 551,338 prints; 28 ground negatives and 150 enlargements. Each Multiprinter did over 240,000 prints and the hand printers did 58,000 prints. It was while the Unit was at Castiglione that the King visited 285 Wing. Owing to the high pressure at which the men had been working, they were excused the Wing parade on the aerodrome and they continued operations as usual. For the great spate of work was unabated.

The Wing M.O. declared that the men could not keep it up; and the Unit C.O. sent out an urgent appeal for reinforcements to make a three- shift system possible and also to allow rest for men who had had no leave for 12 months or more. Being human, many of the men probably made things worse for themselves by a sight-seeing in their free time. But with Perugia, Assisi, Cortona and other famous old hill towns of Tuscany in the neighbourhood, who shall blame them When No. 3 M.F.P.S. left Castiglione it left the worst of its troubles behind. There was still plenty of work to be done, but the conditions improved in two ways - reinforcements arrived to share the burden and the choice of sites proved very happy from the men's point of view. Particularly blessed was the removal to Malignano, near Siena. It entailed a rough dusty journey of 6 miles (which "A" party made on August 1st and "B" party on the 2nd), but was it worth it! The men felt like the Children of Israel leaving the wilderness for the Promised Land. Here was a beautiful site on the bank of a river suitable for bathing. Relays of photographers from 232 Wing enabled parties from No. 3

M.F.P.S. to enjoy short spells by the sea at Cecina, while those remaining with the Unit worked hard and played hard amid pleasant surroundings... Water polo became popular, and matches were played against various units. Thanks to a nucleus of experienced players, No. 3 M.F.P.S. generally won with ease. Another relaxation took the form of a dance at a neighbouring village, organised by the Unit and with the unit quartet providing the music, a huge number of young people from the district accepted invitations to attend and the occasion was a great success. A wine shop near the camp also provided a popular resort for relaxation.

The war moves on – This picture tells several stories. The Germans have fallen back and 3 MFPS moves on to a new site. In the centre, refugees with possessions piled on a bullock cart. On the right the French North African Ghoums are moving up

Another peacetime shot at Vasto. Fishermen take in their nets. The catch will be small but food is scarce.

.

Vasto fisherman carry on. War seems far removed from Vasto where these fishermen haul a boat onto the beach.

Legends and Heroes | 162

"All work and no play – "….So we played hard as well. At Malignano water polo was popular. After a dip it was pleasant to sunbathe and watch the others perform.

Tubby looks as though it hurts!

3 MFPS baseball team:-
Back row:
LAC's Place; Fox; Sharp; Chamberlain; Allen and WO Cox.
Front row
Sgt Thornhill; Sgt Selby; Flt Lt Mathews; LAC Kitchen; Cpl Mason.

Then there was Siena itself, only 10 miles away, lovely old town, almost untouched by the rough hand of war. Little wonder that the men of No. 3 M.F.P.S. look back on this period, and we were three weeks at Malignano, as one of the high-lights of the season. Practically the whole of the last week of August was spent by the Unit in re-crossing Italy in conjunction with the "secret" switch of the Eighth Army back to the Adriatic. It was an exciting time. "Hush, hush" was the order of the day, and the name of the Unit was blotted from each vehicle. When the time came for the move the unlucky drivers found the roads choked with other convoys also participating in the switch, and both "A" and "B" parties had to endure two long arid arduous days travelling over roads good and bad, but always dusty, and involving another trek across the mountains that form the backbone of Italy. Our destination was Chiaravalle (near Ancona) and the distance was 270 miles. After the luxury of being static for three weeks, again there was the bustle or loading and packing and pulling down tents, followed by a night in the open, a dawn call and a snack breakfast. The convoy was away by eight o' clock, but it was eight o'clock that night before all the vehicles had reported to the staging post at Foligno. Off again at seven o'clock to tackle the mountains. It was exhilarating, that climb over the pass; for the road afforded a long series of spectacular views - for the passenger. For the drivers (a reminder here, that they were mostly auxiliaries who had volunteered for the job) it was somewhat different! Despite the difficulties of the day's journey there was only one serious casualty. An old Fiat three-tonner, which had been picked up earlier and had roared its way lustily for many a mile during that season, had to be written off and abandoned at the roadside and its load transferred to other vehicles.

The convoy reached Chiaravalle after dark, staged in a convoy area, and moved on to the new site next morning. Back went three three-tonners to help "B" party carry stores (the Unit never had sufficient carrying capacity). "B" party moved at six a.m. on August 27th. A prompt casualty was again the office articulated vehicle, which fell out as early as Siena, but which caught up during the day. More serious was when the steering of a three- tonner came adrift near Perugia. Out of control, the lorry swerved into a ditch and there lay on its side. There were several men aboard, but luckily no-one was hurt. Repairs to this and other vehicles span out the day, and it was an hour short of midnight when the last driver clocked in at the staging area at Foligno. Nineteen, hours on the road, in an Italian August! And an early start next day - at 5-30 in fact. It proved worth while for, despite a long detour over a very dusty dirt track near Jesi, all the vehicles reached the site before 1900 hours. But more than one had to be incessantly coaxed over those last few miles. The complete Unit was operational by 10 o'clock next morning (August 29th) - but on August 31st, "A" party moved to Piagiolino (32 miles away), followed by "B" party next day. Despite the dislocation caused by moving, the Unit put up impressive figures in meeting the August demands made on it:

13 sorties, carrying 48,633 negatives; 491,752 prints (8,669 on the multiprinters and 43,083 by hand), in addition to 27 ground negatives and 72 enlargements. The peak day was August 14th, with five sorties (2451 negatives) and 26,983 prints.

Piagiolino was almost as pleasant as Malignano, for a tree flanked stream ran along the foot of a well-wooded hill. But in some respects it was a vicious site. Before retiring, the enemy had sown the area thick with shu mines, and more than one man had a foot blown off within sight and sound of where the Unit was encamped. Another legacy from the late campaign was that the trees along the stream had been badly cut by shrapnel, and the high wind that sprang up on several nights brought great boughs and one or two whole trees crashing down, sometimes within inches of the tents. But the site was enjoyable, and it was here, too, that the heat of the summer at long last gave place to the more temperate warmth of approaching autumn. Blessed relief, for work was still very heavy. On Sept 17th the Unit made another short step forward, to Cassandro, 27 miles away. The site was approached by a narrow track and most of the artics lay down in the ditch either on their way in or when they left for the next place. The section was set up in a farmyard, enabling the airmen and the farm people each to see how another half of the world lived. For their part, the airmen saw youths tread grapes and women use scissors to shear an unfortunate sheep; Indian corn spread to dry in the sun and tomatoes converted into puree. The Unit moved 10 miles on to Rimini on September 25th, and that move provides a convenient point at which to interrupt the story of the season's tour, for the weather was breaking and the work began to assume more reasonable proportions. What happened at Rimini and beyond, then, can be left for another chapter. And this present chapter, into which I have tried to compress all too much, can be brought to a close by quoting the impressive production figures for September: 71 Sorties, 32,000 negatives, and 444,170 prints.

Music while you work –

The Unit has its own quartet, LAC's Jones; Bateson. Buchanon and Tyce (with his home made double base) rehearse al fresco.

The Desert Air Force orchestra, (which at that time included LAC s Robertson and Baker from 3 MFPS) visited the Unit on Vasto beach.

Legends and Heroes |

Cassino and Rome – 3 MFPS passing through the dust of Cassino in early June 1944.

June also brought the Unit within reach of newly fallen Rome. The Coliseum and St. Peters were popular objectives

The hills and towns provide many a test for drivers. Leave parties travelling to Florence found snow and ice on the roads to add to the difficulties of negotiating hair pin bends

Those hill towns and those hills –
The hill towns of Italy are world famed
A view from San Marino

The aerial view of San Marino (independent republic) gives a good impression of the hill towns of Italy and the tortuous roads that lead to them.

Winter's Tale

As I have already indicated, the move to Rimini toward the end of September really marked the close of the hectic season that had opened when the Unit left Vasto beach at the beginning of June. From, this point the burden of my song is worsening weather and lower production (though many a day still saw the prints shoot well beyond the 20,000 mark and each month the total was generally at least double that of the corresponding month in the previous winter). There were fewer moves and consequently longer halts, the transition from tents to billets, and a development of what might be called social activities. One thing the autumn and winter sites did not provide - a comfortable distance from Jerry. At Rimini "A" party were entertained by the shelling of a road uncomfortably near the airfield; several nights brought air raids (during one of which a number of men on a neighbouring squadron were killed) and there were the inevitable mines to walk warily of. The airfield was particularly thickly sown - and unhappily Jerry reaped a good harvest. During the first few weeks nearly every other day saw a vehicle blown up, though fortunately the personal injuries were not often serious.

The weather at Rimini was bad. Tents were erected and the rain and the ground first became ankle deep in mud and then in many places knee deep in water. The section was housed on the concrete of a shattered hanger and the adjoining buildings offered billets for some of the men, while others sought refuge in a half-wrecked farm-house. The rest were eventually accommodated in villas half a mile away. It was at Rimini that the Unit started its "Wranglers". An average of 30 men (out of a total f 8o) met once a week to hear a talk and then discuss it. An occasional quiz proved popular too, while another feature that established itself at this time was a bar, the "Getsum Inn", where demon vino was dispensed under the management of Corporal Mervill. Football was played; occasionally there was a show by a travelling film unit; and few of the men neglected to visit San Marino, whose peaks dominated the skyline to the west. All these activities helped to compensate for the worsening weather. Then, on November 7th (after a stay of over a month), the Unit moved 10 miles up the coast to Bellaria. Unluckily, the billets the Unit had hoped to secure were not available. A good farm house sheltered a few parties; a big barn took quite a crowd; the rest were in tents. At Bellaria, where the Unit stayed until December 2nd, there was a development in the non-operational activities. The authorities were pressing the claims of education. Correspondence courses were promptly taken up, and similar keenness was shown in supporting language classes, taken by LAC Griffiths, a newcomer to the Unit. English, French and German classes were almost equally well attended. It was at Bellaria that the Unit lost Warrant Officer Cox, who returned to San Severo and was replaced by Warrant Officer Horsfall. The last move of the winter gave some of the drivers the experience of being strafed. The immunity from strafing that had been enjoyed up to this point is eloquent testimony to the air superiority gained, by the Allies: moving in convoy is sufficiently difficult without embarrassing attentions from enemy aircraft. The winter site also held one or two other unpleasantness's. It was about five miles from the front line, and we took a poor view of the consequences. It was not nice to hear overhead the whine of German shells on their way to the aerodrome a mile farther back. Bad enough in the day: a thousand times worse at nights But an even greater disturber of sleep was the barrage regularly opened up by British guns sited near the unit. We were also close enough the front line to benefit from an occasional hit-and- run raid by enemy aircraft. Several times the processing of films and the production of prints were carried out in vehicles uncomfortably close to the bomb-bursts, while the noise of flak added itself to the music of the machines the men were minding. But things got better. The enemy was eventually prised out of Faenza, and, as he was pushed back, so the noise of battle receded. These weeks saw a further extension of social activities.

A "gen" room was opened, furnished with war maps, news bulletins, official photographs, scrap book, Unit cartoon and Unit "Scandal" Sheet. Also, the prospect of being static for some time encouraged the engagement of a local priest to give lessons in Italian. Again, the entertainments committee was busy, with a series of gramophone recitals, brains trust, mock trials, quizzes, darts competitions, and on. Sergeant Marsden, sports officer, got a boxing school going, his adherents being known as the "Marsden Maulers". When weather permitted, a football team competed in the Forli League. Indeed, it seemed at times that there were almost more activities than a small unit could support, for there was still a good deal of work. But, somehow, things were kept going surprisingly well. The steady flow of work is indicated by the following figures, and there is also the unexpected fact that one bright day in January brought the Unit no fewer than 12 sorties, containing 4,680 negatives. This is a record both for sorties and for negatives. A latter-day increase, by the way, in the number of ground negatives and prints is mainly due to the Unit being required to produce nearly 2,000 identity photographs for various R.A.F. and Army formations. LAC Ward, responsible for this work, also found himself involved in a new development. He had to give instruction to a series of parities of two or three men from various units ('including Polish) that were establishing photographic sections. Needless to say, his trailer became known as No. 3 S.O.P. (Nos. 1 and 2 Schools of Photography being in Britain).

The production figures, then, for these winter months: October: 51 sorties (19,362 negatives), 266,021 aerial prints; 6o ground negatives, 250 ground prints.
November: 65 sorties (23,187 negatives), 364,684 prints.
December: 62 sorties (22,932 negatives), 252,710 prints; 282 ground negatives, and 664 ground prints.
January: 75 sorties (30,859 negatives), 223,579 prints; 124 ground negatives, and 248 ground prints.
February: 75 sorties (30,877 negatives), 245,151 prints; 51 ground negatives, and 120 ground prints.
The grand total for 1944 was 3.350,000 prints.

And, if you will insist on laying them end to end, you will have to travel as far as from London in Aberdeen to do it. To close the story here is by way of achieving an anti-climax. But it cannot be helped. Since I started I have been wishfully thinking that the European War might end before I had finished, and so provide a climax. But the great god Mars has decreed otherwise. There is still plenty of fighting to be done before we can celebrate that unconditional surrender of Germany. And when it is all over, perhaps No. 3 M.F.P.S., (as happy unit as the R.A.F. can show will be disbanded and its members scattered far and wide, some to Civvy Street, some to the East, some - who knows where? But that will not be the end. We do not intend to emulate the old soldiers and simply fade away. Plans are being made For a No. 3 M.F.P.S. Circle, with an annual reunion, at which we hope to recapture something of the spirit that has animated the Unit during its life "in the field".

© *Leading Aircraftsman C. L. TAYLOR*
(Northern Italy, March 1945)

Cutting sandwiches for Christmas, 44

Camp Life is many sided –
Air Chief Marshall Sir Arthur
Ludlow-Hewitt, Inspector General
of the RAF, visits the Unit at
Ballaria and is seen here with
Group Captain Millington and Flt
Lt Mathews.

A "celebration" in one of the tents:-

Putting finishing
touches to a home
made stove

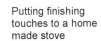

Don Leo and his language class

One side of the vino business –
Grape gathering in an Italian vineyard may make a pretty picture -
and some of the gatherers are not exactly
unattractive.

But there is another side –
The sight of grape treading is likely to put the stranger off. But these little Sicilians seem

The process is not much more appetising when the treading is done in tubs as here.
But the repugnance soon wears off and Demon Vino comes into its own again

Legends and Heroes | 173

Woman's work –
The woman's work is never done.
Here is a peasant spinning.

Typical farm yard scene with the women taking on a
big share in the stripping of the corn from the cobs.

A very common feature of the Italian countryside. Wherever there is a stream there is
a "dhobi" woman. And what would the serviceman have done without her.

Legends and Heroes

The Italian peasant with his ox plough.
A cloud of dust drifts away as the plough
share turn the light dry soil.

The inevitable bullock cart

Italian agriculture is still at the "sweat of thy brow" stage – but it makes for the
picturesque. A team of men and women cutting corn with sickles.

Postscript - May, 1945

Various circumstances have held up production so long that V. E. Day has come and gone - and so 1 can briefly round off the story of the Unit up to the time hostilities ended. Forli can now be named as the town in which we spent the winter. The last two months there - March and April - were remarkable for a return to a scale of print production comparable with that reached during the height of the previous summer, indeed, while March provided 51,889 negatives and 439,884 prints, April went one better with 51,659 negatives and 604,191 prints - more prints than in any previous month. "Perché?" as our Italian friends might say. The projected spring offensive is the explanation.

It brought Army demands on an unprecedented scale, particularly for cover of the Venetian Line. But the enemy crumbled and soon came the great news of the unconditional surrender of the Germans in Italy, which was quickly followed by a general collapse throughout Europe, leading to the long awaited V. E. Day on May 8th. Meanwhile, No. 3 M.F.P.S. had resumed its mobility. The first move was to Ferrara on May 1st, a journey of 71 miles. It was here that news was received of the German surrender in Italy - and it found the Unit almost "dry". Oh, calamity! On May 6th the Unit moved forward 8 miles to Treviso - which spelled Venice and all that Venice offers in the way of the spectacular. Many of us were lucky enough to celebrate V.E. Day in a gondola on the Grand Canal. A more orthodox celebration followed in camp that night... Shortly the breakup of the Unit seemed imminent: attachments were warned to pack for a return to their parent units, while the rest were to prepare for San Severo. But at the last minute the plans were changed, and the Unit was to accompany 285 Wing on its northerly trek. Accordingly, on May 16th No. 3 M.F.P.S. moved to Udine, under the shadow of the Alps and within easy reach of Austria.

© *Leading Aircraftsman C. L. TAYLOR*

Glossary

A guide to the RAF terminology and slang used in the story

artic – Articulated vehicle

bods – Man power

contact print – Exposing a print in close contact with the film

contrast - Tonal range of the image from black to white

CPU – Continuous Processing Unit / machine for roll film

erks – Aircraftsmen

hand basher – Photographer processing by hand methods

kite – Aircraft or aeroplane

Multiprinter – Printer and processing machine for photo paper

PR – Photo reconnaissance (Spitfire PR = Spitfire PR aircraft)

panchromatic – Film sensitive to all of the visible spectrum

paper grade – Low, medium or high contrast printing paper

recce – Reconnaissance

stereo – 3 dimensional appearance from two consecutive
pictures with 60% overlap

tiffin – Tea or lunch break (originally Royal Navy slang)

Chapter 6

Wing Commander Adrian Warburton
DSO and Bar,
DFC and Two Bars,
DFC (USA)

"The most valuable pilot in the RAF"
Marshall of the Royal Air Force Lord Tedder
when AOC-in-C Middle East

Born 1913 in Bournemouth, he was educated at St Edward's public school in 1936. He was considered a rebellious loner and a liability. However, he was physically very strong and fought like a lion, an excellent shot and top class swimmer but hated physical exercise. Previous students at the school included RAF aces Douglas Bader and Guy Gibson.

He joined the RAF in 1939 and was described as "a below average pilot" in his early days. It was also reported that he did not "fit in" with his colleagues, had difficulty with landings which were described as "more like controlled crashes!" and found to be always away from base on "training". Other comments on his report included: "Fraternised with other ranks too much" and had "embarrassing financial difficulties". He married a girl from the local pub, Betty Wescott for "all the wrong reasons" in 1939.

In 1940 his CO, Australian born Flt Lt "Titch" Whiteley had faith in young Flying Officer Warburton and gave him the chance to prove himself. Warburton was given the task on worked on opening up a route to Malta and despite Warburton's problems at home, he showed brilliance at navigation and flight planned a route from UK to Malta, which turned out to be used by many who followed. He took off in an American Maryland aircraft from England to Malta and became very adept with this particular aircraft. In September 1940, his Maryland aircraft provided long range reconnaissance and in the November he photographed the Italian fleet anchored at Taranto. Despite the extreme danger he flew in 3 times very low and under intense fire. The success of his mission resulted in the launching of an attack by Swordfish aircraft from HMS Illustrious which sank one battleship and damaged two.

In June 1940 the Island of Malta was under intense attacks from bombing raids and became a beleaguered island. Perhaps because of this he fell in love with Christina, a beautiful dancer, stranded in Malta. Their love affair become a legend and Christina made every effort to assist the islanders in their plight, so much so that they became referred to them as the "uncrowned King & Queen of Malta". He was akin to Lawrence of Arabia in looks, temperament and stature. He was certainly a bit of a loner yet of deep caring for his airmen and one of the bravest pilots in the RAF.

In February 1941 he was awarded the DFC and in the following September a Bar to the DFC. He flew 155 sorties in just 12 months, some of these included bombing raids. Whilst at a "rest" unit in Egypt he contrived to join No 2 PRU at Heliopolis and flew sorties over Crete and Sicily. He returned to Malta whilst the island was under intense air attacks. In November 1941, he continued his reconnaissance sorties with new targets – Tripoli, Messina, Palermo and Taranto bringing back the vital aerial pictures ensured the successful invasion of Italy. After 6 weeks of intense operational flying by Warburton, the Air Officer Commanding in Chief, Air Vice Marshal Hugh Pugh-Lloyd awarded him the DSO in the March of 1942. His crew of brave photographers who flew as voluntary unofficial aircrew were also rewarded. In a most exceptional and unusual award, Cpl Norman Shirley   and LAC Ron Hadden were awarded the DFM by AVM Hugh Pugh-Lloyd. The DFM is normally only awarded to official aircrew.

He converted to Spitfire PR IV's in 1942 at Heliopolis and sought out new targets which included Athens, Pireaus, Salamis, Rhodes and other Greek Islands. He also joined with USAAF "Halpro Force" based in Egypt. By 1942 the island of Malta however, was under siege and almost starving. It was desperately short of all supplies. Relief finally came by a convoy of ships which had fought it's way from Gibraltar under operation "Pedestal". Many ships had been attacked and sunk.   Warburton's return coincided with this operation "Pedestal".   Italian cruisers threatened to sink the surviving ships in the convoy. He took off to search for the enemy cruisers and found them west of Sicily. He directed Wellington bombers to attack the cruisers forcing them away from the convoy. In the November of that year he was awarded a second Bar to his DFC.   Flying over Algeria, his aircraft was damaged by German Me 109's. He managed to reach an airfield at Bone and got a lift back to base with the vital camera film magazine. He shot down a Junkers 88 during the second sortie to Bone and was promoted to Wing Commander.

The Spitfires of 69 Squadron were formed into 683 Squadron under Warburton as CO and in February 1943 as preparations for the invasion of Europe embraced the RAF and the USAAF PR squadrons including 60 SAAF Squadron. It was during this time he was to meet one Lt Col Elliot Roosevelt (son of the US President) commander of this new wing at La Marsa, near Tunis. The invasion of Sicily became a top priority in July 1943 and true to form, Warburton brought back astonishing low level pictures of the heavily defended island of Pantalleria. General Sir Harold Alexander and Air Marshal Sir Arthur Cunningham award Warburton a bar to his DSO.

The success of the Sicily landings in 1943 was directly attributed to Warburton's aerial photos. Conferred by the President of the USA, the Americans award him their DFC in January of that year. Air Chief Marshal Sir Arthur Tedder called him: "The most valuable pilot in the RAF". On the 8th September 1943, Italy surrendered. Warburton had completed 390 operational sorties and was given command of 336 Wing at La Marsa, Tunisia. The new wing had the best photo reconnaissance aircraft available: Spitfire PR Mk Mk9's and 19's, together with Mosquito PR Mk 4's and Mk 9's. sadly on 26th November 1943, Warburton's luck ran out. He crashed off the road while driving a jeep presented by Lt Col Elliot Roosevelt, and fractured his pelvis. As the weeks pass he is inevitably he is relieved of his command and the following January (1944) Elliot Roosevelt is moved to England as a full Colonel to help preparations for the Invasion of Europe.

The US Eighth Air Force strategic reconnaissance capability was formed under Col Elliot Roosevelt using Lockheed F5 reconnaissance versions of the P38 (Lightning) fighter and some Spitfire PR aircraft. 106 (Photo Reconnaissance) Group was formed comprising both USAAF and RAF strategic Squadrons. Col. Roosevelt asks for Warburton who is then appointed his deputy at Mount Farm, Oxfordshire, close to the RAF PR Headquarters at Benson. He became the RAF Liaison Officer to the US 7th Photo-Reconnaissance Group and despite latent effects of his injuries in the accident, he arranged to fly on an operational mission in the F5 Lightning. The date was the 12th April 1944 when Warburton took off in a Lockheed F5 (Ser no 42-67325), target: Schweinfurt, a ball bearing factory. Captain Charles Chapman accompanied him in second aircraft, his target was Regensburg, a Messerschmidtt factory making the new Me 262 jet fighter. Both pilots were supposed to rendevous at a position 100 miles north of Munich but Warburton failed to keep the rendevous, Chapman waited and circled, calling on his R/T but there was no reply, nothing. Chapman had no option but to continue his mission and flew on to his next location, Alghero, Sardinia and then returned to base at Mount Farm.

Warburton was never seen again. His disappearance was a complete mystery for many years. Warburton's widow Eileen was presented with his medals at Buckingham Palace. She generously gave them to his parents. He was recorded as having "no known grave". No public adulation was accorded to him as with other "aces" of the RAF. Reconnaissance was to remain a sensitive subject, especially after the war and the forthcoming "cold war", perhaps this was the reason.

Nearly 60 years later in early 2002, Dr Anton Huber made an intriguing discovery from documents he had been studying an eye witness report on wartime events at Lechfeld, a secret testing base for the Me 262 (a German jet fighter). On 12th April 1944, at11.45 local time, on the same day an American aircraft (Lightning F5) was seen over the airfield. The American aircraft was shot down by anti aircraft fire and crashed into a nearby field. The Wehrmacht found the wreck but decided to push the remaining parts on the surface into the crater. Some of this wreckage was cleared in 1951/52 during land consolidation work. Interest in the site was rekindled by German historian Dr Anton Huber who was familiar with the story behind the disappearance of Warburton.

On August 19th 2002, an excavation at this recorded site was begun. Lockheed F5 (Lightning) remains were uncovered near Lechfeld airfield, also blue fabric, possibly RAF uniform and a length of film (from a K17 camera). Human remains found at the site were sent to the USA for DNA testing with samples from Warburton's relatives. In April 2003 the DNA samples were indisputably confirmed as being from Warburton. If Warburton had seen the activity of the Me 262 jet aircraft on the base at Lechfeld, it would have been in Warburton's nature to cover this target with his cameras, his final sortie as it turned out. So nearly 60 years on his final resting place had been discovered, but that is not the end of the story.

On May 14th 2003, the Queens Colour Squadron of the RAF bore his remains with full military honours to his new resting place at Durnbach cemetery, attended by his widow, 91 years old Mrs Betty Wescott, along with surviving members of his squadrons, were present to witness the emotional event.
The rumours and mystery were finally dispelled.

Dave Humphrey 2013

References:-

"Malta Pilot"

The story of Wing Commander Adrian Warburton
DSO & Bar, DFC & 2 Bars, DFC (USA) –
"The most valuable pilot in the RAF". – Lord Tedder

The story of Warburton's fearless bravery and achievements were the subject of a BBC TV documentary shown on Channel 4, in October 2003. Produced by Mike Wadding, the documentary includes interviews with many associated with his life, and those who have researched his story. Submissions to the programme included Roy Nesbit, RAF Historian, and members of the "Medmenham Club", Mike Mockford OBE also curator of the Defence Intelligence Museum, Chicksands and Dave Humphrey curator of the Military Photography Museum at the RAF Museum Cosford. These among others have becomes fascinated with the lives of PR Pilots whose lonely and unarmed sorties into enemy territory have remained unsung for so long.

"Warburton's War" - Tony Spooner DSO DFC

The author, a pilot who served in Malta with Warburton, has been in touch with nearly 150 colleagues, including many of the ground crew who were so devoted to Warby.

The following extract is taken from
"Warburton's War"- by Tony Spooner DSO, DFC

Wing Commander Adrian Warburton (known to all as Warby) was one of the most highly decorated pilots of WW2. Fearless in the air, he won fame in Malta for his invaluable photo reconnaissance work at Tarranto, Sicily and North Africa. So invaluable that he was ordered not to make detours to shoot down enemy planes, yet he shot down nine!
Earlier he had been below-average misfit with 22 Squadron of Coastal Command. Sent to Malta to avoid trouble in the UK, and guided by an understanding CO, Australian Flt Lt "Titch" Whitely, Warby quickly became famous. Known at first as a loner, he was given his head by AOC Air Vice Marshal Hugh Pugh Lloyd. The spectacular results he achieved

enabled his unconventional behaviour to be overlooked. With his glamorous girl friend Christina, the two became part of Malta's legend, symbols of the Islands resistance. Still in Malta, Warby later became CO of first 69 and then 683 PR Squadron. After contributing greatly to the success of the Sicily landings, for which he was personally thanked by General Alexander, he commanded 336 PR Wing in North Africa.

By then he was working closely with the Americans with whom he got on so well, as he did with the Canadians and South Africans. After a serious car accident which caused him to be grounded, he returned to the UK and, thanks to his friendship with Elliot Roosevelt, the President's son, took up a liaison job with the US PR Groups at Mount Farm. On 12th April 1944 Warburton departed in an American aircraft on an unusual mission over Europe, both plane and pilot disappeared without trace, giving rise to a host of rumours that his disappearance was intentional.

William Kimber & Co Ltd – 1987   ISBN 0-7183-0661-9

-oOo-

"Eyes of the RAF" –
A History of Photo Reconnaissance
– Roy Conyers Nesbit

An accomplished author and historian on the RAF, he was approached by the Association of RAF Photography Officers to write the history of air photography *(Eyes of the RAF),*

This prompted his research into the legend of Warburton. In his article "Death of a Maverick" published in the December 2002 issue of the "Aeroplane", he reports that on August 19, 2002, a German historian in Landsberg, Dr Anton Huber began to excavate a site in a field south east of Egling near the airfield where the ME 262 was being tested during the war. It is now believed that this may be the site where Warburton crashed after being shot down by an Me 262. Relics have now been examined and sent for DNA testing by the American authorities. Among the items found were a length of 10" wide film (typical for the American K-17 camera which used a 9" x 12" format) and some parts of blue-grey coloured clothing. Subsequent DNA testing completed in the USA proved this was indeed the site where Warburton had crashed after being shot down. The mystery had been solved at last, nearly sixty years after the event.

Alan Sutton Publishing Ltd – 1996   ISBN 0 -7509-1130-1

Legends and Heroes | 183

Wg Cdr Warburton
in Malta during the
siege of the Island

Colonel Elliot Roosevelt,
son of the US president,
head of the
US photo-reconnaissance
at Mount Farm

A Lockheed P38 Lightning similar to the F5 US reconnaissance
version in which Warburton went missing April 1944

The camera installations of the Lockheed F5 aircraft

Warburton's Australian CO
in 1940,
Flt Lt "Titch" Whitley

Warburton's
photographer
Cpl Norman Shirley DFM

F24 hand held camera

Wg Commander Warburton finally laid to rest with full military honours at Durnbach Cemetery

The final farewell from his widow Mrs Betty Wescott aged 91 years

Legends and Heroes | 187

The women in Warburton's life

Betty Wescott,
whom he married in 1939

Christina –
the dancer with whom he
fell in love in Malta

Warburton's aircraft

The Martin Maryland he used for photo-reconnaissance
(the crew included photographers: Cpl Norman Shirley DFM
and LAC Ron Hadden DFM)

An American Spitfire Mk IX at Mount Farm, Oxfordshire

Chapter 7

Cpl Norman Shirley DFM

Warburton's photographer

In a letter written in 2000 to wartime colleagues Norman Shirley relates his story of the unusual award of his DFM:-

My working life has been almost entirely in University: my discipline has been Metallurgy. Photography has been an underlying theme in Radiology and Crystallography. Still a photo man you see! I took anatomy and did some original research into metal inserts into the human body, such as hip replacements. Now the answer to your query about the award of the Distinguished Flying medal (The DFM):

I had done 22 operational sorties before I arrived in Malta which, as you will recall, was under siege and there was a constant patrol of enemy fighters somewhere in the shies above and around the island. We arrived in a blaze of ack ack and dogfights, one of our pilots sailed down in his 'chute in front of us calmly lit a cigarette and just strolled away. That was Luqa in Malta. I went on to complete 13 more sorties, number 13 with F/Lt White and we were shot down by an Me109 whilst landing. We had been attacked prior to this and although I tried to persuade him to remain airborne as we were faster at sea level than a 109 (I had learned a lot front F/Lt Warburton) My pilot, Flt Lt White decided to land. As I expected they came in about halfway through our approach, I saw part of the rudder fly off and a piece of the wing then a terrific bang in front when the armour plate of the Very Light Box exploded and I was hit in several places including the left lower abdomen, which was painful. I was also hit in the teeth and spitting blood, quite unable to talk to my pilot. Benjie White landed well considering but I was busy putting out fires caused by the exploding Very Lights. I was about to leave when I saw that the air intake behind him was ablaze and he was sitting in his seat staring at it and not moving so I went along the plane put the fire out and shoved him through the cockpit sidelight. When I tried to get out myself my legs wouldn't work so he pulled me through. All wasn't over then. The IOP's sprayed both of us and also the first aid rescue services whom I thought were marvellous.

The Beaufighter did not explode and I was able to receive some treatment on the ground beside the plane before being rushed by stretcher to the Medical Room and then by ambulance to hospital. I was in a hospital bed with my legs sand-bagged apart unable to see clearly. I had just had surgery to remove a splinter of cannon shell from my left eye and my right eye was weeping in sympathy, neither could I speak properly through swollen gums and the stumps of my departed teeth.

Through the haze and pain I saw a group of officers at the foot of the bed. One of them pinned a medal on the front of my pyjamas and I was told that I had received the immediate award of the DFM. Apparently it has to be awarded within three days of the incident and is the same as the King awarding it in the heat of battle. I do not know how true this is but as you can see there is no death and glory stuff about this incident, I give it to you straight off the cuff. I apologise to you both for the rotten typing and for the presentation. I feel that we are not of this 'e-mail' generation.

Sincerely yours,
Norman.

Norman Shirley, DFM

Chapter 8

LAC Alan Fox DFM

"The Forgotten Army" –

This was the title adopted by the soldiers, sailors and airmen who fought far away from the spot light of the European campaigns. Lines of communication were vastly different from today's "instant" reporting. Apart from families of those serving in the Far East very few people at home were even aware of some of the campaigns being fought in such difficult and dangerous conditions where oppressive humidity and disease were rife. Many of those who bravely and proudly wear the Burma Star and other Far Eastern campaign decorations are quick to point this out. We include a few extracts from those who worked in the field of photo reconnaissance to illustrate the conditions which prevailed constantly. This is our tribute to those brave photographers and PR Pilots who took the fight to capture intelligence information right into the territory occupied by the Japanese Invaders

OPERATIONS IN SOUTH-EAST ASIA 1942

Extract from "ABOVE ALL UNSEEN" by Edward Leaf

LAC *Alan Fox, the* third *and last 'other rank' within the field of PR to receive the DFM during the* Second *World War, which he was awarded after flying 75 operational sorties over enemy territory.*

In India plans were laid to form a photographic reconnaissance unit from their own resources. Christened 5 PRU by Air HQ India, and commanded by Flt Lt Pearson, the unit was officially formed at Dum Dum on 11 April 1942 around the remnants of 4 PRU and those that had survived the retreat from Burma. In the absence of any other suitable aircraft 5 PRU was equipped with five Mitchell B25Cs. These aircraft had been part of an order from America for the Dutch Air Force, but the military situation in the Dutch East Indies had prevented their delivery and they were appropriated in Ceylon by the RAE They were then sent to Bangalore where all their armament was removed (the mid-upper turret was replaced by an astrodome) and mountings for three cameras were fitted in a fan over a circular 3 ft open hole cut in the fuselage floor, behind the bomb-bay fuel tank. A fourth camera was installed still further aft. Besides two pilots and a navigator, whilst on operations the aircraft also needed an extra crew member to supervise the cameras and change the magazines if necessary. Since there was no specific aircrew trade to cover this role, volunteers were called for from amongst the unit's ground-based photographic section. Of those that stepped forward, four were chosen for flying duties — Cpl R. S. Blackburn, AC G. E. Smith, and LAC's Alan Fox and B. Weighell.

In his book "*A Very Late Development*", Alan Fox describes what it was like to fly on operations:- "Most of the sorties were a mixture of monotony, some fear, aesthetic pleasure and discomfort. The B25 had its severities for the camera operator. He was isolated from the rest of the crew (first and second pilots and navigator) by the bomb-bay fuel tank, which left no more than a narrow access tunnel on top that could be wriggled through but only with a struggle. And it was difficult to feel wholly nonchalant about those 2,000 gallons of high-octane fuel sloshing about at one's back. Moreover, however grilling the heat on the ground, the temperature at operational height of around 26,000 ft was bitterly cold — especially given the large open aperture in the fuselage floor — and the full wool-lined flying clothing and boots were required, together with parachute harness on top. An oxygen mask of American design had a rubber bag in which condensed droplets of breath were apt to freeze and blow about rather disconcertingly One was often glad, too, of the leather helmet, since one of the photographer's functions, apart from being responsible for fitting his electrically operated cameras, changing magazines if required, and coping with stoppages if any, was to keep look-out through an extremely draughty astrodome at the mid-upper point in the fuselage and notify the pilots over the intercom of any threatening dots in the sky.

The AOC, Air Chief Marshal Sir Arthur Tedder, was prevailed upon to release some aircraft for PR use in South East Asia. The first Hurricanes from 2 PRU arrived with 5 PRU in April. Tom Rosser, a Spitfire pilot who began his PR operational tour on Hurricanes and also later flew some sorties on B-25s, recalls:

"The PR Hurricanes were simply fighters with the guns removed and a modified fuel system comprising a series of tanks of various shapes and sizes fitted into whatever space was available in the wings. In order to avoid airlocks, refuelling of the wing tanks began at the wing root and moved out towards the wing tip which required the use of a special funnel that could be screwed into each tank in turn. When petrol began to run into the next tank the funnel was transferred, and so on. The prudent pilot got onto the wing and supervised the process personally. The metal wings of an aircraft standing in the Bengal sun became almost too hot to handle so that by the time the refuelling was finished the pilot was soaked with perspiration, and that was before he got dressed for flying. There being no cockpit heating, he had to put on woollen socks, heavy sweater, overalls, gloves and fleece- lined boots, etc. His state as he took off and headed east can be imagined. As he gained height he became progressively cool, chilled, and finally very cold. He would have to stay that way, in his wet clothes, for at least three hours".

On the 13th May 1942, No 5 PRU was moved to a new location in Bengal which was described by Alan Fox as:-

". . The unspeakable Pandeveswar in up country Bengal. In this furnace-like plain, tents were pitched under clumps of trees, with big open latrine pits straddled by bamboo poles on which the performers propped themselves with extreme care. What bully beef was to the First World War British infantry, soya sausages were to us, and there was a general feeling that whether it proved to be a long war or a short one, it was certainly going to seem long.

Maintenance problems were severe. Every movement of wind carried sand with it and made life difficult not only for camera fitters but also for engine fitters, riggers, electricians and the other skilled trades. Temperatures of up to 115 degrees made heat exhaustion or worse a constant threat for those working on aircraft, and lesser penalties were the daily run of experience. After midday the metal of an aircraft exposed to the hot-season sun burned whoever touched it, and a fitter struggling with a tricky adjustment could feel the salty sweat stinging his eyes and the pulverizing sun draining the strength from his arms. Anyone working inside an aircraft would pray to get everything right at first time - there is not much careful patience left in a temperature of 100 degrees plus and maximum humidity."

Footnote:
Despite extensive research this seems to be one of the few personal records of a photographer which has come to light covering the war in the Far East. If anyone has further information to complete our records it would be gratefully received.   Dave Humphrey 2013

LAC Alan Fox, the third and last 'other rank' within the field of PR to receive the DFM during the Second World War, awarded after flying 75 operational sorties over enemy territory.

F/O Rothwell DFC in the cockpit of a 3 PRU B25 Mitchell. By the insignia on the fuselage side, it appears that this aircraft flew 50 PR sorties

Legends and Heroes

Chapter 9

Sqdn Ldr Howard Lees
(Photographic Officer)

No.8 Group (Pathfinders)
An interview attributed to the Bedford Museum

My name is Howard Lees, I'm 97 which perhaps accounts for me being too old for air crew during World War 2. Nevertheless I've flown in 12 different types of RAF aircraft on experimental work and managed to put in one vary moderate operation. Things didn't get really serious until after the war was over when I was machine gunned in Java and fired on doing a photo reconnaissance in a Beechcraft with Colonel Van der Post. The war was over by that tune. But coming back to the war I'd only been in the Service Just over 12 months when the Pathfinder Force was formed and at that time I was serving on an Operational Training Unit at Litchfield. Operational Training Units were used for training aircrew prior to them going on Operations. My role was to train them in the art of navigation, gunnery and bomb aiming by the use of photography rather than the actual weapons of destruction themselves. I had acquired a bit of reputation as a bit of a rebel. I got into trouble with the Station Commander for introducing my new methods without telling how but nevertheless they were approved by Bomber Command and when the Pathfinder Force I was appointed to take over the post & Photographic Officer, the Intelligence Officer at Litchfield said to me, 'What have you been up to Lees? I said, 'Nothing, why? He said, 'You must have put up a back to be posted to that man Bennett bad luck old boy!'

That was the reputation that Air Vice Marshal Bennett, who at that time was just a Group Captain, that was the sort of reputation that he had acquired, quite wrongly as it turned out. I found him a very kind and considerate man provided you did your job properly and you did it with all due modesty. One of the methods for training air crew in bomb aiming was the use of infra-red targets. We had infra-red lamps installed at various positions throughout the country; there was even one in Hyde Park, another in Benbecula, another in the yard of a tweed factory in Aberdeenshire and so forth. These infrared lights could not be seen from the air and the job of the Navigator was to find his way to these targets. And then the Bomb

Aimer took over and bombed them by operating the camera which was set to tick off the time interval for a bomb to be dropped from the prescribed height. And it recorded this flash which was in Morse code so that every infrared target could be identified differently, they recorded on the film and where the record finished was the point where the bomb was intended to strike the ground and they were assessed on those photographs accordingly. There was also a method of tracking them by day photography, similar idea. The camera was set to lake three photographs, one on release, one to link up with the first and the third, and the third one, the centre of the photograph was supposed to represent the centre of bomb strike. Now when it came to actual operations it was a different story. I'd be talking now about practicing over neutral territory where the natives were friendly but to try to do these things over enemy territory when they objected to you doing so and fired at you and tiled to bring you down was a different story entirely. Consequently night photography, which was the main object of my work in Bomber Command and with the Pathfinder Force, was a completely different story because after bomb release the obvious tendency of the crew was to take evasive action to avoid the flak and weave. Unless they were straight and level at the time when the photo flash exploded the centre of the photograph which was assessed as the point of bomb strike wouldn't be the true point because it might be taken at an oblique angle.

Shortly after I joined the Pathfinder Force a New Zealand officer came to me and showed me a close focusing device for a Leica camera and said, "How do I use this?" I explained to him how it was operated and he said "Well, I've done that and it doesn't work" I said, "What are you trying to do?"

He said "! Can't tell you, its top secret". I said "Well I'm sorry I've gone as far as I can unless you show me what you are trying to photograph, I can't help you anymore". So he went away. He came back shortly afterwards said he'd had a word with the A.O.C., that was Air Vice Marshal Bennett, and was to swear me to secrecy and show me what was called an H2S set. This was top secret at this time, it wasn't used on Operations. It was a device by which radio signals were sent to the ground, rebounded and were recorded on a cathode ray tube according to the reflection, the reflective power of the radio signal, the illumination on the cathode screen varied. For instance if these signals struck water they would be absorbed. If they struck a building they would rebound with full strength, if they struck fields, moderate strength and so forth. So they formed a picture on the cathode ray tube, a very rough guide of the ground beneath. It was to be used by navigators to find their way to the target. Anyway, I told him were he'd gone wrong and fixed it all up and that was that. It wasn't used for some time afterwards because strangely enough although it was a war winning device it daren't be used In case the enemy got hold of it so it seemed rather pointless. But it was eventually brought into use and I remember very well the first night it was used on operations. I drove to three different Pathfinder Stations, collected eight Leica cameras that we'd bought on local purchase because we hadn't got a special camera for the job. There are pictures of them with these rings that 1 had made. I collected eight cameras and had the films developed. We produced 41 negatives and that night I produced 287 enlargements, loft each - that was 5'x5' prints from 35mm film plus contact strip of three rows of titling which had to be done as a separate operation.

I had to get one set of these photographs to Donald Bennett at RAF Wyton by nine o'clock the following morning for him to fly down with to Bomber Command, which was accomplished. The other operation was night photography, which I regret to say I criticised on my training session at the School of Photography at Farnborough. I had the audacity to say "That is a bit Heath Robinson, isn't it?" I was very firmly put in my place and they said, "That's how it says in the book and that's how you do it.!" Well it was just stupid because you could not possibly say that the centre of a photograph was where the bomb strike would be, because it was d done by timing. The timing was upset by weather conditions, by evasive action to avoid flak and the behaviour of the photo flash. Now the photo flash was device about 40 inches long and about 4½ inches in diameter which was set to explode at 0.6 of the height of the aircraft with a with a trail angle of 60° of the angle of view of the lens - flash and illuminate the ground and when the photograph was taken. The aircraft returned and the photograph was printed. The interpreters plotted the centre of the photograph as the point of bomb strike.

Well of course the aircrew were very indignant indeed! They knew jolly well they'd hit the target or said they had, but the centre of the photograph was probably some fields, about three miles away due the fact that it had been taken at an oblique angle. I went to the Station at Graveley, and went over the bombing range in daylight to drop a flash and see how it misbehaved because I had my own theories about it. Now the Halifax has a door which is curved partly underneath the fuselage and is ideal for hanging one's head down outside to see what goes on, which I did - very securely tied in! And looked underneath the aircraft and watched the flash emerge from the other side and as soon as it cane out into the slipstream it cart wheeled.

Now the flash is operated by a propeller on the beck which has a pin through the shaft. The shaft of the propeller had a hole in it with a pin through it. And so that pin is attached to a lanyard which is secured in the aircraft. And when the flash falls out of the flare chute that tightens - pulls the pin out, leaves the propeller free to revolve in the slipstream. And when it is fully released and flies off, it releases the firing pin to start the fuse which is preset according to the prescribed bombing height of the aircraft. But it didn't quite work out like that, because when this cart wheeled the propeller would go that way but when the flash was going through the air that way the propeller would go back the other way. So the timing was completely upset and to plot the centre of the photograph was just stupid. So I went to Air Vice Marshal Bennett and said, "Could I have a flash produced to be dropped with the bombs, streamlined, shaped like a bomb, with the same ballistics and he said, "Lees, bomb hooks are used for killing Germans not for taking their photographs!" So that was that.

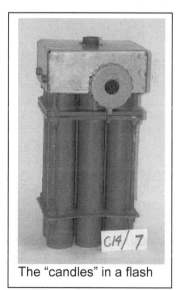

The "candles" in a flash

Then I had the idea! Target indicators which we used for marking the target are dropped from the bomb bay, from bomb hooks, why not have a

Target Indicator incorporated with the flash? Now the Target Indicator was a bomb casing of 250lb. a boot casing containing 60, what we called "candles" - they are like roman candles, fireworks which were either red, green or yellow according to the colours of the night They were ejected from the rear of the cylinder, of the bomb cascading to earth and marked the target. So I asked Bennett if we could have sonic of these candles removed and a flash put in their place and he thought that was a good idea. We had 20 candles taken out leaving 40 to mark the target and the flash put in the place of the other 20. The flash was ejected with them and instead of bursting after the aircraft -it burst in the view of the lens. And wherever the flash burst was recorded on the Win and the point over which the Target Indicators cascaded and that gave you an accurate indication - even if the flash was recorded in the corner of the photograph, we plotted that — and not the middle. So that was one idea. I had a car that was used throughout the war for staff duties and when I invented this Target Indicator photo flash and it was ready Bennett sent for me. I went to his office and he said, "Lees, your toy is ready! Pick it up from Wyton bomb dump take it to Feltwell and have it dropped on Rushford range and let me have a report on it". So I drove all the way to Feltwell, over very dilapidated state of the roads in those days with this bomb bouncing up and down on the back seat!

The F 97 Night camera with two lens units

Another idea that I developed - these are whet you call fire tracks (looking at an aerial print of multiple fire trails in the night sky). The Photographic

Officer from Bomber Command visited me one day shortly after I'd joined Pathfinders and said, "Have you got a suggestion for overcoming the problem of fire tracks on night photographs?" And I thought for a minute and I'm not usually very bright but for some mysterious reason it just came to me immediately. "Yes, why not have two shutters, two lenses. Two shutters operating alternatively. Instead of leaving the shutter open for eight seconds, during which time you get these fire tracks recorded and the more fires that there are on the ground the less chance you have of recording any ground detail. Instead of recording these as lines they'd be cut down to the length of time it took one shutter to expose and energise the solenoid of the second shutter which would take its turn. The two would operate for a period of eight seconds, alternatively, so that either A or B or as we called them, the Master or the Slave would record the flash and get the photograph that would reduce all that interference. It showed the actual location of the fires on the ground and that's how it worked out. But coming back to Air Vice Marshal Bennett, I mentioned that he had a reputation of being a bit of a tyrant but in actual fact he was a very kind man and very considerate.

Once he sent for me and said that he wanted me to take a summary of evidence from an Officer who was confined to his quarters because he was suspected of not going to the target, what we called LMP (Lacking Moral Fibre). I protested- I said, "I'm sorry sir, but it's not fair to ask me to do this because I've not been through what he goes through. I've no experience of Operations. If you'll let me go on an Operation, I'll be better qualified to take a summary of evidence". And he stood up behind his desk and thundered at me end said, "Lees, it's your duty, men are dying every night" and he said it with a real passion. That man felt, in fact I've seen him almost in tears when we've had a very bad night, a lot of losses. He felt it personally and that was the true nature of the man. I was very proud to serve under him. He worked 24 hours a day; he never took any leave at all. We had to follow he example. I had seven days leave and that was sick leave alter a quinsy and I worked seven days a week, 14 hours -24 hours a day and we all did and we were proud to do for that man - that was a true man!

What I remember of VE Day is Don Bennett's Personal Assistant said, "You are wanted, Lees". So I reported to Bennett's office and there was the Senior Air Staff Officer, three or four Wing Commanders and Mrs. Bennett. And Bennett said, 'For you Lees, the war is over". And that was aft I knew about VE Day. I didn't even have a drink of water let alone champagne. He was a teetotaller and we just dispersed aid went back to work. The following day I tried get to Peterborough with three navigation officers. Take them in my car to Peterborough for a bit of a spree and got stuck on the Al with my master cylinder gone and the car wouldn't move. That was my celebration of VE Day!

Howard Lees

Author's note:

This story was taken from "Flashback", the RAF Photographers Association Newsletter, summer - 2006

On March 16th 2006 Howard Lees died aged 98. His main claim to fame as far as the Royal Air Force goes must be that he was the Photographic Officer to number 8PFF Group, The Pathfinders. Because of his work to further and enhance aerial photography during WW2 he became a close friend of the Pathfinders founder, Donald Bennett. In order to assist in proving kills' from Bombers he developed a 2 shutter camera which enabled the target to be clearly seen after a raid. He also developed a means of photographing the screen of the H2S, the radar device which greatly assisted navigating to the target in the first place. He had always been interested in photography from an early age and frequently had articles published in photographic journals. He played a major role in helping us to win WW2.

Two legends: Howard Lees with Jack Eggleston

Chapter 10

Group Captain Peter Lewer OBE FBIPP
(Photographic Officer)

The desperate need for a man to continue and improve the quality of aerial reconnaissance both during and after the second world war was embodied in the experience and brilliance of Group Captain Peter Lewer.

Group Captain Peter Lewer
OBE FBIPP

A man of great vision, he came through the early traumas of the war as an air photographer and an air gunner. In 1942 he was selected for a commission and completed the technical officers course. Soon after he was working in India on air surveys, also designing and installing reconnaissance systems in Liberators for long range operations. Some of the work involved clandestine operations for intelligence acquisitions over the Indian Ocean. He also became involved with research and development work for the Royal Navy on gradient assessment of beaches for potential landings. It was during this time that among his many achievements he started to apply himself to the production of environmental control systems for reconnaissance exploitation laboratories. In 1945 he achieved a rare distinction (in those days), in being appointed to command a flying unit as a technical officer. The unit was the Reconnaissance Systems Development Flight in Ceylon, which was equipped with Mosquito aircraft. His work included design of reconnaissance systems and the use of infra red and colour separation principles. He was also designing hazemeters and airborne exposure meters whilst investigating the effects of atmospheric haze on optical systems.

After the war he returned to the UK with Coastal Command but was soon selected for an exchange appointment with the Royal Canadian Air Force as 2nd in command of the Reconnaissance Development Establishment at Rockliffe, Ontario. He then went to work on the design of systems for Lancaster Aircraft covering the African Surveys in conjunction with the Director of Colonial Surveys, and this was followed by an on site review of the German opto mechanical industry. The objective being to exploit and develop the potential to produce high altitude and long range surveillance cameras. The introduction of the Canberra PR 3, 7 and 9 soon followed. The mid fifties found him designing and producing a fleet of mobile imagery exploitation laboratories for use with the five reconnaissance squadrons in Germany, in conjunction with the Von Lienen works in Bochum, Germany. It was to be the foundation stone of things to come. The Malaysian and Borneo campaign placed heavy demands on updating maps and charts with the Directorate of Military Survey. It was during this time he co-operated with the Royal Australian Air Force in the development of imagery exploitation systems.

By 1960 he had risen to the rank of Wing Commander and then returned to Germany, providing technical support for the reconnaissance force and its mobile exploitation laboratories. He oversaw the acceptance trials of the new low level, high speed cameras using auto exposure control and image movement compensation. Four years later he was on the staff of the Assistant Chief of Air Staff (Operations) and undertook to reorganise the reconnaissance system and support services in the RAF. As a result of his efforts the Air Force Board recognised the profession of photo technology and formed a new and separate branch under the Director General Engineering. A new structure of training, standards and career patterns was formed for technicians and operators. In 1967 he was promoted to Group Captain as the first Deputy Director of Engineering (Photo Technology) (RAE). He was now responsible for the direction, management and training of some 2,000 officers and technicians. In 1969 he became the Commanding Officer of No 4 School of Technical Training as part of the Air secretary's policy for broader based appointments. This culminated in a move to HQ Training Command responsible for dealing with 500 courses in ten schools of technical training and the RAF College, Cranwell.

He retired from the Royal Air Force in 1973 to pursue a new career as the Training Director of the Multi Occupational Training and Education Centre (MOTEC), the residential training centre of the Road Transport

Industry Training Board. He became a consultant in management, recruiting, industrial relations and training. His operations were primarily in the UK but included Europe, USA and Australia. It is a fitting tribute to his Royal Air Force career that during his service with the Royal Air Force it became the most efficient, versatile and mobile reconnaissance system in the world.

The following pictures were on display in the Museum and illustrated key moments in WW2 photo reconnaissance achievements:

The "Freya" radar unit on the French coast at Bruneval
Scene of the first combined operation in WW2

Sqdn Ldr Tony Hill, who provided the vital pictures used in the raid at Bruneval

The F 24 camera used by Tony Hill being fitted to a Spitfire

Flt Lt Constance Babington –Smith the photo interpreter who finally identified the V1 and V2 launch site at Peenemunde

Post strike photo
showing the bomb
damage to the
V1 and V2 launch
site at Peenemunde

The iconic post
strike photo of the
Möhne Dam by
617 Squadron

"Behind the Lens"

Luce Scribimus - we write with light

A lifetime in military photography

"Behind the Lens"

Contents

Author's Introduction

"Behind the Lens" - *A lifetime in military photography*

The official crest of the RAF School of Photography includes the Latin inscription "Luce Scribimus" which translates to "we write with light". The primary objective of the military photographer is to reproduce an image through a camera system which is permanent, accurate and reproducible, whether that image is produced from the "wet film" or digital process.

I became part of the photographic (and reconnaissance) world back in 1957, when I joined the training at the then RAF School of Photography at Wellesbourne-Mountford, near Stratford-on-Avon. The mechanical cycle of the F 52 air camera gearbox and the early marks of the F95 air camera were faithfully memorised. The MPP 5 x 4 press camera using double dark slides was my first introduction to "ground" hand held photography, soon to be replaced by the Rolleiflex twin lens roll film camera. This was the age when monochrome was king and colour photography was an infrequent luxury, not considered practical (or cost effective) for military everyday purposes. And it was not until many years later that colour became a serious contender for every day public relations and operational needs.

I was also privileged to be an Instructor for 23 years at the School of Photography. I recall the magical birth of the digital age with the introduction of the first Kodak digital camera, which cost about £15,000 and used a very small mega pixel CCD chip! It now resides in our museum collection. The capacity of the digital camera and its massive potential for military use started as a trickle and then became a torrent of progress and a phenomenal asset to the training capabilities. Since retiring in 2004, I have been astounded even further by the advent of the UAV reconnaissance systems as seen with increasing revelation by the world's media coverage of current conflict zones.

Some of the young students who attended the school are now themselves instructors and some hold senior management posts there, looking after the interests of the new generation of trainees. It is also a fitting tribute to the disciplines instilled by the early founders of the training school in 1915, whose bench marks were the firm foundations on which the highest standards of image quality achieved today, remains as it was then, just 100 years ago.

Dave Humphrey 2013

Chapter 1 - Formative Years

I was born too late to take part in the Battle of Britain being six months old at the time, but I can lay claim to being a war baby and all that this entailed... Rationing was in full force and our "Anderson" shelter had pride of place in the centre of our back garden, the smell of damp sand and hessian sacking still brings back vivid memories of the sand bags around the shelter entrance. The Pheasey Estate and Tynedale Crescent was a privately built enterprise by Henry Boot located in those days within Staffordshire County. The local Collingwood Drive School was the home to the US army G Is billeted there and became the centre of attention around Christmas time when they held parties for the local children. It must have been 1944 when I attended one of these and I recall being given a large pink candy bar. I had no idea what it was and spent a while testing it for breakage on the nearest object before I was shown the error of my ways by a chap who unwrapped it for me to eat. Seriously, it was the first time I had seen that kind of sweet as my mom usually made toffee apples at home. There were a number of unkind tales about a blonde lady called Mrs. Walter who lived in our street. She was perhaps more hospitable to the US servicemen than others who were quick to criticise but eager to share the cigarettes and nylons she generously distributed, not to mention the extra food and sugar she also gave away to anyone she felt in need.

This was a time of extreme austerity, obesity being unheard of and utility standards being the bench mark of all manufacturing for home consumption. Powdered egg and "Pom" potato mash powder were often the necessary substitute if you did not grow your own or have chickens in the back garden. Collingwood Drive School was still being used in 1945 by the last remnants of the US Army before repatriation back home. The day of their final departure I well remember. We were stood around watching the huge trucks load up as the soldiers were climbing aboard slinging their kit bags over the tail board. When they saw the crowds gathering they began to empty their pockets of all their loose change and hand it out to the children watching. A huge soldier came near and I must have caught his attention with my wide eyes staring as he was as black as coal and the first coloured man I had ever seen in real life. His took my two tiny hands in his huge fist and plonked a stack of coins into them. I could barley hold them and they were all large silver pieces amounting to more than ten shillings, a small fortune to us (if you think a man's wages were then around £4 a week!). It was typical of their generosity and despite the popular myths of those less informed, in our experience their manners and behaviour were always beyond reproach.

In the 1940's and 1950's class distinction was much more prevalent than today. How I ended up passing the eleven plus exam for the grammar school, was in itself a bit of a drama. From 1945 until 1951, my primary education was at a tiny Roman Catholic school called "Maryvale", at the bottom of Oscott Hill in Great Barr, Birmingham. It was recently exposed to International fame due to its connections with Cardinal Newman and the recent Popes visit to the UK. The headmaster in 1950 was Mr. Wright, a tall, balding man with horn rimmed glasses, who always appeared wearing a grey suit. He was a strict disciplinarian (as were most teachers in those days), whatever he said and decided, stood unquestionably. His "co-pilot" in the school regime was a Miss O'Conner, with a like minded disposition. She was very large, ("broad beamed" as my father would say) with a mouth, which I recall, resembled a JCB bucket. She wore mostly tweed skirts and heavy brogue shoes which she pounded on the ground to warn timorous pupils of her impending passage. She was rightly feared by all (including our compliant Headmaster) having a very domineering personality. She was a self appointed censor, determined to filter all potential candidates for the 11 plus entrance exam to grammar schools with only those, she would decide were certain of success.

To this end any weak performers were dismissed as lack of guaranteed results, which also included those who had missed some measure of schooling through ill health. I was deemed to be one of those as I had suffered greatly from the age of two, with mastoids, an extremely painful disease of the skull bone behind both ears. Every winter the cold had wrought havoc with this painful condition and penicillin injections three times a day became the cure all. It almost became the kill or cure as I developed a nasty allergy to it after many years of being stabbed with the huge needle necessary to deliver the thick liquid. After eight operations on my head, I contracted an abscess on the mastoid when I was just turned ten. This, for some mystical reason had stopped the annual recurrence of the problem. Many years later when I met my second wife Carole in 1995, she was also a victim of this crippling pain from mastoids as a child in 1945. She is the only other person that I have met to have suffered from this disease. My long suffering mom was appalled when she heard that I had been excluded from the list of the 11 plus candidates because of my ill health. She had always been ready and willing to hear the other point of view when faced with any form of confrontation ("life's too short, anything for a bit of peace and quiet"). So to my utter amazement she descended on the school to fight my corner. I was called to the headmaster's office where the headmaster and the thunderous Miss O'Conner were emphatically stonewalling my mom's constructive arguments as to the injustice of their decision. To my shock and horror she stood up and declared she was not about to see my chances of a decent education be rolled into the ground by an "overzealous and pompous pair of idiots". I will ever remember the slack JCB bucket jaw of Miss O'Conner dragging itself up to a closed position in stunned silence as she turned a into a vivid beetroot colour around the face. Mr. Wright was also pretty stunned but I suspect was more fearful of the imminent explosion form his "co-pilot" and chose to follow the rule that discretion was the better part of valour. He made mutterings (or was it spluttering?) about the school not being held responsible if I failed the exam and left the office before the walls imploded. What I did not know at this time, was that my mom had previously visited the Birmingham Education Offices and discovered from a very sympathetic school inspector, that I was perfectly entitled to sit the 11 plus, (as was every other school pupil). Some weeks later my mom received the papers saying I had passed the 11 plus (along with just one other candidate from Maryvale School) and I would be granted entrance to St Phillips Grammar School. I think it was the proudest moment of mom's life and my mom went up ten fold in my estimation and has stayed there ever since. The new school was located next to the Oratory and again had historical connections with Cardinal Newman, so it also became a point of call on the recent Pope's visit during the beatification procedures towards sainthood of the famous Cardinal.

It was January 1952, the year that Princess Elizabeth became Queen Elizabeth on the death of her father George VI. It was also the time that my mother gave birth to my brother Martin. It must have been a difficult time for my mother, as the social climate in those days was not so supportive to women having children later in life. The twelve years between me and my brother meant she had to abandon any ideas of a working career to help support the family in the austere times of post war rationing (which in fact continued through to 1954). My father managed to find extra work at weekends with a man who ran a bicycle shop and lived on a small farm in Doe Bank Lane. "Uncle" Frank Wheelock as we were obliged to call him seemed to spend most Sunday lunchtimes in our home and I always resented his somewhat patronising attitude. He considered himself a sort of landed gentry (which was far from the reality) but he put on airs and graces to the point of ridicule. My sister Marion had a remarkable gift for mimicry and she would have us in stitches after his post Sunday lunch departure with uncanny replay of his ludicrous upper class behaviour. My poor brother Martin became the butt of sibling rivalry at times, understandably, his needs demanded most of our mother's attention and I suppose we became a bit frustrated as children with not too much patience to spare. All in all however, we became a pretty cohesive bunch against the odds and unified against any external threat to the family wellbeing. Some years later, my brother proved to have unique qualities in writing for commercial journals. He also had the patience of Job later in life, when he chose to look after my mother and father throughout their elder years whilst working effectively from their home. He successfully combined his lifestyle with their needs in care and comfort, remaining with them throughout the rest of their lives. It is the best tribute I can place on record as without his sterling effort we would all have been in difficult situations.

My days at St Phillips were filled with hard work, lots of sport and more somewhat severe discipline. Corporal punishment in those days was quite normal and no student as far as I know became a mass murderer, sadist or paedophile from our school. Frankly we didn't have the time or energy left! My art teacher, Mr. Goethe was very clever at getting us to appreciate all manner of art and craft along with many other teachers who were exceptionally gifted to inspire and educate through their imaginative patience and enthusiasm. It was probably these influences which kick started my interest in photography through the wonder of geometry, physics, chemistry and art, a very useful combination as it turned out. The school also encouraged students to join its own Air Training Corps Squadron which allowed me to indulge in my passion for aircraft, flying and the RAF. My father had regaled us with many stories of his wartime experiences as an engine mechanic working on Spitfires, Wellington and Lancaster bombers. At the outbreak of the war he had started at Cosford, Tern Hill and Prees Heath, before landing in North Africa and then moving up into Italy. I found out many years later that he had worked on the photo reconnaissance Spitfire Squadrons which my colleague and mentor Jack Eggleston has also been attached to as a photographer in the RAF. My story is full of many such coincidences which have always given me great pleasure to relate. My two elder sisters; Annette and Marion were probably the leading influence in my interest in all things RAF as they were members of the W.Aux.A.F. the weekend auxiliaries who trained to support the regular RAF. The were "stationed" at Castle Bromwich, an airfield just opposite the factory site where the Spitfires had been assembled during the war and tested by the famous Squadron Leader Alex Henshaw. They trained as radar plotters and thoroughly enjoyed the role especially as it often gave an opportunity for an experience flight in the Airspeed Oxford aircraft used to act as invading targets for the radar units. I do recall their favourite films of that era. "Angels One Five" was a fictional story based on the experiences of many stations during the Battle of Britain. It starred John Gregson as a young fighter pilot and Jack Hawkins as the stern Group

Captain. Another favourite was the American production "Twelve O'clock High" with Gregory Peck as a Commander of a bomber squadron and Dean Jagger as his loyal deputy adjutant set in the Cambridge area of East Anglia. Like many teenagers of their time they swooned at anything which was remotely connected to their film idols and I suppose it became an infectious fascination for me, though being just 14 at the time understandably, I was not always included in their social world. I was however; very fortunate to be allowed to join an experience flight in an Airspeed Oxford on one Sunday morning and I can still remember the thrill of being invited into the co-pilots seat for the whole mission. As a young easily influenced lad, it made my day when the pilot (and I still remember his name: Flt Lt Oliver) told me to take over the controls whilst he went to relieve himself after a long leg of the flight. I was absolutely mesmerised but had enough nous to remember my experiences in the Link trainer (a crude simulator which taught the rudiments of flight control). I am not actually bragging when he remarked that I had a good aptitude for flying and he kindly let me keep control for what seemed to be a very long time, changing course each time to his directed new headings. I don't remember the bus journey home but I knew from that moment on I would someday follow my father into the RAF.

Chapter 2 - 1954 Latent Images Develop!

My early childhood memories are of the privations of a wartime Britain, with rationing and little or no spare money available for any of today's necessary "luxuries". Furniture and materials were in very short supply with the mantra of "make do and mend" being the normal thinking everywhere. All items manufactured during this time had to be marked with a special "utility" standard label or marking to show that they conformed to Government rules on minimum wastage and maximum functionality. "Designer" labels were never heard of! Frugal was more the in word then. This life style continued for many until 1954 when rationing was finally withdrawn and rare commodities came from "under the counter" to be placed on sale to everyone.

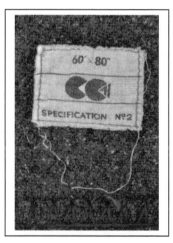

The wartime "utility standard" mark on a blanket

I was fourteen then and the world was at my feet, or so I imagined. My mom had bought me a Kodak Coronet camera for my birthday which had a plug in detachable flash gun. It was a simple solid shiny black plastic camera with no adjustments and a white shutter release button. I can still recall the almost comforting smell from the plastic safety coating of the little magnesium flash bulbs ("PF14" I think they were called) There was no boss on the camera for a tripod to be fitted so I made a crude rigid wooden three legged version with a hardboard plate on the top. It didn't need a tripod at all because the shutter was fixed at a standard 125th of a second duration, but I felt it made me look the part a bit more, so I would plonk the camera on top and walk around my subjects as if I had some idea of what the hell I was doing. Frankly I did not and most of my musings were a form of posturing in a desperate attempt to impress (mostly, my dear old Mom, who indulged my whims so generously). Mom was a very special person in my life and like most of us I did not really appreciate at the time, the enormous sacrifices and stress my "whims" and demands made upon her. Mom was actually far more intelligent than I realised as a young lad. My father was a self educated "scouser" who had passed for grammar school but his parents were unable to consider the costs to send him there and so he had spent a great deal of his young life reading all manner of books (probably borrowed from the library and friends). He was able to hold well informed conversations "above his station" and surprised a number of those who would judge him by "class" distinction.   We often went up to Liverpool to visit my Grandma (my father's mother) who lived in Alverstone Road, Wavertree, just around the corner from the now famous Penny Lane. Her home was a wonderful place for us as children, full of ancient and beautiful items from the Victorian era.

She was a wonderful person with the most tolerant and loving disposition. The house stood in a terraced row with three stories available including the attic. The front door had a huge round brass knob and a highly polished brass letter box which the embossed word "letters" had been almost rubbed away over many years of careful attention. The door step was also a place where Grandma had knelt for years scrubbing it clean and rubbing it red with the "Cardinal" red polish. Set in the door was the most wonderful stained glass, which became spectacular in our eyes when the sun shone through it. The "parlour" however was a very special place only to be visited under the closest of supervision. So naturally we would sneak in there to ride on the wonderful large turtle shell she used to cover the huge fireplace. It made a wonderful "boat" or whatever we cared to imagine it as. However we never got away with it and for many years we thought Grandma had psychic powers to be able to tell we had sneaked in to play. She told me many years later that she used to sweep the carpet in one direction with the carpet sweeper so when she looked across the pile she could see any footprints in the pile! She had been absolutely resolute in resisting the new electrification introduced many years previously to all other homes in the road. She was terrified of what "they" may put down the wires. She always called it "electrickery". Eventually she had the only gas lit home in Liverpool. Her greatest attribute was her wonderful cooking which she conducted on the "black leaded" cast iron cooking range. She kept it immaculate and always in full working order. We loved the wonderful "scouse" stews she would leave simmering for hours on end. When she died at the age of 94 her home was a living working tribute to Victoriana and I was so upset when the council dismissed its unique quality for the sake of "progress".

Chapter 3 - 1956: A Working Lad

By the time I was 16, I finished school and I joined the "Nicholls Dorrity" advertising agency in the now famous jewellery quarter of Birmingham as an illustrator. I was of course head tea boy and "gofer" for the production manager Roy Langford an ex RAF Mosquito fighter pilot (complete with handlebar moustache) who regaled me with many fascinating tales of his exploits during the war. He was a very kind and understanding man who often protected me from the dreadful ribbings of the established artists in the illustrating department. He would have been around late thirties, slim and endowed with "dashing good looks" as they said in those days. He also had a great sense of humour and suffered my incompetence with gracious patience and paternal fortitude. The bosses, (there were two) Nick Nicholls and Mr. Dorrity, were wonderful characters, both so very different yet a wonderful complimentary team. Mr. Dorrity was a short wavy haired middle aged man of a stocky build and yet always wore very well cut smart suit and enjoyed a high standard of living.

The old Nicholls Dorrity advertising agency studios
in the jewellery quarter, Vittoria Street, Birmingham

He was definitely the business "brains" behind the company and knew a great many important people in the TV and "media world" (as we would now call it). Nick Nicholls was a tall elegant and pedantic man, with features not dissimilar to those of Sir John Gielgud the actor, he was probably near his late fifties with a wonderful laid back disposition. He was highly tolerant of the mad artist staff (and just wanted to be one of the boys on the illustrator's bench really). He was a fantastic artist in his own right and I vividly recall him demonstrating to me how to draw a near perfect circle completely freehand.

"When you can do that, old son, you can call yourself an illustrator".

I was always impressed as to the ease which all the illustrators could draw typefaces and company logos with such deadly accuracy and apparent ease. Unlike today's "graphic designers" who need complicated computer programmes to accomplish the same.

I was also seconded to the in-house photo studio, which gave me wonderful opportunities to see some really creative photography. I was really smitten with this side of the business and craftily wangled every opportunity to spend time there. It was around this time I acquired a Vespa scooter, complete with tan duffle coat and "Corker" crash helmet! I felt like a real trendy teenager fresh out the college campus! I changed it's colour to a very bright red body with glossy black lumps which covered the engine and gear box. I got hold of a length of new black plastic hose and carefully cut it lengthways so it could be pushed over the edging of the leg shield to give it a black contrasting edge to the fire engine red. It almost resembled a ladybird insect but it was a fantastic little bike and I have never seen another with such trendy looks! I was also allowed to join the team at the ATV studios in Aston Road to see Noelle Gordon presenting a programme called "It's a Woman's World" in which she promoted our clients products ("Barbers Tea" was one I recall). I also had the privilege of meeting Kenneth Horne (the director of Chad Valley toys at the time) at these studio sessions. All in all it was pretty heady stuff and although I was only earning £1 10shillings a week, I was gaining some very useful experiences in what is now termed "people skills".

My yearning to become more involved with photography pushed me into seeking alternative employment, which, with the wisdom of hindsight, was a hasty move born of youthful impatience. So I searched the local papers and took up an opportunity to join a small photography studio under a Mr. Reg Cave, in Solihull on the southern outskirts of Birmingham. As the studio assistant, making tea, fetching and carrying heavy kit and being the general dogsbody seemed to be my lot. My foreman and working boss was a chap called Arthur who was very patient and had a knack of explaining things simply and effectively. I managed to learn the rudiments of the photo process quite quickly with his guidance and trust I also acted as "back up" photographer at wedding locations. I was not impressed with the behaviour of some of the wedding guests at these functions. There was always an amateur photo chap (usually a relative of the family) who crept up behind the official photographer and tried to scoop the picture through the professional efforts of Arthur. I felt quite angry that these cheapskates would try to cash in on the efforts of others but he was always firmly patient and polite. I respected him greatly for this and the fact that he was really taking quite a chance on me. Reg the boss, however, was beginning to moan about "the high cost of training has to come out of profits". I was also introduced to the workings of the VN folding plate camera which I think was a German manufacture and used a high speed focal plane shutter. The glass plates were half plate in size and used a metal dark slide holder to fit in the back of the camera at the focal plane.

I was however very thrilled when the boss announced we were going to the Rover testing circuit to cover a special event, the trials of the first ever gas turbine jet propelled car in the world!. We collected a ton of kit and I was allowed to load up a very nice Ilford Envoy folding camera which I had become proficient with as the back up man. It was a remarkable experience and I managed to consume six rolls of film in rapid succession as the huge black Rover coupe (which is the only way I can describe its appearance) screamed round the banked test circuit sounding just like the jet fighter aircraft I had seen at Castle Bromwich air displays. We were not allowed to photograph the engine or detailed bits but the pictures we came back with still stick in my memory and sometimes I see the car again on TV documentaries of the old motoring days. I have always been intrigued as to why the jet car was not developed into a viable product, as it was an awesome beast, to say the least! There was one day which I declare as my day of triumph over arrogance. We were covering a high society wedding and the boss had got it into his head that we could be the first to provide the fastest processing turnaround in the country. He had adapted the little Ford van as a miniature mobile darkroom to process the film and thus save an hour or so as we travelled back to the studio. Wonderful idea, but not tried and tested as my foreman tried to argue. The boss was having no dissent and appointed me as the on board processor, only because I was then small enough to squeeze inside. The kit was carefully stowed and the van checked for any light leaks which were quickly covered with black bodge tape. The roll film processors and plate processors were put into their fitted racks (made by the boss the night before!) processing solutions and temperatures checked, wash/rinse tanks topped up and off we went. The day went well with your truly acting as back up man using ten rolls of film which I kept unprocessed in my bag as it was unlikely they would be used for the client (as usual). I suppose it was because of my unstressed demeanour that I really felt I had some winners "in the can". It was a pleasant summer's day as we started back with me fumbling around in the back of the little van. Despite the rocking and rolling movement I managed to load the roll film processors and the plate processing tanks but I was aware that the temperature in the van was now very warm (with no ventilation!). The journey took a lot longer than planned due to traffic congestion caused by a football match! Shortly before we arrived I had the films fixed and rinsed so we were able to open up and I just about fell out, suffering from cramp, bruising and heat exhaustion, not a happy bunny by any yard stick! The boss dismissed my state of health as part of the learning curve, which I thought was a bit callous. Arthur was much more sympathetic and fed me gallons of water (as an old soldier he obviously knew I was in a bit of a state). The boss was dashing about getting the films into the proper wash when he finally got a chance to view the images.

I will always remember the wail emanating from the processing room as he screamed at me "Where's my bloody pictures you imbecile!"

I was aghast, as was Arthur, when we saw yards of clear film and plates of clear glass being carefully washed in the darkroom. Not even a faint latent image was apparent! Arthur being the experienced operator that he was dashed to the Ford van flung open the doors and examined the processing tanks.

"Here's your bloody pictures Reg, in the bottom of the tanks, it must be over 100 degrees in there".

The rising high temperatures, the long delayed journey and the constant rocking of the van as it journeyed back was enough to melt off the photo emulsion coatings and leave them in the bottom of the tanks like a grey slime!

I thought the boss was going to need an ambulance until Arthur said quite calmly "Well Reg, young David has no doubt got some good stuff in the bag. I watched him duplicate all our shots, so let's see if that high cost of training has paid off".

It had, sounds a bit conceited, and I apologise for that, but Arthur had given me the best he had to offer in encouragement and patience, and to his credit, not really mine it really had "paid off". The boss just fell silent, but to his credit I did earn a fat bonus for "saving his bacon" as it were. Sadly I could not see much of a future with Reg Cave and his studio but I was grateful for the experience gained which stood me well in later life. The opportunity to join a specialist reprographics company in the centre of Birmingham at Newhall Street came by way of an advert in a newspaper.

R W Brown created huge photographic prints by special projection enlargers on rails for exhibitions such as the annual British Industries Fair held at the Castle Bromwich Industrial site. My first introduction to this method was courtesy of Alan, a Scottish chap in his mid thirties, who had suffered a withered arm from polio as a child, but he was more than capable of producing some outstanding work with this huge enlarger and processed the giant rolls of exposed photo paper (40" wide) by holding one end and hurling the rest of the roll down a very long processing sinks, each filled with a 4" level of developer, stop bath and fixer. He then frantically rolled it up creating the appropriate agitation and then upended the roll to turn it over and repeat the process until he judged it was "cooked". I was mesmerised by his ability to manipulate his withered arm with such poise and dexterity during this processing cycle, that it changed my judgmental attitude to disabilities for ever.

My first "live" run at such a task came when I was told to enlarge a sectioned drawing of a nuclear reactor built by British Thompson Houston which was going on display at the aforementioned industries fair. Alan showed me how to use smaller test strips of photo paper in critical positions likely to require some form of shading during exposure, dependant on the image being projected. We had to stand on steps to reach these areas during the exposure which would often take 30 minutes or more. For this reason the negatives used were made into a very large glass plate negative to prevent any curling or distortion occurring during these long exposure times. We then had the exhausting task of pinning large rolls of photo paper into position on the wall like wall paper (without the paste!). Keeping the material flat and working in very dim amber safelight was not without its discomfort. By the end of the exposure you would know where you arm sockets and leg muscles were as the ache and pain quickly reminded you. Alan, of course was a lot more used to it all and would chide me as, being a fit youngster, I should be able to manage better than him. Then came the processing, like I said it was all physical and you had to time it just right or you would be in serious trouble with a roll of under or over developed 40" wide paper up to 15 feet in length, costing more than a few bob to say the least. But Alan knew all the tricks of handling such cumbersome rolls which had to avoid paper stretch and distortion, which to the unwary, could be as much as 6 inches over a 15 feet length roll. He was also a very patient and good teacher. I must have been very fortunate on reflection and without really realising how much good experienced knowledge these guys were passing on. To their credit it stuck and stuck well as I was to use every ounce of this experience in later years. I loved to work on these large projections with the huge negatives. There was something very satisfying about seeing your handiwork on display in a huge exhibition hall and hear the comments of people around you. Up to that time I certainly had never seen photographic print images measuring 30 to 40 feet wide by 15 feet high. After many discussions with Alan I realised just how much I still did not know and the task of acquiring the necessary skills seemed intangible. At that time not many colleges ran courses for budding photographers and those who did were located too far away for me to reach. The impending prospect of National Service was also uppermost in my mind and I certainly did not relish the thought of a career with the army as a clerk or footslogging infantryman. Alan suggested I looked at volunteering to join the RAF as a regular for a three year stint and I could possibly get to choose a trade as a photographer. He assured me the training was probably the best on offer and at least I would be doing something I wanted to do.

Chapter 4 - 1957 Per Ardua Ad Astra

The RAF influence was still as strong as ever and the only barrier that could have prevented my ambition was my old arch enemy mastoiditis of the ears. Even in those days (the late 1950's) you had to be fit to be accepted into the military (even in National Service). So it was with some trepidation that I went along to the initial medical inspection after going through the recruitment office procedures. To my horror the medical officer dismissed my enthusiasm with a terse "Not fit young man, so that is that!" I was absolutely deflated as the prospect of ambitions vaporised. I went home and told my Mom, who just looked at me and said "You don't give in that easy if it's what you really want do you?" She contacted the recruitment office and asked if there was any alternative medical expert available who they would accept as verification to my fitness. They suggested a consultant from the ENT hospital in Birmingham who turned out to be the surgeon who had operated on my mastoiditis many years ago in Bromsgrove, his name was Dr Schneider. I did not expect him to remember me as it was so many years ago since we last met. To my utter surprise he recalled exactly why, what and when he had operated on the back of my ears. He made a very thorough examination and I began to feel that I was not going to fulfill my ambition.

After writing many notes on the forms he just looked up and said "Well you're clear and perfectly fine as far I can tell, so best of luck and I hope you like the RAF".

I thanked him profusely and promised to let him know how I got on (which I actually did, for once!). A few weeks later I received the papers of acceptance with instructions to use the enclosed travel warrants to report to the induction centre at Cardington.

On our arrival at Cardington I was looking for a particular hangar which my father had told me about. The famous R 101 airship had once been housed there in a huge hangar and sure enough, the huge hanger was still there, sadly, the R 101 was no longer to be seen. It was all very cordial though a little something was not quite there. No big welcome aboard or anything like that, so I was a tiny bit suspicious that things were going to change fairly soon. We were divided up into groups of around twenty. In one of our groups was a chap from Scotland called Andrew who seemed to be quite a bit older than the rest of us and later when we were kitted out he was certainly treated with some sort of deference compared to the rest.

Some of the clerks were keen to flex their muscle of "authority" and one leading aircraftsman took pleasure in ensuring we called him "L.A.C." I was aware that he really was just a classic pratt and deliberately referred to his rank as L.O.C. which gave him a bit of a fit, especially when I walked away pretending to be half deaf and oblivious to his ranting. Later, in the wooden billet, we sat around sorting out our kit and trying to ensure we could steal a march on our next part of the "process" i.e. shining our hob-nailed boots and buffing the brass buttons. Andrew was very accomplished at this and within a short time he had "spooned" his boot toe caps (using a heated spoon as a hot smoothing iron) and used spit and polish to bring up an amazing mirror like gleam. It was when he started to open the issue "housewife" (a handy set of needles and cotton wrapped in a green material folder) and sewed on a couple of medal ribbons that it dawned on me. Andrew I found out later, was an ex soldier who had fought with the "Glorious" Glosters in the Korean War as the Korean UN war medal clearly showed. He had said nothing of this to any of us but curiosity eventually won the day and we plucked up the courage to ask him about the medals and why he was now in the RAF. It turned out he left the army a few years ago but could not settle or find a suitable job. He was married with two children and he had tried to persuade his wife to agree to him re joining the army, but after his luck had held previously she insisted he joined a less dangerous occupation and the RAF seemed to be the best compromise in every way. He was going to be trained in the RAF Regiment as a gunner, a form of soldiering, which he thought would make the best use of his skills. Needless to say he was a mine of useful information and we eagerly soaked up every morsel of hot tips and don't do's.

We finally completed the initial induction process and were lined up for despatch by train to the various basic training camps. Rumours were abound as to which camp was the worst "boot" camp. Some said Padgate, others said Bridgnorth, neither of which were familiar to me. Wearing our stiff new uniforms and boots we approached the train carriages struggling with our cumbersome kit bags and were unceremoniously bundled aboard in a nasty portend of things to come! My destination was Wilmslow, about which I knew zero! However on of my co travellers was keen to tell us that the WRAF was also trained there so we did have our anxious spirits lifted by this news. The crescendo of yelling and screaming came to us out of the blue as the train pulled to a standstill. A mad whirling dervish dressed in RAF uniform flashed by our window, crashed through the door and literally began hauling us out onto the platform where boots and big sticks (pace sticks) flashed around our rear ends and heads as we tried to escape the venom of these lunatics. I saw two stripes on one blokes arm and a white belt around his waist, but that was almost the last I saw as I was thrown into the back of an RAF 3 ton lorry followed by my weighty kit bag which took the wind out of me completely. We scrabbled around in the back of the lorry trying to find our own hats and kit bags as we sped up the road at what seemed 60 mph. "Welcome to Wilmslow" someone said in the truck and we started to see the funnier side of it all, not for long however, as the lorry came to a deliberate crash stop and flung us all up the front. The reverse procedure followed and this time I managed to stay on my feet as I landed on the gravel roadway, some of my fellow travellers were not quite so lucky and got a painful gravel rash as a souvenir! The ginger haired Corporal Drill Instructor stood ramrod straight waiting for the groans and moans to subside and then he started. The usual soldierly expletives I shall not repeat but we were all illegitimate and useless "pouffs" fresh from the teddy bears picnic. The rage continued for a short while then he screamed indecipherable orders which none of us understood (as was the intention) which gave him the excuse to deliver more of the same.

Eventually the tirade subsided and we "double marched" (ran like fun) up this hill which slowly became a mountain as our breath ran out and our energy levels faded. We reached the wooden huts which were to be our home for the next eight weeks (always assuming we actually survived of course). Crashing through the doors we collapsed on steel framed beds (nothing else was on them!) and we lay there sucking in air at such a rate, had there been curtain, we would have swallowed them whole! The ginger haired tyrant stepped into the room behind us, carefully placing his mirror shined boots on the gleaming brown linoleum floor.

"On your feet, NOW", he screamed.

We jumped and forgot to ask how high on the way up.

"My name is Corporal Allen, I was born with that name", he paused for effect.

"You will never forget it". He was right, I never have.

"When I speak to you, you will listen. You will say "yes corporal" or "no corporal. You will not speak to me unless I demand it, is that clear?"

A chorus of "Yes corporal" followed, but was not loud enough for him.

"What did you say, I can't hear you" he bellowed, followed by a chorus bellowed "Yes corporal".

"I have no mom and dad, so that makes me a complete bastard. Take my word for it, you will have no doubt about that, by the time I'm finished with you".

Again he was absolutely right, he was the most complete illegitimate sod I ever met. We were not privileged to wear the RAF uniform yet as we were not considered "trained" airmen. Instead we wore a green all in one boiler suit and marched everywhere in columns of three. At meal times we marched to the cookhouse with our issued "irons" (knife, fork and spoon) and white ceramic mug held in our left hand behind our back. This left our right hand and arm free to be swung up to shoulder height whilst marching and of course available for saluting (should we ever meet an officer).

Physical training (or PT as it was known) required us to change at lightning speed ("You have 30 seconds to get changed into PT kit starting ten seconds ago") when we arrived at the gym. We were introduced to the "medicine ball" during these keep fit sessions. This was a huge and heavy leather covered round solid lump (probably filled with sand, we thought) which you had to pass to each other with increasing velocity until your arms fell off or you collapsed, whichever came first, often at the same time! I had an amazing and lucky escape on one occasion. It was during an exercise designed to teach us a bit about escape and evasion, though I was never quite sure where I would be to need such skills, in a photographic darkroom perhaps? It was freezing cold and we wore the appropriate clothing, blue PT shorts, white PT vest, thick socks and hob-nailed boots, ideal for stealth when escaping and evading! We were dropped off the back of a 3 tonner (lorry) in the middle of nowhere, divided into teams of two, given a map and compass to get back to base, best we could without being caught by the Land Rover mounted patrols out looking for us. They forgot to switch off the sun for that day, but there was no melting of the snow and we had one option to keep warm, keep moving, ever so fast if possible! My mate Bob and I were bobbing along a country road at a fair rate and looking for suitable hides continually to avoid the disgrace of being first to be "lifted", not to mention the rumours of what might befall you if you were caught. We were well into our stride and had covered a good mileage when it was time for a compass and location check.

We were sitting on a low wall which we thought would be useful if we heard the approach of the dreaded Land Rover patrol. Bob was a good navigator and I picked up some very useful ideas from him so we were feeling pretty cocky when we heard the distinctive sound of the Land Rover engine cruising somewhere in the distance. We listened harder and suddenly we heard it coming round the bend. Bob rolled over the wall backwards without a second glance, I was slower to react and saw that it was a farmers Land Rover, so did not follow Bob. I leaned over to tell Bob who was now lying twenty five feet below the wall and very, very still. The farmer pulled up as I frantically waved him down and told him what happened. He quickly found a rope from inside his cab and I shinned down to see what state Bob was in. He was out cold and could have had broken limbs. The farmer, bless his cotton socks knew there was a phone box down the lane and drove to it. He came back with some blankets and a first aid kit which was sufficient to tend Bob's cuts and bruises but we needed

Behind the Lens |

professional help and quickly as the falling temperature were adding to the emergency. Right on queue the RAF Land Rover patrol turned up and out jumped Corporal bloody Allen. I was expecting the usual tirade of abuse and had it in my mind to lay him out if he started. Instead he weighed up the situation in a glance, and without a word, cleared the wall and literally dropped the twenty five feet or so landing without harm as a paratrooper would and checked Bob over just as the ambulance bell sounded its arrival.

They were pretty switched on and had notified the fire brigade who arrived as well. Corporal Allen was obviously a very experienced first aider along with his other hidden attributes and, not one to miss an opportunity to instruct, showed me how to apply splints to Bob's one broken leg, just as the medical boys climbed down to add their expertise. They were impressed, but not so much as me. I still hated the sod, though. By the end of the eight long weeks, he did manage to turn a shambling bunch of complete stumblebums into a cohesive well-organised team whose drill choreography would have made a West End Show producer proud. As time went on at Wilmslow we learned that Corporal Allen had joined Wilmslow boot camp fresh from the Queens Colour Squadron. His knowledge and performance of drill routines was actually a delight to behold and he almost succeeded in turning us into a poor mans replica of that Squadron. I have to say we were the best drill team seen to pass out from Wilmslow for many years and I do feel grateful for that (I was privileged to be the right guide and marker, a key position on that occasion).

Chapter 5 - 1958 – The Learning Curve

The trauma of "square bashing" and the return to normality was a great relief, especially as I was about to start on my chosen career of photography with RAF in the Trade Group 14 as a photographer. In 1958 the photographer trade was divided in to that of: general servicer or "GS" as it was known (dealing with the needs of general photography); reconnaissance servicer or "RS" as it was known (loading, fitting, unloading and servicing of air cameras for aerial reconnaissance); and bulk processor or "BP" as it was known (processing and printing aerial films and prints by machine equipment). So here was I as a trainee AC 2 (Airman 2nd class) about to be launched as a Reconnaissance Servicer along with nine other shiny raw students. Experienced airmen who had completed a number of years in either of these trades returned as Senior Aircraftsmen (SAC's) to complete a "Photo II" course which was designed to create an all round operator incorporating all three of those basic skills of the "splinter" trades as they were referred to. These students could then be selected for eventual promotion to the Junior NCO level. The advanced "Photo I" course was designed for those Junior NCOs to be eventually selected for promotion to Senior NCO levels. I have always found it strange that the RAF (and the military in general) like reversing numerical sequences from 2 to 1, as they did with the ranks of the Warrant Officers i.e. WO II being a lower rank than WO I. I have never discovered the reason for this illogical system! After my baptism of fire at Wilmslow, the real business of why I joined the RAF began.

The RAF School of Photography was located near a lovely village called Wellesbourne Mountford, quite close to Shakespeare's birthplace at Stratford-on-Avon. It was one of the older training stations with wooden huts for accommodation and the mess hall on one side of a country road and the "technical site" on the other. Winters in those days however were harsh and bitterly cold in the wartime wooden huts with only a central pot bellied stove fuelled by a meagre ration of coke, not the easiest fuel to light up as we novices were to soon discover. We were obliged to march everywhere again but this time we were accompanied by a Sergeant Liddy, the "discip" SNCO (discipline, senior non commissioned officer), who sported a huge handlebar moustache and had a round jolly face to match. He would have made a wonderful Father Christmas. On "sports afternoons" we could choose what sport to take up but sometimes it would be a compulsory cross country run through the local woods at Loxley. The odd crafty student airman would "skive off", sneaking back into the billet and if they heard the discip Sergeant approaching they would hide in their wardrobe.

On one occasion I recall the Sgt went into the billet knowing full well there was a "skiver" or two hiding in their wardrobes, so he took a load of pencils out of his pocket and jammed it across each of the wardrobe catches securely imprisoning any "skivers" hiding inside. He returned about half an hour later to release the near collapsing "skivers" who did not repeat the exercise again!

The Royal Air Force
School of Photography
– based at
Wellesbourne-Mountford
1948 to October 1963

Our training began in earnest and we were treated to sessions of physics with a suitably qualified officer in the education branch. We learned all about the properties of light, refractive index of glass, chemistry relevant to our processing chemicals and brushed up on Maths and English into the bargain. I have to say it was some of the best training we could have received. I was lucky enough to have covered a lot of it at my school but it was a good reinforcement. We also learned the basic principles of aircraft electrics (DC) as we were going to service and fit aerial cameras to aircraft as part of our job. We were introduced to a range of aerial cameras (including the F24, F52, F95 and the huge F96) which we had to learn inside out, literally reciting the cycle of the gearbox sequence, by heart and the shutter operating principles. There was a range of ancillary equipment such as test boxes, used for servicing the cameras, and camera control boxes which the pilot used in the cockpit. We also had to learn the methods and alternative arrangements for fitting the cameras inside the aircraft with all the safety procedures, again by heart and we were examined on a regular basis to ensure we achieved each objective. The technical training started in earnest with many aspects of the basics covered in periods similar to normal schooling. We were also introduced to the optical qualities and principles of the lens, how images are formed, the structure of photographic films and paper. The mysteries of the chemical process for developing and fixing the image into a permanent state on both films and light sensitive papers were revealed. We were then taken into the darkrooms and taught how to load and unload camera magazines, double dark slides and how to find our way around in total darkness and work as a team in safelight illumination for the printing processes. Although it seemed so difficult at first to operate without sight and by touch alone, we soon realised there were useful methods and systems which we needed to accomplish these seemingly impossible task.

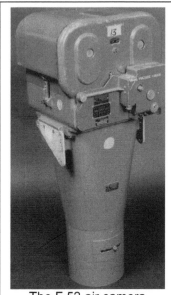

The F 52 air camera

Using a strict order of layout for equipment and tools and working from left to right in a constant sequence made life much easier. We soon became proficient at threading the large and small rolls of film into complex camera magazines without damaging the film. As the training progressed we began to operate the continuous film processing machinery and the multi printer machines which produced thousands of feet of film and paper prints, like our predecessors, using the same machines they used in WW2. We also learned how to prepare the hundreds of gallons of developer and fixer solutions required to maintain these hungry beasts. This was soon followed by introductions to multiple air camera fits required for the current aircraft and how we would be expected to install and maintain them. It was a fairly steep learning curve with periodic tests at various stages to ensure the learning curve had been accomplished. Sadly this was not always the case and a few friends were lost along the way, albeit they often had the opportunity to "remuster" to another trade deemed more suitable to their abilities. I do recall my instructors; they were a Sgt Butler-Davies and a Chief Technician George Parry. A Chief Technician was a technical version of a Flight Sergeants rank. They were excellent instructors, always very patient, caring and ever encouraging us to be the best. They must have been good because I still recall the various bits of the F 24 and F52 aerial camera gearbox; the heart shaped cam which raised and lowered the pressure plate of the camera magazine in between exposures; the gap wheel which was cleverly engineered to drive the focal plane shutter into a set position and then release the capping blind via the sprig pawl. The whole system was driven by a 24 volt DC motor coupled to a flexible drive connection via a clutch mechanism. All this knowledge and expertise was carefully built up in stages of accomplishment (practical objectives) and I have to say the instructors were so innovative in designing visual aids and mock up installations, it really did remain in my colander-like skull for a very long time; to their great credit. It must have been impressive as I later turned to instruction as my chosen speciality and thoroughly enjoyed every minute of it. The Commanding Officer of the school in those days was a Squadron Leader Berry and I recall he drove a very unusual American car. It was a Studebaker in pale blue with a very pointed front end which looked almost like a jet engine. I also recall a young Corporal instructor called Al Cousins who owned a Heinkel "bubble" car which was his pride and joy. He was in charge of a billet inspection one Thursday morning and he decided we were not cleaning the place properly so we had to do it all over again on the Friday night for inspection on the following Saturday. This blew away our weekend for going home to girl friends, so we were not happy little airmen.

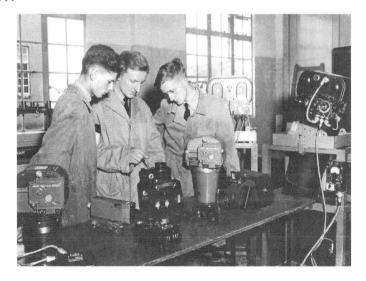

RAF School of Photography, classroom Instructor Cpl Gerry Payne

Behind the Lens | 233

I remember it well because on that Saturday morning it poured with rain, almost torrential and Cpl Cousins must have left the canvas roof open on his "bubble" car and it just about filled up with rain all day. He accused us of deliberately sabotaging his car, which we might have done admittedly, but on this occasion we were truly innocent. We spent the rest of the day in hob-nailed boots running around Loxley woods on a cross country run, not as a punishment of course, just extra training! Many years later our paths crossed again and I tried to convince him we were innocent but he still didn't believe me! Frankly I can hardly blame him as we must have seemed like we were a wild bunch of rebellious students when I recall some of the antics and daft things we got up to in the name of a bit of fun. Our Instructor pointed out a young advanced student (who was actually much older than us by at least three years!) as being a very intelligent and exceptionally bright lad. "You will see him as an officer before long, mark my words" and he was right this chap was Graham Saxby who became a Chief Technician very quickly (years before anyone else) and soon afterwards an Education officer teaching the advanced courses in physics, chemistry and maths. He later became absorbed with holography and as far as I know was a leading authority in the UK on the subject. I understand he lives in Tettenhall, Wolverhampton but he must be retired for quite a while now.

On the social side we were very lucky to have the beautiful town of Stratford-on-Avon on the doorstep and the spring time brought young lady visitors from all over to enjoy the famous theatre and boating on the river. Needless to say our somewhat restricted finances were no match for some of the young ladies accompanying jet set lads with their flash MG open topped sports cars. The local ladies were more amenable and we usually enjoyed ourselves at the many pubs, cinema and jazz club outlets. Our exams were numerous and nail biting as there were no sympathies to a failed student, three strikes and you were out. No appeal would be sufficient to alter that. One practical task was to be able to produce twenty matched contact prints from a given strip of air film with suitable shading to enhance the required exposure. This was achieved by use of tissue laid over the glass plates stacked in the body of the lamp house to act as a light diffuser. We actually used toilet paper which was imprinted on every sheet with the legendary "Government Issue" lettering which was carefully torn off of course before pushing the tailored sheets in position for best effect. Processing all twenty sheets of exposed photo paper in the developing dish required very adept manual dexterity if you were not to lose the sequence critical to producing a consistent overall density level. The practical exam on processing a roll of film in total darkness using the continuous processor was an art in itself when it came to splicing the film securely to the threaded leader in the machine. I doubt it would be allowed today under health and safety regulations, as it involved using a very sharp knife in total darkness, using only the sense of touch to locate the clamps securing the film flat on the leader and securing it with a binding of special tape! This processing machine was known as the CPU Mk 5 (designed and built by Williamsons before WW2). Mr. "Bill" Bailey (an ex RAF NCO) was the instructor in charge of this phase and a stern taskmaster at all times. If we happened to drop one of the stainless steel rollers down into the bottom of the tank he would make us drain the whole system to recover it and of course refill it afterwards. We knew he had a pair of special long reach tongs which he could have let us use but he felt it would make us more careful in handling the rollers without dropping them. He was right, but we all dreaded being the one with "butterfingers". I was among those who were lucky and never did drop a roller. We were also expected to take our turn at guarding the armoury, though I never did find out why, as it was securely clad in steel doors and plates over the windows, so only a tank could have blasted their way in. The Main RAF Police Guardroom was nearby at the site entrance and the RAF Policemen were very skilled at blowing their alarm whistles with deafening results (there were no armed guards then, we had to fend off invaders with a pick axe handle). We were sceptical even then as to the real value of this roving patrol but we were always told it was "character building" and necessary to build our stamina in holding back the red hordes we were assured could decide to invade at any time, day or night. The prospect of facing a fully armed "Ivan" with an unloaded pick axe handle did cross my mind as akin to a Japanese "kamikaze" pilot. but with much lesser effect! Mind you we were severely tested one dark winter night when my friend Des Bennett, who was a very tall ex police cadet, and I had drawn the short straw for being on armoury guard patrol.

We had been out for a couple of hours or more in the pitch dark and the bitter cold had well and truly permeated our hob-nailed boots. We were suddenly confronted by a young officer in uniform, holding what appeared to be a revolver! He was quite close and had obviously intended to surprise us having a crafty fag.

He bellowed "I am the enemy! What are you going to do?"

Des was like lightning and brought his pick axe handle across the arm holding the weapon, which flew into the dark as the officer screamed in agony. I thought Des had broken his arm for certain. He was now on the floor rolling in agony and I sprinted to the guardroom to fetch help. The duty RAF Policeman was agape when I told him what happened. However our luck was in as he was a Sergeant and a worldly wise one at that. He told his Corporal to send for an ambulance and the duty Medical Officer and ran to the scene with me in tow. Des was standing over his victim and threatening to lay into him if he moved!

"No one ever pulls a gun on me, ever!" he shouted down to the young officer still moaning in agony.

The Sergeant told Des to back off and look for the gun. He checked over the victim and decided he had not received a broken arm just as the medics turned up. They confirmed it had received a nasty bang but not broken. The young officer was bundled off to the sick bay and Des found the "gun" in the grass a few yards away. The sergeant took it and it turned out to be a well carved "pistol" shaped from a piece of wood.

"Well son, this could be a bit awkward, but it does look like the real thing in the dark. You two get back on patrol for now and I'll be back shortly"

An hour later we were relieved and taken to the Guardroom to make a statement and report the incident. So much for our four hours kip between patrols! We finished writing up the paper work and crashed out, although we didn't really sleep with fretting about what might happen to us. The following morning we were sent for by the Adjutant at the Station Headquarters. He asked us what happened in our own words and listened impassively until we finished.

"Right, that's it is it?" he asked.

"Yes sir" we both replied in unison.

"You are a right pair of bloody imbeciles, but in this case you were right. Now you will keep your mouths shut about this. If I hear one whisper on the subject you will be posted to the worst hole I can find after being immediately removed from training. Is that clear enough for you both?"

We were absolutely fazed for a second or two, expecting to be at least court martialed for assaulting an officer and here we were scot free... if we kept schtumm!

"Yes sir!" we again replied in unison.

The relief was almost euphoric. Later we learned the young officer was actually with the local ATC Squadron and suffering from the effects of a bit too much socialising in the officer's mess. He was determined to see how effective his wood work carving would appear to two unwitting airmen. Well he found out the hard way! He was told not to return to the camp for the foreseeable future and referred to his superiors. I often reflect on this early lesson of my RAF career. It showed me that if you are right, you have to do what is right, sometimes you may not be treated fairly, but that is down to the standards of those in charge and no-one is perfect. It did restore my faith in how the RAF, even in those tough days, could be seen to be fair and practical with a measure of common sense when it mattered.

In those days the military were striving to increase the manpower and National Service was still in operation, although we had all become aware that it was to be concluded in the near future. I always felt great sympathy to many who were not suited to military service. The mistaken mantra that National Service "straightened" out less desirable young men is usually voiced by those without the benefit of military experience. Our final days at Wellesbourne loomed and we were now getting pretty exited as to where we would be posted. Most of us had preferences, I just wanted to go anywhere abroad and soon the day came when our "postings" were detailed.

The Guardroom at RAF Wellesbourne-Mountford

Chapter 6 - Troop Ship to Germany

The completion of this course on our passing out day heralded our despatch to pasture new (it was my sister Marion's birthday, May 8th 1958, which is why I remember the date so clearly). Some of my colleagues were sent around the UK, but I and my friend Des Bennett were told we would be going to Germany as part of the BAOR (British Army of Occupation on the Rhine), and so began my adventure abroad. We were packed off by train to Harwich where we joined a troopship sailing across to the Hook of Holland. This was quite an adventure for yours truly having set my heart on travelling the world. The Army were of course in charge of these troopships (don't ask for the logic, it doesn't exist!) A big barrel chested WO (Warrant Officer) was in charge of our group, which was a mixed bag of Army and Air Force. We were instructed to put on the "Mae West" life jackets and get into the hammocks slung across frames set up down in the hold. It was not exactly "P & O", more like a cattle ferry. The "Mae West" had to be inflated as we lay in these hammocks which meant if you suffered from claustrophobia, you had a bad time, with your face about an inch from the sagging hammock slung above you. This was of course an early form of the Health and Safety because we may have hit an iceberg in the Channel and we could have lost valuable seconds getting it on before the ship sank. The fact that you could hardly move with it inflated and half jammed in the hammock and the likelihood of successfully getting up the many flight of steps to the open deck would have been nigh on impossible, but "orders was orders" and you did not question them in the days of latter day national Service.

The Army lads were a very mixed bunch as usual, mostly national Service and there were a number of characters I would rather not have found myself in the company of by choice. This of course was my original primary reason for signing on as a "regular," so I could choose my trade, and the service with which I served that time. After a sleepless and dreadful night of rolling in the Channel across to Holland we were finally disembarked onto the quayside where we ushered onto the "blue train" (I never did find out why it was so called), which took us through to Germany and the line actually ran into the RAF base at Wildenrath near the Dutch German border. The RAF chaps were ordered to get off and we were taken by lorry with our kit to the mess hall where, in those days, you were told which RAF unit in Germany you were to be posted to. Des Bennett was to remain at RAF Wildenrath but I was to move on to RAF Geilenkirchen, a base even closer to the Dutch border, as I was to find out. I remember a couple of lads with me who were national service and we got to comparing notes after getting to know each other. The older chap (almost 20!) was a draughtsman and had worked with an aircraft manufacturer; he had been trained for his time with the RAF as a cook! The other chap was a medical assistant and he fortunately had been given a nursing trade. This was quite common and sometimes I think there was some evil sod with a twisted sense of humour in charge of fulfilling quotas as I came to find numerous "misfits" who were very skilful tradesmen pushed into the daftest waste of their talents for their national service duration. There are many who advocate the re-introduction of national service. Forgive them, they know not what they do! Believe me, there are far better ways, and much more effective ones, of maintaining discipline. It begins with earning "respect", usually by example, not just the wearing of badges of rank, hard won though they may be. So here I was at my first posting in foreign lands, far from Mom and Dad. My squadron was 96 Squadron, a night fighter unit with old Meteor NF 11 jets. I do admit to it being a bit of a let down for me at first sight, as I was hoping to get a reconnaissance squadron like Des Bennett, who had 17 Squadron at Wildenrath with Canberra PR 7's, the cutting edge of our reconnaissance force. My Corporal in charge of our little squadron outfit was Charlie Coppins, a benign, kindly soul, who was more of a friend than a boss. He was of average height and thin as a rake, with very wavy hair and aquiline features. My co-worker (there were just three of us altogether in the section) was Leading Aircraftsman Len Potts, a national serviceman, who somehow had managed to get into the photo trade. How, I do not remember but he was a knowledgeable chap, quite tall and came from "down south" somewhere near Reading I think. I was soon to find that the other ground crew boys on the squadron were a mix of national service and regulars, but with a few characters with an exceptional sense of humour.

I had never laughed and been so happy for a long time. Their wit was razor sharp and the aircrew officers had a great deal of respect for them, often "fraternising with the lower ranks", by drifting into our crew room on some pretext of other to enjoy a good ragging from the "comedians" in the ground crew. The boss was Wing Commander David Farrar, a mature and highly decorated pilot from WW2, who looked a bit like the film actor Peter Finch. He was a very caring and natural leader, strict without being overbearing. He had seen a lot of real action and knew all about his men and how to lead them. We were paid in "B.A.F.S." (British Armed Forces Service Vouchers), these were printed paper money notes in Sterling denominations, right down to three penny notes and printed by Thomas De

La Rue (the playing card manufacturers). The idea was to limit the Deutschmark currency being used by the forces to the minimum. With a wallet full of three penny notes you could feel like a millionaire, if only in pennies! Of course you were allowed to exchange your BAFS for German currency but it was limited and mostly un- necessary as we had no cars and used the NAAFI (Naval Army Air Force Institute), for most of our needs. Even so we ventured off base as soon as we were organised and felt confident enough to "break out". My pay at his time would have been about £7 per two weeks and we actually managed to spin it out quite well but of course the national service lads were only paid £1 and 10 shillings (£1.50p) a week so it lasted about half the time of the "regulars" pay. We were all usually down on our luck by the middle of the second week and tried to make our own entertainment by getting involved in all sorts of capers. It would be at this time, the second week after pay day, that our boss would suddenly turn up at the billet with a mini bus (a VW crew bus) and invite us down to the local pub in Geilenkirchen. Despite our protests at not having any money, he told us we could take him out the next time we were flush, and he would stand for the tab on this occasion. We always did the noble thing and returned the compliment the following pay day, which of course turned into a bit of a heavy night for him and we would almost carry him back to his wife and their MQ (married quarter home). She was also of sterling stuff and despite chiding him and us; she would then set about making a "brickie's" breakfast for us all.

We were very grateful and very impressed that they would care so much about our predicament, especially the national service lads. Our aircrew officers were very conscious of the need to get the best out of their team and to their credit, they were always to the fore on this. Sadly some of the "shiny arse" non-aircrew officers had a bit of a bob on themselves in those days, and had yet to learn the gift of true leadership. My role in all this was to fit and maintain the cine gun camera recorders. These were placed in front of the pilots eye line so that a "graticule" image was projected up onto their plate glass gun sight and the image recorded by the camera above it. This camera was called the G.G.S.R. (Giro Gun Sight Recorder). Another recorder was fitted in a covered space inside the left (port) wing so the lens could also record the results of the gunfire when needed. This was called the G 45 B, an older design of camera first used during WW2. This camera had to bee harmonised to line up with the guns from its location near the root of the wing. We worked very closely with the armourers ("plumbers" in RAF slang) on these occasions and we were often called to assist them in the event of an alert or "flap". We were quite happy to do this and other tasks such as marshalling aircraft into position and helping the armourers load the guns, they were using our muscles really, not so much doing the clever stuff, just help in the general team spirit of such occasions. This is also why many small photographic units were often accommodated above the armoury on the station. However our station was quite new in comparison with older stations in the UK, so we were housed in the corner of the hangar in our own special workshop with the aircraft and where the rest of the maintenance bays were located to support the squadron. We also were responsible for processing the 16 mm film from the camera magazines after the pilot landed his aircraft. This was done in the main photo section for the station and we had a darkroom set aside for processing these cine films. We had to unload the films from the magazines and lace them onto a frame about 3 feet square with rubber collar separators spaced out along the top and bottom rails which was designed to keep the film flat and separated as it was wound onto the frame. The frame was clamped between two upright arms with a central spindle and clamping spigot which held the frame central and able to revolve as we wound on the film in total darkness. We then had to manoeuvre the frame into position above a narrow deep tank filled with developer and agitate it for the prescribed time and then pass the frame into the rest of the chemical tanks in sequence and at the appropriate time intervals. The process was undertaken in total darkness until the film had been in the fixation chemical tank (number three) for twice the time it took to clear, around 3 minutes at the correct dilution. All the chemicals the developer, stop bath, fixer and wash tanks had to be maintained at 68° F (or 20°C). The front of each processing tank had a series of large indented bars (like giant Braille) to signify the first (one bar) the second (two bars) and so on to ensure you aligned the tanks in the correct sequence of processing. We always worked from left to right as a standard safeguard and good practice and this was how we were trained from the photo school. There was one occasion when for reasons best known to him alone, the Sergeant in charge of this photo section decided to re- arrange the layout in contrary to this standard practice and of course he failed to notify us at the squadron when this was done.

I remember this well because my boss on the squadron had a film from one of his flights which he required processing urgently. I was not told what the target was, but it may have been an "intercept" of a Russian aircraft which frequently tested our reactions. I dashed to the processing section and completed the film process. When I turned on the lights to view the film, to my abject horror there was only clear strips of film with absolutely no images on it at all! I knew there was a serious problem because the camera usually leaves some sort of darkening at the start even if the shutter system failed on the camera. This was clearly (pardon the pun) down to the incorrect processing of the film by yours truly. It had somehow gone into the fix tank before the developer tank which would

Behind the Lens

completely clear any form of recorded image from the film. When I looked at the identifying bars of the processing tanks I realised what had happened. Someone had swapped the tanks around contrary to standard practice. I was then told by the Sergeant (who has a silly grin on his face) that he had ordered the tanks to be relocated in the reverse order because it "looked" better that way for the forthcoming annual inspection by the Air Officer Commanding. I was absolutely speechless and incredulous that such a stupid action by a Senior NCO in charge of our department had caused the total loss of vital film images. How I did not knock him senseless on his arse is a credit to the installed discipline of my "boot camp" training. He knew that I was furious by the white anger in my face and my silent fury which left nothing in question. True I should have double checked by feeling for the indented bars, but we had been told by the same Sergeant that we had sole responsibility for this particular darkroom facility. When I reported back to my C.O. with the bad news, he questioned me very thoroughly as to how and what had happened. He showed no anger, other than the obvious disappointment at getting evidence of a live Russian intercept. I was fully expecting him to blow a fuse and rip me to shreds, but then I was a bit young to understand his pragmatism after coming through the hell of WW2. He did however pay a visit to the Sergeant and, as I learned some time later, advised him to refrain from making any alterations to the processing department which he saw as part of his squadron facilities without his express permission. Coming from a full blown Wing Commander I think the Sergeant would have wound his neck in a bit swift, if you follow my drift. From that moment on the Sergeant remained discreetly in his office with the door closed when we entered the facility for processing. Yet another lesson and important experience had been tucked under my belt.

Our squadron had been reformed as No 3 Squadron and re-equipped with the Gloster Javelin fighter aircraft. This was a much larger aircraft with massive power and an "all weather" night intercept role. It sported large radar in the nose which improved the capability very much from the old fashioned Meteor NF 11. It also had an ejector seat for both pilot and navigator. We had to learn to be very respectful of this as anyone setting off the seat by accident would almost certainly be killed. There were special locking pins which were very carefully removed after strapping in the crew, just before closing the canopy and replaced in position after a flight as the canopy was opened to release the crew. We were all very careful when entering and leaving the aircraft to test systems as we knew the implications of negligence would prove fatal. I was resting in the billet one night when the squadrons were conducting night flying exercises, which did not require our cameras or us to participate, but we got an urgent call to report to another squadron hanger immediately. When we arrived it was obviously something very serious was happening as the police, ambulance and lots of other staff were rushing about in a state of anxiety. We were told to collect hand cameras and film from the main section and report back to the hanger as soon as possible. We were back within minutes and a senior MO (medical officer) took us to one side and told us he wanted us to record every detail which he would point out to us on one of the aircraft in the hanger. It was then that I looked up and saw the damage in the roof caused by an ejector seat from the cockpit of the aircraft beneath. My heart sank and my stomach did somersaults as I dreaded having to photograph the remains of what may well have been someone I knew. My face had shown what was going on in my head to the MO. It was then that he filled me in with the most incredible lucky escape I ever heard of. The airman had unwittingly rearmed the seat and then somehow inadvertently tripped the ejection system. In the micro second before it shot up into the roof, he had somehow crammed himself forward into the tiny space around the control column and the seat had just caught his back without causing fatal injury and he had lived to tell the tale! Some time later we photographed every combination of thin people available to try and re-create his posture in the scenario, which proved impossible. The only explanation offered was that sheer fear had allowed his body to compress in such a way as to avoid the worst injuries imaginable if the seat had caught his body in its upward trajectory. I have never heard of anyone since surviving such accidental ejector seat malfunctions but I have unfortunately recorded some of those who didn't. This is the darker, and not so pleasant, side of our profession in military photography.

It was also during this first "tour" (a term used to describe a period of overseas posting) that I witnessed an unusual incident which stuck in my mind at the time and became clarified many years later. We got the word that an American aircraft was in trouble in our area and coming in as an emergency landing. Curiosity got the better of me when I learned it was a Voodoo fighter. The Fire and Rescue team were deployed along the runway and the RAF Police suddenly appeared in large numbers in a nearby revetment bay (a sort of concrete u shaped pen). The aircraft appeared and landed safely, the wise airframe technicians informing us that it probably had a false hydraulics alert and the pilot played safe. As the aircraft parked up in the nearby revetment, the RAF Police formed a highly visible cordon around the aircraft. This did nothing but raise our curiosity as to why this was necessary. I fetched a set of binoculars in our camera room which someone used for bird watching and went to get a better view. A large hand gripped my shoulder and a voice in my ear said "I will take those now, nothing for you to see here today". It was an RAF Police Sergeant and he walked away with the binoculars and no further explanation. It was many years later, I learned that some of these Voodoo aircraft were used to carry a tactical nuclear weapon and I now recognise that the security was probably because it was one of these rather sensitive issues that the US take lengths to protect from unwelcome viewing including their allies!

Chapter 7 - Supplementing Incomes

It was also during this tour that I began developing a sense of business which has always led me to create finances other than the "kings shilling". My national service colleague and co photographer Len Potts was also a good mechanical engineer in his own right. It was at his behest that we visited a local scrap yard filled with many decent looking German cars. One had caught his eye as being a bit special. It was a BMW two seater (in red leather) open topped sports car, which had triple carburettors and centre lock wheels. It looked very much like the Jaguar XK 120 in shape and the silver body was all aluminium. I have always been suspicious that this is where Jaguars got their styling ideas for the XK series from, but it may have been coincidence. Len's idea was to supplement his meagre income by doing it up and putting back into a roadworthy condition. We bought it for the equivalent of £13 and got it moved to the camp. Len had a lot of friends in the MT (motor transport) section and they helped us to get the spraying redone and the engine tuned to a satisfactory standard. This we accomplished in a few months and we were approached by a young officer from the squadron who wanted to buy it and ship it home. Len managed to keep a straight face and stated he wanted £150 (a king's ransom to a national serviceman!). Well he was more than happy to pay that which did wipe the latent smile off our faces, and we were suspicious then that he knew a lot more than we did, but a deal is a deal and we made plenty out of it. I saw the same car last year advertised in a classic car magazine for around £80,000! Some deal eh? If only we knew then, what we know now!

We repeated the exercise with a lovely Mercedes 170V saloon which had been owned by a doctor during the war as there were documents to this effect which were translated for us by a German worker called Gunter who we got to know on the camp. This was in much better condition than the BMW so we had to pay £50 for it but we did sell it to a local German garage owner for £250 thanks again to the help of Gunter who began to build quite a good relationship with us. This was a bit unusual for us as our experiences of many of the Germans we had come across in the town, was less than friendly and somewhat sullen to the RAF lads. With the wisdom of hindsight, we should have realised that the war was still very fresh in their minds (being ended just thirteen years before) and they must all have suffered greatly under the RAF bombing raids as we had from the

Luftwaffe back home. Len had also managed to secure a job as a projectionist in the Astra cinema on camp which doubled his regular income to £3 a week. He asked me to join him in this venture and soon we were both adept at running the show from start to finish. We used Einemann IX projectors with carbon arc illumination sources which I came to use again during a later tour in Germany. I can still remember how to re-etch the two sets of "Q" dots in the corner of the 35 mm picture frames towards the end of each reel to warn the projectionist to start up the number two projector for changeovers. We also spent many hours repairing damaged bits of film lengths before and after each showing, which meant you had to cut out the damaged frames and re-splice the film. This is why you would sometimes see a person apparently jump across the screen where the damaged bit had been removed! These were times when every little venture helped to secure a better standard for those less fortunate than our counterparts in the civilian world. All things considered we did well enough and it was enjoyable as well as very rewarding, which stood us in good stead later. My first detachment came when we were sent to Orly airfield in France to provide a demonstration of the Javelin for some kind of international air display. I had also qualified for the next rank up and proudly wore the badges of a senior Aircraftsman (SAC). I went along as the squadron photographer, my first real public relations job since training, so I was really excited at the prospect of doing a "proper job".

The twin lens Rolleiflex
camera circa 1960

I had the use of a Rollieflex twin lens camera which used 120 film size (6 cm x 6 cm format) and a whole bundle of films. I remember the boss being introduced to a very special French lady, whose name I do not recall, but she was a pilot! Now it seems almost normal today, but in those days it was a bit like meeting Amelia Erhart in person. She turned out an aerobatic display on the big day, which our own pilots were in awe of, so she must have been really something. We also managed to get a trip to Paris, where we did the usual tourist sights. It was fantastic for me, a young 19 year old kid in his smart uniform getting curious looks and lots of smiles from young girls. I was in heaven and determined to enjoy every minute. It was during this time that I had returned home for a spot of leave and even my old dad (who was always a bit critical of me in earlier days) showed me off to all his fellow workers and friends. It was during this leave that I fell in love… with a BSA Gold Star 650 cc, gleaming brand new and I just had to have it. I managed to persuade my dad to sign the papers (over 21 in those days was the legal age for HP contracts!) and I paid my hard earned cash as deposit. This gleaming monster, all black and gleaming chrome was mine, to have and to hold from this day forth, I was untouchable and indestructible and had quite a job keeping the very heavy beast upright when it wasn't rolling! I was not used to such power and she was oh so smooth. I quickly learned all the skills needed to keep the beast under my control, thanks to my Dad's help and advice form his experience with bikes.

Travelling back to Germany was an absolute dream. Aboard the ferry crossing my bike drew a number of admiring glances from other bikers and this was shades of things to come. Passing through Holland I had to take a nature call and parked up at a roadside café for a breather and a coffee break. When I came out of the café, my bike was surrounded by a bunch of lorry drivers and bikers. I had not realised that the "foreigners" were so keen on our bikes, but it was of course the latest and greatest machine out of the BSA stable (it had the new Burgess silencers which gave it a wonderful powerful growl). I managed to part the group and sat astride the bike fiercely trying to look "cool" as they say in modern parlance, but I couldn't stop the Cheshire cat grin of sheer satisfaction as she kicked into life and swooped on the highway, me of course opening up the throttle that extra bit (a lot!). Oh, the vanity of the young male on full testerone injections! It was a few weeks later I really did fall in love with a very beautiful young lady on one of my "sorties" into Holland. I had teamed up with a colleague from the Squadron, Graham Pool, who owned a German "Horex" bike, so we tended to get away from the local area, spreading our interests a bit further into Heerlen, Venlo and Maastricht. We came across a very nice looking café / restaurant at the side of a highway not to far from our usual touring patch. We had called in for something to eat and we were served by a very lovely young lady who I quickly found out was in fact from Poland. Her name was Anna and I was smitten from that moment and she knew it too. I hoped she had similar feelings but it was too much for me to dare to hope. She had the most wonderful blue eyes, long flowing hair and she was very "petite" (as they say in France). Needless to say we made regular visits as Graham also had his eye on the owner's daughter, a very vivacious looking brunette called Ria. Our relationships grew to a point where I was beginning to get serious feeling for a permanent situation.

Both our worlds were about to get a "reality check", as happens sometimes when things are going so sweetly. Graham had gone out on a run with Ria, and I was at the café talking to Anna, when they re-appeared from down the road going very carefully and something was obviously wrong. Ria's arms and face were bleeding from scratches and scrapes and obviously very upset. Graham was white faced and obviously in some distress. They had somehow come off the bike, fortunately at a fairly slow speed but the damage and shock to them both was pretty frightening. We got them both to the hospital and the medics were very good at patching up their wounds but Ria was frightened that her face had been permanently scarred. Her father and mother were very understanding about the whole thing and were just as concerned about Graham who had really fought like hell to minimise the injuries and damage, taking most of the collision force on his arm and shoulder. Ria was actually very lucky in that her scratches and scars disappeared after a few weeks with no real visible traces. It was a sobering time for all of us and the euphoria of the bikes was somewhat diminished for a while.

Shortly after this time Anna had received a letter from home in Poland asking her to come back for a visit as her family were missing her. This was of course at a time when the Iron Curtain was firmly in place and the prospect of her going back to Poland alarmed me very much. She assured me everything would be fine and she would talk to her parents about us and our relationship which had become quite serious. I was just turned 20 by this time and wanted to get engaged but she would only agree with the blessing of her father. I had no choice but to hope for the best and after a week or so I was anxiously waiting for her first letter telling me of how she had got on. It did not come, not after the first or the second or the third week. Ria's father had contacted the authorities and asked their advice as he was anxious for her well being also. The Dutch Embassy had contacted the Polish Embassy and they were still waiting for a response. None came and for the next few weeks, which turned into months, my heart was crushed and broken. I tried through the channels of our UK Embassy in Cologne and was met with the same response, nothing, she had seemingly vanished into thin air. I think at that time I felt a white anger at the stupidity of all things political to create such meaningless obstruction for ordinary people who simply wanted to get on with their lives and were no threat to anyone. It has stuck quietly in my heart ever since and I can never forgive those responsible, whoever they may have been. You have no choice under such circumstances, but to get on with your life. Eventually, after some time had passed, I managed to do so with mine.

Many years later I passed through the same part of Holland and I still found that heartache feeling well up inside, as if it were yesterday, wondering where she was and if she ever remembered me. I had been a fully fledged Senior Aircraftsman for a couple of years now and I was due to return to the UK for a training course to learn other skills within our trade and so become a Photo II tradesman, which meant I was supposed to be able do any of the three main shills such as Reconnaissance Servicer (R.S.- as on my original training course), Bulk Processing (B.P. - processing all types of film and printed images from the aerial cameras) and General Servicer duties (G.S. - a strange name given to those involved in general photography such public relations and studio work). Why the RAF could not simply call it photography was beyond any of us, but then the minds of those above worked in mysterious ways. So it was back to Wellesbourne Mountford again for a few weeks learning to do the jobs we had all probably been doing unofficially any way, but now we would be officially qualified! Of course it was also an essential step if you were ever to be considered for promotion to the dizzy heights of non commissioned officer rank (N.C.O.). When I arrived at the rail station in Wildenrath for the journey back to the UK, standing there was my old pal Des Bennett (the pick axe slasher as he had become known!). I was so pleased to find he was also on the same course, I knew then we could take on the world of Wellesbourne with confidence!

Chapter 8 - 1960 SOP Again!

We duly arrived and found ourselves confronted by a new face as the discip Sgt, one Sergeant Mcklusky, a rather lean and abrupt Irishman who disliked "experienced" airmen. Probably because we were a little more worldly wise and did not have the same fear threshold as the raw recruits fresh from boot camp. The Commanding Officer (C.O.) was a Squadron Leader Peter Mayle who was light years ahead of hair fashion as he was completely bald, not by nature but he chose to be that way! We should have known there was something a bit weird in his make up from this and so it proved. He spoke with that false, ever so friendly voice, which really meant you were about to have the wrath of an insane hairless fanatic descend upon you. He was fanatical about B.S. (bull shine – a close enough spelling) and his own appearance was that of a newly manufactured manikin, immaculate from head to foot with super gleaming shiny shoes to round it all off. He carefully explained how he had just returned from teaching the Americans how to march properly. We were aware he had just returned from a "cream" posting in the USA. He just knew we all loved Saturday morning parades, where we could show off to the wide open countryside how well we could march up and down in our immaculate uniform despite the pouring rain and near gale force winds. "Certifiable" would be the understatement of the year. On one such occasion we were absolutely soaked to the skin again, when the Discip Sgt Mcklusky acted totally out of character, ignoring the CO and gave the order to right wheel off the square as we were making one of many passes up and down the tarmac area. We needed no second bidding and followed his order, but not so Squadron Leader Peter Mayle who continued on his own, marching down the length of the square as we left him alone in his own tiny world. We never did find out if this performance was at all intentional, or a joke, but it did reveal to me that there were some people who took life a bit too seriously for the good of the rest of us and thanked God for the eventual break through of a bit of common sense.

I made a lot of new friends at Wellesbourne and many of us compared notes as to our experiences and exchanged stories. It was the continuation of building up a long list of fellow tradesmen, many of whom are still around and in touch even now. There really is no substitute for the camaraderie and "espirit de corps" which grows from these relationships. As always, the training we received, was top dollar and we did learn a whole bag of new stuff, some more useful than others. My main recollection was using the MPP Micropress camera which was a hand held plate camera (similar in appearance to the Speed Graphic cameras used by press photographers). We were obliged to use it with a battery powered flash gun using giant PF 60 flash bulbs, which would be considered lethal in today's cotton wool environment. It was really a "field camera", mostly used in a studio environment but for some reason it was considered good "character building" if you could handle one of these on the hoof, like the reporters in the old black and white movies were often seen to do.

The MPP field camera (complete with PF60 flash unit) used 5 x 4" cut film dark slides, circa 1955

To be fair our training was very careful and we knew how to handle these flash bulbs safely. It was only when the excitement of the moment overcame logic and normal thought processes, as it was with me that day I went blind! I had loaded the plate holder in the camera and was about to fire off the shutter at one of my "technical subjects", a huge bulldozer of the Airfield Construction unit housed in the hanger when I thought it would look much better with a dollop of fill in flash. I turned the camera round started screwing in the PF 60 flash bulb into the flashgun with my hankie (thank God for small mercies!) when the world went terribly bright and that was the last thing I saw for about two weeks! I had stupidly looked at the gun whilst fiddling to get the bulb in place and somehow triggered the flash, probably by knocking the shutter release on the camera lens in my haste. I spent the next 10 days or so with my eyes covered, stuck in the sick bay and hoping there was no permanent damage to my eyes. The MO (medical officer) had assured me it was temporary but it would be best to leave them covered for a while. I found out how different life was for someone to lose their sight. Thankfully mine was very temporary. I could actually tell by the sound of footfall which nurse was walking by and I could feel the sun on my arms and hands changing the room temperature. Fortunately I was used to feeling my way around darkrooms and I was able to get around surprisingly easier than I thought possible. Your memory and senses do reach new levels of acuteness and awareness. However thankfully mine was short lived and it was soon time to open up again to the world. I have always had a great fear of blindness since this accident and I have the greatest respect for those who are less fortunate. I am particularly careful about leaving things in places where the unsighted may come to grief for one example. I do get especially angry at people parking cars on pavements for this reason also. My delay in the sick bay proved not too difficult for me to catch up with the training and I managed to successfully pass the course, perhaps with less high scores than would have liked. For Des Bennett and me, it was back to Germany to finish our tour of duty and we were pretty thankful to have survived fairly unscathed.

Members of 61 Advanced course May 1960
Jeffries, Pardue, Wallis, Poulson, McIvor, Humphrey
Bennett, Smith Cpl Brouard, Mattocks Proudlove, Mair

Chapter 9 - Return to Geilenkirchen

I had not been back at Geilenkirchen for long when I learned the squadron was going up to Norway to a place called Trondheim for some gunnery training. We flew there in a Norwegian Air Force transport aircraft made in the USA, called a "Packet". It had two enormous Pratt and Whitney engines which were deafening, as we sat for the long journey on the edge of very uncomfortable fold down seats wearing a parachute and a life jacket which did nothing for your confidence. Eventually we landed and I do still remember the wonderful smell of pine trees as he doors were finally opened for us to fall out onto the tarmac. It took a long time to force my legs into movement and even longer before I could understand a bloody word anyone spoke! The hospitality though made up for it all and we had a fantastic time. We actually won the gunnery competition and beat the USAF into third place behind the Norwegians. Fortunately for us it was in the late spring and early summer, so we had the benefit of not experiencing their extremely cold weather, that was to be my good fortune some many years later!

We did manage to get to Trondheim and I think we visited a lovely place called the Tiergarten but I am afraid we enjoyed the local brew a bit too much to recall it with any real clarity. On our return to Geilenkichen, I was resigned to get back into the old routine when my old friend, the smiling Sergeant sent for me. I was slightly perturbed since I had studiously avoided his company since our "brief encounter" and his meeting with my Wing Commander. However, to my surprise, he was genuinely happy to see me. "Good news for you, old son", an expression I was suspicious of immediately, "You've got your tapes, congratulations!" I had been promoted to Corporal and he actually pumped my hand like he was my father. The modern expression is "gob smacked" and so I was, speechless, until it sank in fully. I was so over the moon, and quickly dashed off a letter to home. I knew my Mom would be so pleased as yet again she had been proven right after all her efforts to get me past the MO all that time ago. My father was also very happy to know I had at last made something of myself and he was genuinely pleased to see me, on my return home on leave. Like all young people my main objective on leave was to socialise as much as possible so money did not last as long as one hoped. To this end I decided to see if I could earn a few bob helping out at my local pub, "The Hare and Hounds", where I had seen a notice asking for bar staff to help out. For me this solved the finances and allowed me to socialise, albeit from the other side of the bar. I met the landlord Bill Edmunds and we seemed to get on quite well. He was an ex army Warrant Officer and the pub echoed his military methods. Everyone had quite specific detailed assignments and not much was left to chance. Fortunately my mental arithmetic was well up to speed thanks to my very useful education which proved essential as it turned out. We were still using the old sterling denominations of pounds, shillings and pence, i.e. 20 shillings to the pound and 240 pence to the pound etc. So when you consider we also had to separate the cash taken for cigarettes and catering from the beer and drinks served, it became quite an agile brain exercise to serve at rush periods, especially just before "time gentlemen please" was called at 10 pm precisely followed by the legal 10 minute "drinking up" time in force then. I was also shown how to tap a barrel (known as a Hogs head) and vent the peg which acted as a valve. I managed to learn how to strip and clean the "engine" of the pump which pulled up the beer from the cellar through yards of polythene pipe and how to "stoop" a barrel, carefully tilting it to gain the maximum output. I really enjoyed the work, tiring though it could be at times; there was a certain satisfaction at having made a few bob, along with the tips of course.

I met a lot of very different people from all walks of life (and a few rogues who worked on the wrong side of the law). It was during this time that I also met the landlord's wife, Elsie. She was a very outgoing person who was an excellent cook. They had two daughters, Patricia (as she liked to be called) and Valerie, the younger of the two and about the same age as me. Pat was married to a chap called Ray and he was not unlike the film star Paul Newman in general looks (which is why I privately suspect Pat fell for him) and worked at the Rover car assembly plant at Longbridge. Valerie still lived at home (in the accommodation upstairs at the pub that is). The pub itself was quite a large mock Tudor post war structure extending along the main road from Kingstanding to Hawthorn Road in the Great Barr area of Birmingham. It had a very pleasant terraced garden area at the rear which also accommodated the local bowling club. The Kingstanding area name comes from history, when Charles II assembled his forces in the area during the civil war (hence Kings Standing). Unknown to me, Elsie had been keeping a sharp eye on my progress and had decided that I might be a potential candidate for her daughter Valerie's hand. I suppose she was also considering the potential of her daughter's future with a fellow from the RAF, and as it turned out, she was not far off the mark. I had to return to Germany for the last few months of my tour and I do confess I was still thinking about Elsie's daughter Valerie. I suppose it was probably on the rebound from my sadness with losing Anna.

Chapter 10 - Summer of 1960 - JARIC

It was in the following summer that I returned to the UK and my first posting to the Joint Air Reconnaissance Centre located at RAF Brampton near Huntingdon in Cambridgeshire. I was now of course a Junior NCO (Non Commissioned Officer) and as a Corporal I had a rather different perspective of life in the Royal Air Force being not quite at the bottom of the heap any longer. I was afforded a few benefits, the privacy of my own room in the barrack block, for example and a number of staff to look after including some members of the WRAF. I had been thoroughly "vetted" by the then security service, as to my leanings towards the communist party or homosexual tendencies (or "left wing pouffs", as they would so eloquently put it in those days) and having being found lacking in either department, they considered me a reasonable security risk. Being duty bound to the "Official Secrets Act", I would not dream of revealing anything untoward the security of this wonderful country of ours, but it is in the public domain that we worked closely with our Allies in these matters.

The Joint Air Reconnaissance Intelligence Centre.

The unit was recently closed down at RAF Brampton

I was looking after the re-production of maps and plots of aerial coverage of unknown areas (there was no way for us to know what country or specifically where it was from under the "needs to know" policy). For this task we used a machine known to the commercial world as a "Photostat" document copier. It was really a large book holder with UV lights either side and used very slow UV light sensitive thin bromide paper to record images of originals which were then wound off into the dark room side and processed by hand in conventional chemical solutions. I suppose the machinery would have been at least thirty years old judging by the engineering and ancient mechanisms. However it was reliable and simple to operate, so perhaps that was the key to its longevity in the service of the RAF. We were also required to print images from aerial films using a very clever electronic printer made by a company called Cintel. This was a glorified contact printer which used a cathode ray tube to provide the light source and the scanning "spot" could be controlled in such a way as to give a useful form of "shading" (increasing or decreasing the illumination to adjacent areas affected by cloud shadow on the target area) without affecting the overall contrast or exposure level for the rest of the format. I loved this particular machine as it was in those days the cutting edge of our technology and a very successful printer which gave pretty reliable service overall. Most of the work required high numbers of reproduction and so our skills at being able to produce matching copies were always in high demand.

When I look back on my early days of experience in these times, I realise that the real skill came from the training given to us by those who knew a lot more about "Sensitometry" (a form of photographic quality control) than I ever did at the time. Sensitometry was to provide a fascination for me in later years and I still believe that the man responsible for its proper introduction and application to the training was Jack Eggleston. Jack was a Warrant Officer when he retired from the RAF but he continued his career with the Air Ministry as an instructor at the School of Photography until he retired. His profound knowledge and expertise in this field, I have always felt, was greatly undervalued in the wider commercial world of photography, to their loss and the military gain, I hasten to add. He wrote a wonderful hand book on the subject called "Sensitometry for Photographers" just before he retired and it won a prize for him, I am very pleased to say. It should have been re printed at least a dozen times but then publishers are not always aware of the value they have at their disposal. I had started an interest in the Radio Brampton relay broadcast which we used to entertain a few hundred listeners with music, record programmes and stories read from suitable snippets of local news and interesting subjects. We even had a go at a bit of a radio play, a doing a radio version of the film "The Hasty Heart" which starred Richard Todd for those old enough to recall him. We created our own sound effects and managed to acquire some sound effect tapes from the BBC to supplement our efforts which sounded too much like rubbish. It was quite a success, even from the usually philistine youngsters who would normally switch off at any suggestion of culture! It was during this time that my life changed dramatically as I became more than just a friend to Valerie (she of the "Hare & Hounds at Kingstanding). Our romance had blossomed over the year since my return to the UK. We had spent a week together with her father and mother and other friends on a trip down to the wonderful town of Carbis Bay in Cornwall. I was very impressed with a number of those friends who were fellow licensees, including Horace Stokes and his wife Joan from the "Tyburn Arms" pub near Castle Vale and Leo and Eileen Wood from the "Tennis Courts" pub on the Walsall Road near Perry Barr. Horace was a very outspoken and direct man who was not always careful about what others in the company may feel or think. This had caused a few ripples in their relationships with some friends but he was the sort of man who did not bear a grudge and would be equally surprised if anyone else did. I was to find out after many years that Horace had an incredible past as a much decorated war hero in the Special Forces during WW2. To his great credit, he had never ever told anyone outside his family of this and I will always value the memory of his friendship to me personally, for ever. Valerie and I became engaged in the February of 1961 and we were married in the March of 1962. The ceremony was held in a beautiful Catholic church in College Road Erdington, Birmingham, and the reception held at the Stockland pub in Erdington. We had bought a small Austin A35 van at the time (brand new at £450), as it was an economical and practical vehicle for us to run. We had taken up renting a flat in Peterborough as we did not yet qualify for Air Ministry housing on the base at Brampton.

Chapter 11 – 1962 The Cuba Crisis

My CO (commanding officer) at this time was Squadron Leader "Ricky" Waite who I always managed to get on well with. My immediate boss was a wonderful character called Warrant Officer "Doughy" Baker. He was a much decorated chap with a lot of experience and walked with a pronounced a limp. He and his wonderful wife lived in a large married quarter (MQ) on the base site at "Belle Isle" a sort of satellite area just away from the main site (which was originally a park surrounding a beautiful mansion belonging to a Lady Elizabeth Sparrow). He had a very large family of about seven children, if my memory serves me well, hence the need for two houses which adjoined each other with a connecting door leading into each. I was in charge of the massive collection of aerial films housed in a special building called the "Film Library". Many of these films dated back to the Second World War. We were called on to locate inspect and despatch selections to wherever they were requested from the Registry at the main site for JARIC. It was an interesting task for me as I was always fascinated to view all kinds of territories from around the world in detailed photographic images and I suppose fed my interest in the historical aspects of reconnaissance at the same time.

We also played host to a group of American Air Force lads who arrived at our site with some photographic duplicating machines designed to copy a large amount of films we held there. Soon after they had completed their task, we became aware of the reason for their visit by dramatic world events which shocked all of us out of our complacency and near sedentary existence there. I arrived for work one morning to find an American Air Force lad fully armed at our gates who flatly refused to allow me in without authority from his superior (who was of course no where to be seen!). To say I was a bit indignant would be a bit of an understatement and I let him know in no uncertain terms. The sound of his weapon being brought into a loaded condition and pointed in my general direction persuaded me to agree to wait for his boss! Eventually our Warrant Officer appeared on the scene together with the American Sergeant who had been supervising their stay in our site. As soon as we got inside our enclosure, we were briefed on a situation which beggared belief at that moment. It was of course those fateful days in May 1962 that the confrontation between the USA and the Soviet Union came to a head over the Russian missile sites in Cuba. We realised that this was no drill, no boring exercise, this was a real prospect of a dreaded nuclear all out war, and we really were all in a very serious situation. The photographic evidence of the missile sites at San Cristobel appeared on TV and the UN Security Council were provided with this indisputable evidence. The US President, John F Kennedy introduced a blockade of the island and the Soviet leader Nikita Kruschev warned the USA of dire consequences. The world held its breath for those critical seven days in May. To his eternal credit, the US President's ability to negotiate a deal finally provided a break through which allowed a saving of face for all sides and the world was allowed to breathe again.

The San Cristobel missile site in Cuba

The American U 2 spy plane

The "hot line" became a reality to try to prevent any future similar conditions arising between the super powers and the power of photo reconnaissance to also prevent wars became a corner stone for its place in history. In the autumn of 1962 we were allowed to move closer to the base in what was called an official "hiring" at "Eaton House", Eaton Socon, near St. Ives in Cambridgeshire. A "hiring" was a private dwelling / flat apartment which the RAF rented from the owner to help subsidise their on base quota of housing, and those qualifying would then pay rent to the RAF (at a reasonable rate). The "landlady" of this apartment was living in the adjoining building and the apartment was supposed to be self contained. We found out later that she had entered our apartment on a number of occasions without our consent. She was a rather strange person and very inquisitive, perhaps without malice, but certainly a bit more than "nosey" if you follow my drift.

It all came to light one winter of 1962/3 when the whole country was in deep freeze and our apartment like many others lost water supplies (the water pipes to our apartment ran through an old dairy which was tiled and very very cold). Initially she was sympathetic and allowed us a few buckets of water daily from her own ice free supply, but eventually refused our requests when there was no let up in the weather. We were forced to stay with friends who owned a pub in St Ives (and who we were fortunately able to help out when bar staff could not make it in to work). I remember the chap as C. A. B. Richards, or "Cab" as he liked to be called. His wife was called Dee and he was also an extremely accomplished artist, working in oils and water colours with equal expertise. I still have one of wonderful abstract paintings today. Cab had a wonderful full set of whiskers and beard and looked like a Father Christmas understudy, with a disposition to match! They were wonderfully supportive to us during the period of confrontation with the landlady at the Eaton Socon apartment. The RAF brought a civil action against her for breach of contract and eventually normality was restored, albeit a somewhat "frosty" relationship prevailed. In the early spring, I had been sent a document giving me a preliminary warning for overseas duties (PWR) and I was intrigued as to what may lay in store for us. My CO, Squadron Leader Ricky Waite sent for me one afternoon and explained that I was to be sent to a rather sensitive post (called "special duties") at the HQ Allied Forces Mediterranean (located on the tiny island of Malta). I was to be assigned be the personal photographer to the Commander-in-Chief, one Admiral Sir John Hamilton, and assisting in the lithographic printing department when not required for the primary task. To say I was a bit overawed by all this was an understatement, but the kudos and excitement over rode any misgivings. I completed a crash course in lithography and additional training in the public relations role. There was also a very special development in my personal life, Valerie was to become a mother and this was truly the icing on the cake that year.

Chapter 12 - 1963 Malta GC

Malta has a long well known history from the 14th century when the Ottoman Empire besieged the island which was successfully defended by the Knights of St John La Vallette. The Island was awarded the George Cross during the events of WW2 for its valour whilst besieged yet again, this time by the Axis Forces of Nazi Germany and the Italian Air force under the dictatorship of Benito Mussolini. I was aware of some of this history and excited at the prospect of joining this very special unit located in a magnificent old building at Floriana at the entrance to the famous city of Vallettta, overlooking Grand Harbour. We arrived on the island in the March of 1963 and we settled in to a truly wonderful life of social parties and members of the Villa Rosa Beach Club (our NATO recreation facility!).

The NATO HQ in Malta
HQ AFMED

My immediate boss was Commander David Price RN in the public relations department who had a very interesting wartime record, being the pilot of an aircraft which forced a German submarine to surrender. For this he had been awarded the DSO. I also worked with a couple of wonderful colleagues from the US Navy, one P.O. (Petty Officer) Lloyd Ozab and one P.O. Orville Harrison. Lloyd was a lithographer and Orville was the photographer. A Petty Officer was of an equivalent rank to a Sergeant. Lloyd was from New York with a wonderful accent to match. He was a tubby, amiable and friendly character whose English wife Dolly, was also an absolute treasure. Sadly they were unable to have children which were a continual source of anguish for them both, as I later discovered from their US Navy colleagues and friends Charlie and Dorothy Pierce from Florida who also became our friends. Orville and his wife Barbara came from the Deep South along with an also wonderful and completely different accent. Lloyd and Orville both had the habit of smoking the most beautiful huge cigars which they obtained from the PX Commissary in Naples (their version of the NAAFI) and I must confess to being a convert fairly soon. The truth about Americans is they love to be loved and they love to be sociable. They are without doubt some of the kindest and most generous people I have ever had the privilege of meeting. They had the most hospitable "open door" policy at home I have ever seen and it took some getting used to from our built-in English reserve. It was nothing to be in their homes and some friend would just turn up, open the fridge door and help themselves to a beer, a lump of food , whatever, and no-one would turn a hair or bat an eye lid. This was their way of saying simply "you're welcome". Their manners were impeccable, even if their children's behaviour seemed tolerated to a point of indulgence. Their teeth and cosmetic dental care also seemed to be a constant priority in their health care programme, much to their credit and their often beautiful smiles. So this was my introduction to a whole new world of experiences and I was to learn a great deal about their "psyche" and what made them tick. They were fanatical in their loyalty to their country and their flag which came to light one day when the stores Chief Petty Officer (a Royal Navy staff member) put an un-usable US National flag in the rag bag for disposal. There was a near International incident when a member of the US Navy contingent discovered its fate! I soon became aware of this wonderful devotion of their souls to their "mother country" which I have always admired since. I have often reflected what a pity we are not encouraged to hold the same regard for ours. The NATO HQ building housed the Commander in Chief of the Allied Forces Mediterranean and the NATO support staff. My role was to provide photographic support to the Public Relations Officer. It was a very alien position to find myself in, as we were responsible for directly purchasing all our supplies and equipment locally, from a budget held by the PRO (pubic relations office). To this end we had almost a free hand on selecting what we thought was the most suitable kit to do the job, which was just as well as I was soon to discover.

Initially, I found most of the tasking involved operating the printing press equipment to provide documents supporting the needs of the PRO. However I was soon tasked to be out and about following the Commander in Chief and his entourage as they performed the meeting and greeting of many local and international dignitaries. Just for the technically minded, I had permission from the boss to use my privately owned Mamiya C3 camera, which had excellent lens units with perfect resolution for the job. I do owe a great deal of success to this camera as it was soon obvious that the boss had not seen much to beat the image quality we had achieved in a relatively short time. My American colleague was also extraordinarily helpful in recommending the thin based Tri X Pan Professional film (rated at ASA/ISO 400), which we processed in Microdol X developer diluted 1+ 3 for 13 minutes at 20°C, with astounding results on definition and quality. We also used an Omega D2V condenser enlarger which I had not seen before, but created a very crisp image due to its higher inherent contrast properties. Each lens unit of the enlarger had its own set of matching condensers which neatly slotted into its carrier on the illumination head. This was ideal for PR pictures as against the softer illumination head of the Devere 54A enlarger I was used to for aerial photography, where low contrast was essential to retain vital detail in the shadows of intelligence images. I recall my colleague Lloyd Ozab was almost at the end of his tour of duty and was shortly to be replaced by another US navy Petty Officer, Glen Haller, who was a descendant of the Native American Indian Cree tribe from Denver in Colorado. The staff were all extraordinarily patient and intrigued with our different languages, and different they were, other nationalities included; Italian, French, Greek and Turkish! I learned a great deal about their attitudes to the importance of good manners, their national pride and high values of loyalty to their individual heritage. They were also fascinated in all things "English" and we had a wonderful rapport along with the usual sense of military humour common to all military people. When my daughter was born in August 1963 at the RN Hospital in Mtarfa, Glen Haller kindly agreed to be her God father. There were a number of famous dignitaries who visited the HQ including Lord Louis Mountbatten, Field Marshall General Montgomery and the US General Lyman Lemnitzer. We were always kept very busy working long hours, often well into the late night covering official cocktail receptions and the usual meet and greet of local dignitaries, despite our official duty hours being from 7.30 am to 2 pm (normal tropical hours because of the summer heat). There was a useful horse trade in this because we sometimes caught up with our time off when things went quiet. Because we had no official "mess" or club of our own, being somewhat isolated from the usual mess facilities available to the normal service bases on the Island, there was an arrangement with a local club called the "Villa Rosa Beach Club", which had a beautiful swimming pool and club facilities, well above the standard I was used to.

My family and I had rented a very pleasant first floor apartment which overlooked the harbour at Sliema and we often enjoyed a window seat of the comings and goings of the Royal Navy submarines from their depot ship, HMS Ausonia. Glenn Haller was also renting an apartment close by so we often travelled in to the HQ together. Our next door neighbour, CPO (Chief Petty Officer) Tony Kirk and his family, was a submariner in the Royal Navy, serving aboard HMS Tiptoe. We also became great friends over the coming years and he was the instrument of my education into all things traditional in the Royal Navy. My immediate learning curve was the subtle differences between RAF speak and Navy speak. Floor levels became "decks"; walls became "bulkheads"; toilets became "heads"; and many others too numerous to list here. I did learn some wonderful traditional navy sayings and their origins or explanations, which proved eminently useful later in life when I was to join other joint service organisations. My daughter Lisa-Jane was born in the Royal Navy Hospital, Mtarfa on 13th August 1963 and she was a beautiful and treasured gift for both of us. It was just six weeks after the birth of Liza-Jane, in October 1963, that Valerie's father tragically died from a heart attack. To make matters even worse, her mother was staying with us on holiday at the time and had to fly home in dreadful distress. We followed shortly after by the kind generosity of Air Marshall McKinley (the Deputy Commander in Chief of the NATO HQ), who offered us a seat on his staff aircraft which was returning him to the UK for a re-union. Shortly after the funeral I had to return to Malta and Valerie followed on a week or so afterwards. It left a great sadness on Valerie who was very close to her father and she had problems reconciling the fact that he was just 49 years old when he died. The only slight consolation, though no real comfort to the family, was the fact that he was suffering from leukaemia at the time and perhaps would have suffered more until the inevitable had taken him. In those days there was no prospect of a cure for this kind of cancer or many others for that matter. On the brighter side we enjoyed a wonderful social life and made so many wonderful friends in many of the various military services working at the NATO base, and made many local Maltese friends who were wonderful with their hospitality and friendship. My top boss was a wonderful and very powerful man who commanded respect with an almost charismatic aura. He was, by reputation a very stern and precise man, who expected the best from everyone. However, in dealings with the "lower deck ratings" namely me and my kind, he was a quiet and gentle man whose requests were always put in such a manner that you just could not fail or disappoint. Perhaps this was his secret of his success. He personally viewed all my work with a trained and professional eye and knew exactly what he wanted. He also was prepared to listen to the opinions and comments from the likes of me as to how we could best improve the result we needed to achieve. In all my further experiences with "top brass" I have never had a more professionally orientated person who really understood the power of the photographic image in matters of public relations.

It came as no surprise to me in later years that the Royal Navy had the most successful achievements in this field, which also benefited their slice of the Defence budget, something the RAF never seemed to grasp, even today. One morning in November 1963 we had just turned the radio on at home when the programmes were interrupted by news flashes coming in direct from the BBC via the BFBS (British Forces Broadcasting Service) something very serious was going on in America at a town called Dallas and confused reports were pouring in that the American president John F Kennedy had been attacked during a visit there. We realised this was going to be of great concern to my US Navy colleagues and I dashed round to fetch Glenn Haller in case he was unaware. As soon as we got back to the apartment with him we began to hear reports that the President had in fact been shot and critically injured, the rest is history. It was a terrible blow to Glen as he had met JFK in the Pentagon whilst serving there quite recently before coming to Malta. There followed a dreadful gloom which settled over the whole Island for a time and all the Maltese, many of whom had relatives in the USA. The following days and weeks were indeed very unsettling as those responsible were sought out and many media rumours were given airings which bordered on hysteria from time to time. Many conspiracy theories have surfaced (and do still) from attention hungry journalists, the truth, probably being the first casualty after the event. Up to this time my duties had been all shore based (on dry land!), this was soon to change. My introduction to the kind of pressures which would become the norm was my first sea voyage aboard HMS Surprise, a converted despatch vessel which was the C-in C's flagship. Admiral Sir John Hamilton was a tall man with an acute sense of detail and an inborn stature of authority. Despite this aura of power he was also a true gentleman who treated all his crew with a fatherly tolerance and respect, even this lowly RAF NCO. Whenever I was tasked to cover an event, he always made a point of allowing me sufficient time to complete the shoot and seemed to trust my judgment without question as to the location, light and posture best suited. This was a great relief to me in the early days as I had little experience in handling VIP's and dignitaries, but I soon grasped the essence of at least looking and acting as though I knew exactly what I was doing and getting out of the way as soon as done.

Chapter 13 – North Africa

My duties did entail a lot of "sea time" aboard H.M.S. Surprise, the C-in-C's flag ship, and I was enjoying the experiences very much. I also managed to have a couple of tours aboard the U.S.S. Shangri-La, a very old but historical aircraft carrier, and a visit to the U.S.S. John F Kennedy, a more modern fighting ship. One tour comes to mind in particular and that was aboard H.M.S. Surprise. I did not know then but our mission was to proceed to Greece and evacuate King Constantine and his family to safety after the Greek Colonels revolt against the monarchy. We came close to the position of rendezvous, but the RAF had come to the rescue by lifting him and his family out because the situation had become desperate for them. We then turned south to the North African coast and dropped anchor just outside of Tobruk harbour. The object of this visit was to try and persuade King Idris that the troublesome Colonel Ghaddafi was about to usurp his throne and again it was hoped to effect some sort of move for him to a safe haven. When he came aboard I was given strict instructions not to be seen taking pictures directly, but to use whatever subterfuge I could to record the meeting aboard the ship. I managed to use a suitable guest cabin scuttle (Navy speak for "porthole") near the access gang plank designated for his entourage. My presence was masked by a suitably draped coarse camouflage net over the open aperture of the cabin bulkhead scuttle. The coarse weave of the cam netting meant that the lens could record the images without loss of quality.

This was a technique I "borrowed" from army surveillance methods. The C-in-C had an immaculate Austin Princess staff car aboard the ship along with a NATO green Vauxhall saloon back up vehicle, which had been offloaded to the shore for his use at this juncture, but during the process the Austin Princess had been slightly damaged. Rather than risk a further mishap it was decided that the two vehicles would drive overland to our next port of call at Benghazi. I had completed all the onboard processing and printing to the satisfaction of the "boss" so I thought that there may be an opportunity to see some of the places my dad had passed through during the North Africa campaign during the war. I volunteered to act as escort to the Royal Marine NCO drivers to keep them company and act as an extra pair of eyes on the long drive. I was delighted to be given the go ahead and we set off in the early hours for a cooler start for the long journey. It was a wonderful journey along desert roads following the reverse of the route my father had taken many years ago during WW2. We arrived just outside of Benghazi and I was feeling a bit tired from the heat of the journey and chose to sit in the back and stretch out a bit. The Royal Marine Sergeant driver was a great guy and we had talked a lot during the journey about all sorts of things. As we approached to town we had a slight mishap with some kind of small animal which had dashed across the road in front. Mindful of the possible damage, we pulled up and examined the front which was clear apart form a bit of a mess on the canvass cover of the four star plate (which signified the high rank of the rear seat occupant when uncovered). So with no real harm done, we removed the cover and cleaned it best we could until we reached our destination. I had unfortunately not bothered to replace it over the four gleaming stars, which now proclaimed the occupant to be a full blown Admiral! As we approached the Main Guardroom of the Wavell Army barracks, someone must have been on very sharp lookout because we witnessed the fastest assembly of an impromptu guard of honour ever attempted. By the time the Limo had swept past the Guardroom, it became obvious to us the reason for the turmoil we had just witnessed and unwittingly created! Discretion being the better part of valour, we kept going into the base heading for the motor pool to refuel ready for the arrival of the real Boss the following day. It was some time later we learned that the repercussions of our negligence had extended to the officer's mess, who for reasons best known to themselves had decided that Admiral had arrived a day early and organised a swift reception for him! I still don't know how the Royal Marine Sergeant squared it all away to this day, but I kept a very low profile at the Army base for the rest of the visit.

Our next destination was Tripoli and this time I stayed with the ship for the journey there. On arrival at the Tripoli harbour we were tied up alongside the quay where we were able to see the large amount of "farm tractor" supplies donated to the new emergent regime of Colonel Ghaddafi by the Russian cargo ship not far away from us. It was at this point that a young ship's officer approached me and suggested that I put on some civvies and take a walk around the dock side with my camera acting like a tourist and capturing some "very useful" evidence of the contents of the crates. What a jolly jape, I thought, I would really love to spend the next 20 years in a Libyan jail and experience other Arab hospitality, reminiscent of mediaeval times. This I explained to the young officer and I also invited him to accompany me on such an adventure. Needless to say we decided that using a long lens fitted to my 35 mm Leica camera from the bridge would be a more practical solution and this was fortunate as Libyan armed police has just turned up to keep an eye on things at the dockside. History has recorded that the Soviet Union poured massive aid into Libya and other areas of Africa to influence the politics in favour its expansion plans. The pictures I recorded of these "farm implements" on the dockside provided some bits of evidence. As we dropped anchor in Tripoli harbour the brief on arrival was to include a visit to greet the local Muhaffid at his offices in the city. The plan was for the entourage to board the Admirals barge and proceed to the shore to be met by an escort of military police and some local dignitaries. This was the first time I had been allowed in the rear well of the barge (out of sight of course, and well in advance of the boss's descent into the barge from the gangway). The entourage were assembled to be taken aboard the Admiral's barge and I was in the back of the boat with my Mamiya C3 camera, awaiting his departure from the ship and his transfer to the shore. Some distance away we could see the reception party on the quay side with the usual convoy of limousines and Military police escorts all lined up for his arrival. The VIP party came aboard the barge and the barge crew performed their ritual choreography with the boat hooks and we were off. Although I had seen the very adept ceremonial routine by the barge crew from afar, it was the first opportunity to see it in close up. All went like precision clockwork as we pulled away from the ship and made towards the quayside where the convoy of escorts could be seem waiting about a mile away. We were well in sight of the quayside when the unthinkable happened. The Coxswain "barge driver" who was a Chief Petty Officer, had somehow misjudged or misread the tide and the effects of the sand bars between the ship at anchor and the quayside because we quite abruptly came to a grinding halt! No one actually fell overboard but there was a bit of a kafuffle up front and a stream of instructions being passed to the Coxswain who was desperately trying to extricate the barge from the sand bar by turning to port or starboard. However the more everyone tried to contradict his instincts and experience, the worse the situation became. Fortunately the "ratings" barge was approaching from an earlier run ashore and was about to come alongside when the Coxswain ordered it to stand off .He could see that it was in danger of also becoming stuck in the sand bar.

Not far away was the "ratings" barge carrying the ships essential supplies such as a sack or two of vegetables etc., and a working crew escort. To be fair the Admiral's Coxswain tried every trick in the book to get us off the sand bar but it soon became obvious that this was no longer an option. The ratings barge approached as close as it dared without itself becoming a casualty of the same cause. Then a tiny little boat, similar to a "coracle" river boat appeared from nowhere containing a very wizened old Arab, who had decided to seize an opportunity.

"Me take you to the shore, Effendi", he said in his best broken English. No one said a word as the Admiral took in the options and the inevitable delay for any alternative.

"Right, that's it, no choice, let's get this bloody mess sorted without more delay" he declared and the Arab, smiling, manoeuvred his tiny boat to the Admirals barge.
As I raised my camera for the picture of a lifetime, Admiral Sir John Hamilton turned and looked me straight in the eye.

"If I hear so much as a click from your camera, Corporal, I will cut you legs off!" he called out, and my picture vaporised into the ether.
However he did smile at the situation and graciously paid the little old Arab before hopping on to the ratings barge for the final leg to the quay side. There was rapturous applause from the reception entourage and the waiting crowd who were of course well within earshot and missed not a word. For my sins I had to follow him in the same manner and managed to scramble aboard a R.M.P. escort Land Rover just before the rest of the group joined the limousine convoy, after a rescue tow had been affected for the Admiral's barge. If I thought my troubles were over, I was mistaken, because by them, time had slipped by and there was a sense of urgency and confusion among the entourage being met and allocated places in vehicles. I scrambled up on to the quayside and made a vain attempt to clamber aboard on of the escort vehicles designated with my seat which by now had no such room! I turned and saw a Military police Land Rover at the head of the waiting convoy so I sprinted up to the back of it and whistled at the driver to get his attention, at the same time almost hurling myself in the open back seat of the pristine vehicle all decked out with white cushions. It was only when I managed to get upright and look up that I met the steely eyes of the Provost Marshall sitting next to the Military Police driver and caught sight of the gold braid around the edge of his peaked cap and his ceremonial sword at his side.
"Don't you ever dare to whistle at me again, lad, or I'll chop your bloody legs off!" he said through gritted teeth and a near purple apoplectic face filled with rage!
I just wanted to curl up into the tiniest ball imaginable and disappear off the face of God's earth. I managed to splutter out copious apologies and garbled explanations, none of which he showed any sign of taking in but just retorted with a
"Shut the **ck up, sit still, and get out when I tell you to".
For the second time that day, the sword had proved mightier than the camera or words and we took off with flags fluttering and everyone swept out of the way. This was not a vehicle to be challenged by donkey; camel

Behind the Lens   269

oo pushbike and like a knife through butter. Tripoli was neatly sliced open for the VIP convoy to pass through unhindered. We came to a halt outside a great building somewhere in the city centre and without turning the Provost Marshall growled something like

"Get the luck out sonny, you are not coming back with us".

Grovelling profusely, which impressed him not a jot, I saw the boss and the entourage spilling out and into the entrance of the building, which was my signal to get ahead, if I could and beat them to the meeting room on the fourth floor. Unfortunately my luck was not about to change and the lift filled up with many and everyone who needed to be with the boss. I made for the stairs and somehow managed to take them three at a time, just to get there as the backs of the entourage passed into the meeting room. Just before the great doors were almost slammed in my face, a very large Libyan Army Officer (who looked remarkably like Idi Amin, only a bit bigger) smiled at me and held the door ajar to let me in. But by then as you can possibly imagine, although being fit, and the temperature was around the mid eighties, I was therefore a tad overheated to say the least. In my state of near collapse a huge apparition of a gigantic African Army officer appeared and he held out a tray with large glasses of iced orange juice.

"You look like you need one of these" he said with a broad grin on his face which would have put a Cheshire cat to shame.

I was so very grateful and I downed it in one, big mistake! His smile could have lit up the room without the aid of the flash gun on the camera and seemed to be pasted on as it never left him. I took dozens of pictures of all and sundry before "Idi Amin" gently tapped my arm to signal it was time to leave the room. He followed me out into the corridor and asked if I would like something to drink in perfect Sandhurst English. He opened a very ornate cupboard at the wall and there was a refrigerator built inside with all kinds of beverages, (all non alcoholic of course). He poured me a huge glass of iced lemon and orange which went down almost without touching the sides. He must have taken pity on me as my beautifully pressed and polished appearance had all but wilted under the oppressive heat outside and coupled with the Olympic sprint up four flights of stairs, my KD uniform resembled the aftermath of an explosion in a Turkish bath house.

We returned to the ship without further mishap and I was pulled to one side later by the ADC who told me the boss was very impressed with my efforts and especially by managing to keep up with the group under the circumstances. About a couple of hours later, "mother nature" taught me a salutary lesson in taking care not to drink ice cold fluids in high temperatures! I recovered a few days later when life returned to normality. The events in Libya during the following years are well recorded in history but I will always remember that particular baptism of fire in the mad world of public relations. The ship's company was later invited to a welcoming party by employees of the Cable and Wireless Company who had a large base there. It was a wonderful evening where I met Arthur and Cynthia Hammond, with whom I began a long relationship, in the years to come. We sailed for home after a day or two and I must admit that I was relieved to be back with my wife and daughter. After the usual process of docking and coming ashore I handed my classified materials over to the HQ and was given a couple of days off to rest and recuperate with my family. I was astounded to learn that my daughter, Liza-Jane had actually learned to swim during my absence. Not such a big deal normally, but she was only just crawling around when I left. Valerie had gone to the beach for a day out and Liza-Jane had apparently crawled into the sea following Mom and just carried on with a form of dog paddle. From that day on she had no fear of water and we had quite a tough time trying to persuade would be rescuers that she was able to swim perfectly well. Unfortunately it would scare the life out of casual observers when she launched herself into the water at the Villa Rosa Beach Club and we were obliged to fit her with water wings to re assure the company around the pool. There was a fair measure of jealousy from fellow RAF staff at the base at RAF Luqa as I was entitled to duty free supplies (including fuel coupons) as I was working for NATO. This was understandable, as we were all in the same geographical place working for the same Royal Air Force and it did seem to be unfair, even to me as a beneficiary of the system. I was also able to buy a lovely white Volkswagen "Beetle" duty free (which cost me about £450 at the time) and it was my pride and joy for many years. Our neighbours at Pieta Wharf (where we lived in a small apartment) were a wonderful couple; Tony and Margaret Kirk. He was a Chief Petty Officer (equivalent rank to a Flight Sergeant in the RAF) electrical artificer working on submarines not far from where we lived at the submarine base in Sliema.

One escapade was a very peculiar sea voyage aboard a tiny minesweeper, HMS Shavington. This trip was a last minute intelligence gathering mission as a result of the Russian fleet breaking out of the Black Sea and into the Mediterranean, presumably to let Nikita Khrushchev (the Russian President) see what everyone would or could do if he decided to flex his navy muscles a bit more than usual. We set off at some ungodly hour and I had gathered a pile of long lens units, 35 mm cameras, and all sorts of filters to try and grab the best I could get. This being the era of monochrome (black and white stuff!), I needed yellow filters to increase contrast in the shadow detail and hoped this would do the job, despite a reduction in exposure value because of the filter factors. After several days of following the "Moscow" aircraft carrier it became obvious to all and sundry that this tiny minesweeper was not going to be allowed to come anywhere near the big ship and every time we came closer than imaging a large dust spot on the horizon, she just piled on the knots and left us waddling in her wake. Once we were recalled and my mates from RAF Luqa flew overhead in the Shackleton long range maritime reconnaissance aircraft, the skipper allowed me off the bridge and I spent the rest of the trip following up "home town stories" with the crew, taking lots of pictures of the boys at work and writing up the "who, what, where, when and how" for each sailor. The skipper was well pleased when he overviewed my stuff and everyone concerned felt it was at least worth the PR exercise if nothing else was gained. My ego had also grown alongside my experiences and to some extent I was blissfully unaware of the damage being inflicted on my marriage. That is not to say we were both extremely happy with the social side of our lives, but when the party is over the piper has to be paid, which was to prove endemic in later years for all sorts of good and bad reasons.

Admiral Sir John
Hamilton
C-in-C HQAFMED
circa 1963

The fleet at anchor in Grand Harbour, Malta

Chapter 14 - 1964 RTUK

I returned to my old unit at Brampton, The Joint Air Reconnaissance Centre, which was a normal procedure then, probably due to the high costs of security clearance for each of us. I felt quite happy with this as I was becoming quite used to the constraints and procedures of working in high security environments. I was placed in charge of the chemical re-circulation plant and the quality control of the processing solutions which fed the vast complex of processing darkrooms. I had to bone up on my knowledge of chemistry and sensitometric controls. As it turned out I became quite adept at the system, even introducing a few schemes of my own, which I like to think improved the general workings and recovery of the silver from the fixer solutions to the benefit of the environment and the tax payer. I found out that my Warrant Officer was not as appreciative as I might have hoped though. I discovered that he considered my "jammy posting" at the NATO HQ had resulted in my assessment being over rated. I was upset about this as I honestly felt that I had earned the assessments on my annual performance report from my previous boss (a full blown Royal Navy Commander is not given to over assessing his staff in performance). I had to learn to bite the bullet and keep my head down and I was to learn a few other hard lessons in the fullness of time, you cannot please all the people all the time.

I have to say I did enjoy my work there and I have always been so fortunate in this. My experience was widening all the time and I did thrive on challenges at that age as most youngsters do. I was given a free hand to run my little department albeit, there was always someone keeping an eye on how things were going. It was during this time that we found Valerie was going to have our second child in the late summer (of 1966). We had become a bit disenchanted with the continual disturbance of moving homes from private to military hirings and then to the married quarters. We found out that a new estate was being built in Hartford just outside of Huntingdon, and we knew of others at work who had taken to buying a home of their own. With this in mind we decided to take the plunge and secured a simple but useful three bedroom detached house with a garage in Duncan Way. One of my colleagues, Al Simms had also bought a property opposite so we also had someone we knew as neighbours. It was shortly after taking over the home, that my son David jr. made his debut at the RAF Hospital at Ely on September 14th. We now had the perfect family anyone could wish for and we settled into our new home with enthusiasm. It was a lovely area and we had some really good friends and neighbours which made life very comfortable for us. Of course there was the usual nausea from the RAF security services who wanted to know how a humble Corporal could possibly afford the £3,400 needed to finance such a lavish investment. It took some explaining to a very cynical member of the security staff, how the extra 2 guineas (£2 and 2 shillings) a week living out allowance went towards making up the mortgage payments required to meet the £20 a month outlay. I think the maths eluded him as he thought it "highly irresponsible" to commit to paying a mortgage, putting myself in harms way of some enemy agent who could easily use the debt ridden situation to exploit my desperate needs for additional finances. This seriously was the gist of his assessment and I diplomatically explained that the home was in my wife's name and she was not prepared to discuss her personal finances with an organisation of which she was not a member. It was a few months later that I was notified of my PWR (preliminary warning posting) to an "active service zone," namely Aden in the Middle East. No coincidence of course, but in fact it was a very useful opportunity for us to firm up our financial situation by renting out the home to the USAF at nearby Alconbury for the duration of my un-accompanied posting and Valerie was happy to return to live with her mother Elsie, in Birmingham, who also welcomed the children and the company from Valerie. Elsie had been widowed for two years now and was feeling the vulnerability of living alone. She had been given the opportunity to run an off licence in the Erdington area of Birmingham which was a useful supplement to her income. Valerie was able to help and support her in the venture during my absence.

Chapter 15 - Aden – Finale of British Rule

My tour of duty in Aden began in March 1967, as the RAF Brittannia troop transport aircraft landed and came to a halt on the apron of the airfield at Khormaksar. The blast of hot air which came into the aircraft as the doors opened, engulfed everyone, like the inside of a super heated oven. An RAF Regiment WO appeared in the doorway and gave instructions for everyone to deplane as quickly as possible. We were welcomed by a ring of armed troopers from the RAF Regiment who took up defensive positions around the aircraft. We hurriedly disembarked and the aircraft turned around in record time to be filled with lucky chaps who had completed their time in this dreadful place. There was a pungent smell pervading the air from the mixture of sand and oil which reminded me of unwashed feet! I did not like the place and nothing ever did change that view. The romantic notion of the desert and handsome sheiks riding white horses into ornate Bedouin camps exists only on the silver screen. This place was dirty, hot, smelly and had only one thing going for it, absolutely sod all! It was March 1967 and the situation in the Aden Gulf had reached a serious level of deterioration. The British presence for the last 150 years was drawing to a close and the local political unrest had reached levels of unprecedented violence. 1967 was to be the last year of rule from Great Britain, leaving a power vacuum which the NLF (National Liberation Front) and the FLOSSY (Front for the Liberation of South Yemen) were both determined to fill at the expense of each other.

The British Forces based there were, as usual, playing piggy-in-the middle as referee and receiving the violent attentions of both groups for their trouble. The morale was high considering the conditions and the fact that the conflict there had started in 1964 with a hand grenade being thrown in the airport at the British Governor. Since then the situation had gradually deteriorated until we were recording up to 200 security incidents each day throughout the Protectorate during 1967. Harold Wilson, the British Prime Minister had decided the British would withdraw by the end of the year. During my time there the situation became confused, both politically, and militarily, with contradiction from General Tower and Lt Colonel Colin Mitchell of the Argyle and Sutherland Highlanders. The Soviet Union had had a field day stirring up the pot along with many other factions and splinter groups. The title of my unit was ARIC (ME) Air Reconnaissance Intelligence Centre (Middle East). Compared to its other

Behind the Lens | 275

counterparts around the globe it was a small unit with a Flt Lt George Perrella as CO, WO Ron Commons (who was due to be tourex shortly after my arrival) and WO Roy Elliott (his replacement) Flight Sergeant John Cornthwaite, Sergeant Ted Taylor, Cpl's Brian Goodwin, Don Jones, Steve Smith, Mick Ireland and the rest of the crew SAC's Cookie Proudfoot, Ted Edwards, Brian Mateer, Baz Walker and Bob Fothergill. Cpl Dutch Holland was our maintenance man and general fix it mechanic, which he always managed to do. The Intelligence was gathered mostly from unreliable local sources and the patrols of 22 SAS who operated in the area in covert and overt roles. Our small photo section was responsible for the routine support of the engineers, photographing repaired, damaged and defective equipment and aircraft; processing and printing the 70 mm films from the F95 low level reconnaissance cameras fitted to the Hunters of 1417 PR Squadron, and the occasional flight in helicopters using hand held F117B cameras (with 5" wide film). We also supported the Avro Shackleton aircraft of 8 Squadron, which flew with old F24 cameras in the back hatch also fitted with 5" wide film. On top of all this we also had the grim task of photographing the bodies of terrorist killed in attacks on both military and civilian targets. These often included innocent victims, women and children out shopping or travelling to schools who also became casualties of the terrorist campaigns. We found out some time later that an East German assassin had been brought in to despatch specified members of key posts in maintaining law and order, or the essential services such as electricity supply generators or water desalination plants. We were all puzzled at the time as to how the targets had been hit so easily, whilst stationary at traffic lights or petrol stations, and why they had allowed the gun man to get so close, considering their long standing experience in Aden. It was only when the assassin was caught up in a gun battle with covert SAS troopers that the truth came out.

Chapter 16 - 24/7 Work, Work, Work

W
e operated on a shift rotation and all of us were on unaccompanied tours (i.e. no families). We were able to support the other service units whenever and whereever the need arose. So our work varied greatly from supporting the photo reconnaissance Hunter aircraft of 1417 Squadron. This was a very important role as intelligence gathering relied heavily on our reconnaissance images by all the Army units which, during the whole of my tour, included the Prince of Wales Royal Regiment, The Argyle and Sutherland Highlanders, 42 and 45 Royal Marines the Parachute Regiment and 22 Regt, Special Air Service. Whilst it is singularly unpleasant being separated from your family, the security situation gave us at least peace of mind that none of our families in the midst of all this. Only weeks before, one of our colleagues had been injured and "casevaced" home with his family because of in incident outside his home in Tawaii Crescent. The "espirit de corps" and level of job satisfaction was very high and the unit became a well-oiled machine. The quality of the aerial pictures proved very useful to the troop commanders and it began to earn us a reputation of "can do" to coin a modern American phrase, there was no question of demarcation if the situation became volatile.

Hunter FR10 aircraft on patrol over the Aden Protectorate

Those who may have already completed a 12 hour shift, stayed on to support the others whenever the need arose and on one occasion we were issued "stay awake" pills by the MO as we needed to push the envelope into a 48 hour duration. One of the older aircraft based in Aden was the Shackleton maritime reconnaissance aircraft of No 8 Squadron. These huge four engined aircraft with contra rotating propellers could stay aloft for 8 hours or more and provided ideal means of vertical photo reconnaissance, along with the potential to drop bombs, use machine guns against ground targets and generally earn the respect of the nomadic bandits roaming the desolate landscape.

A Saracen armoured vehicle attending an incident at Tawaii

The Hunter fighters of 1417 Squadron were also a remarkable aircraft and their highly skilled pilots produced some astonishing images from the nose and port oblique F 95 cameras. With the security situation worsening week by week, we needed to "beef up" our turnaround time from the aircraft landing to having a processed image available for interpretation. Our Warrant Officer, Roy Elliott had been trying to improve the speed of photographic turnaround for the Hunter reconnaissance aircraft by using one of us as a motorcycle rider to collect the film magazines from the aircraft line hut and getting it to the processing lab in our section. This principle was used very successfully during WW2. So we set up a few practice runs which seemed to improve the time scale considerably and we were all set to make a big impression when the call came in. The first opportunity to put the scheme into operation came shortly after. As soon as we had the "heads-up" the aircraft were in circuit to land, my mate Baz Walker (another fellow Brummie), the acknowledge motorbike "ace", roared off to the line hut to collect the first batch of films. We had the kit all ready and temperatures under control and an eye on the clock, determined to create a new record....and the minutes ticked by. Still no sign of Baz however, and now we began to chew finger nails a bit because it should only have taken him about 2 minutes the way he rode. Five minutes passed and we were now at the gate of the compound, eager to snatch the film magazines from Baz and dash into the darkrooms. Ten minutes went by and anxious glances were now on everyone's face. Where the hell had he got to? We were peering down the road looking for him when a dishevelled apparition came round the corner pushing a somewhat battered motorbike. It was Baz, with cuts and scrapes all over him and the bike in a similar state.

"Those Rock Apes (RAF Regiment troopers) have put a new wire fence up near the line hut and I went straight into it" he groaned.

It was a miracle he didn't kill himself, but he was a tough lad and soldiered on to bring back the magazines. We grabbed the films and made the best of a bad time. When Baz finally stopped cursing and calmed down, he told us that he had taken a short cut across the RAF Regiment compound to gain a few precious seconds on the practice runs. But today of all days, because of the worsening security situation, they had planted a wire fence around the perimeter and he had nearly decapitated himself as he ran into the nearly invisible wire. Fortunately he had the guts and determination to drag himself up, kick the bike into running order, albeit losing some precious minutes and high tail back to us. We had to process the 70mm films by hand on giant spools which held 200 feet of film wound on to the spool in total darkness by an ingenious frame and chute system. We developed the film in Exprol developer (made by May & Baker) and passed it through to the stop bath fixer and a brief dip in the wash tank to be finally dipped in a bath of diluted meths to help it dry rapidly before feeding the film around the A10A drier The whole process took only minutes and we were very proud of the speed and quality we were able to produce. The spools and tanks we used were circular and similar in principle to the normal 35mm film processing tank but of course much larger around 2 feet in diameter to accommodate the spools laid down into them. I have very fond memories of my colleagues in Aden; they were a remarkable collection of very spirited lads with a great sense of humour.

Aden peninsular showing Crater town and Khormaksar airfield

The Hunter FR 10 note the F95 camera port in the nose

The political pressure from the UK to contain the situation was becoming intense for the high command and the media was beginning to have a more involved presence in the affairs. We read reports in the British press from "reliable" sources that our soldiers were giving the locals a hard time and even handling local women roughly during search operations for weapons and explosives hidden in homes and other premises. We were all shocked to read of this as we were often present during some of these operations to record the findings on camera as evidence. I had never been witness to any heavy handed approach by these patrols, in fact considering the amount of grenade attacks and sniping that the terrorists inflicted on the troops, it was surprisingly even handed and done strictly with the minimum of inconvenience to any locals, even those whose homes were found to be harbouring the arms and explosives. It was a very conscientious attitude to win hearts and minds under very difficult circumstances and any transgressions were bound to play into the hands of the terrorists, which every trooper on patrol was only too well aware of. In the end we discovered that someone from the press, who saw pictures of local employees being searched before being allowed into the base to work, believed they were women, when in fact they were men wearing the "longies", a skirt like garment which they preferred due to the extreme climate. It beggars belief that some journalists preferred to report on matters without actually being on the ground, but became armchairs experts from the safety of Bahrain and other more comfortable locations.

I met one reporter who did brave the danger from the Daily Express. He came to cover a "secret" meeting between the leaders of the two main terrorist groups (FLOSSY and the NLF) and the British authorities to try and engineer a peaceful handover after the British withdrawal scheduled towards the end of 1967. He took a number of photos of the group, all sat around a long table in a room with a high ceiling. He asked my boss if he could use our facilities to have the films processed and printed because of their possible urgent significance. He was given permission (very unusual under the circumstances) but obviously political pressure prevailed and he processed the films. Unfortunately when he came to produce the prints, the first results showed the foreground images well enough, but the all important images of the members of the NLF and FLOSSY were lacking in contrast and very dark. He had fired the flash unit directly down the long table and it had diminished in power at the furthest end of the picture. He should have turned the flashgun head towards the ceiling to spread the light more evenly and used a few more shots giving under and over exposure, bracketing the metered exposure, just to make sure. We were always taught to use this method (which we call BLF or bracket like "fun") if there was any chance of losing a picture under difficult lighting conditions. Although we were not exactly enamoured with the press over the recent reports, we could not leave him in the lurch like this and our professional pride came to his rescue. I engaged all my printing skills in shading and dodging the enlarged image onto the photo paper and after a couple of improved efforts we presented him with a suitable balanced image to wire home. He was gushing with plaudits about how brilliant the prints looked and promised to bring a couple of crates of beer over the next day. My Warrant Officer was very pleased with the way we had turned the situation to our advantage, but being a very experienced man he warned us that the press and media often made promises they had no intention of keeping. Sadly he was to be proved right and that was my first lesson in handling the press and media. Do the noble thing, but don't expect it to be returned. My other lesson involving the media came a little later. We were called out to an incident which had occurred on the causeway road which bordered the area outside of the western section of the airfield. It appeared that a local taxi driver had been driving a military person back to the base late at night. The following morning the taxi driver's body was found on the causeway near his abandoned taxi. The assault injuries on the body were so severe, that the head was almost decapitated. Because of the suspected military involvement, we recorded the details of the scene and the subsequent autopsy. The suspect did turn out to be soldier who was later convicted of the murder by a court martial held in Aden.

The subsequent uproar from local indignation reached the British press and they duly followed the events and reported the details. The convicted soldier was to be sent home to serve a prison sentence under the Military and British law as normal procedure. However the local terrorist faction had stirred up feelings and there came a demand for the convicted man to be subjected to a local law trial which would have resulted in the death penalty on conviction. The British press had a field day with their readers who were fed a "sanitised" version of the events which included petitions to "save our soldier". This was not exactly in keeping with the facts or the brutal reality of what had actually happened. The violence that the convicted man had used on an innocent man earning his living was conducive to warrant a plea of insanity in many opinions, including his own colleagues. Had the reporters taken the trouble to investigate the full facts properly they may not have been so keen to portray the convicted soldier as a "victim". I try not to stand in judgment but there are times when the press can unwittingly do a great deal more harm than good in the pursuit of a sensational story to sell. We also played host to 13 Squadron Canberra PR 9 aircraft flown over from Malta to do as much survey and other tasks as they could but they proved a tempting target. The airfield at Khormaksar had been attacked more frequently with home made mortar rounds and consequently the precious aircraft of No 13 PR squadron were deemed to be too valuable to risk being left so they moved to Bahrain for further reconnaissance operations, but of course the front line troops at Khormaksar need more immediate support, so it fell to us to fill the gap. As a result of this withdrawal we were then tasked to do what we could, using hand held cameras, going airborne in "Sioux" helicopters with 45 Royal Marine Commando or 22 SAS pilots. The first time we went out to mount a reconnaissance operation from an army helicopter using a hand held F117 camera, it fell to "Cookie" Proudfoot to do the honours. He was off like a shot, keen as mustard and returned later with great images which we processed on the "Mason" film spool processing unit. This piece of kit was used equally successfully in WW2, and totally reliable so long as you loaded it correctly and counted the number of turns carefully when you did. Otherwise there was a danger of snatching the film off one of the spool ends, which would be almost impossible to relocate in total darkness! "Cookie" regaled us with his details of the flight, during which they came under fire from the ground by some irate member of the local nasty brigade. There were actual holes in the airframe to prove his story and if you know the somewhat fragile appearance of the Sioux helicopter's airframe, it does not bear dwelling on. Although he made light of the incident, it was a sobering thought for all of us as we knew we were to be called on for this kind of operation more frequently.

The Sioux helicopter operated by the Royal Marines

Chapter 17 - Fire Fights RAF Style!

Duing the height of the summer, the situation was becoming difficult and confusing to us, without the benefit of the big picture. This was the occasion when the armoury of the South Arabian Army on the other side of the airfield was overrun by rebellious soldiers who took up arms and fired on the camp area on any likely targets. The violence spilled over into the surrounding areas and a general uprising swept across the local community. I was on guard duty that day, fortunately tucked out of harms way in the guardroom as reports came in of the activity around the airfield. Some of the guards were coming under fire and the RAF Regiment were called out in strength to defend key areas. Our Guard commander, a Chief Technician (equal to a Flight Sergeant) came into the stand down room and told us to get armed up as we going to continue to change the guard as scheduled. He had received no orders to the contrary and therefore he decided to continue as normal until told otherwise! We piled into the open sided Land Rover with him in the driving seat and set off to change the guards. Down the road we went to the first guard point, whereupon the windscreen became crystalline and then very clear as it disappeared in a shower of glass bits. We baled out flat on the ground without any invitation as we could clearly see a bunch of RAF Regiment troopers all around us in similar positions. Their Warrant Officer bluntly asked our "Chiefy" what the hell he thought he was doing, gate crashing into his party... or words to that effect!

Within a few more minutes the situation had calmed down and we needed little encouragement to get the hell out and stay out undercover. It appeared that the RAF Regiments powerful well aimed response had given the opposing team at taste of their own and discretion being the better part of valour; they had decided to withdraw to find less determined responses. I was never more grateful for the genius who decided that KD (khaki drill) was the ideal uniform colour for the Middle east! We were the lucky ones and despite the shaky hands we were none the worse for it all. There was a very black side to all this as the following few days we learned that many soldiers in the town had been caught up in all kinds of fire fights, A number of army personnel out on regular patrol, were caught up in the melee and we lost 13 soldiers on that day. The bodies of those fallen had also been subjected to the courtesies of the locals and it was a grim job recovering them and recording the details on film. There is something manifestly evil in desecrating the body of a dead combatant no matter whose "side" they

Behind the Lens   284

are fighting for and it is something I can never forgive in my own mind. The next day, our team had the grim task of helping to compile photographic records for the post mortems.

Baz Walker, Al Sims, WO Roy Elliott, Brian Goodwin, Dutch Holland, Matt Mattocks, Don Jones, Dave Humphrey, Brian Mateer

The boys had a pretty dreadful time over this but as always they did the job professionally and with the greatest respect. The town of Crater had been closed off by the locals using barricades of burnt out buses and vehicles. We later attended the funerals for the fallen soldiers recording the events for the families and official records. There were no body repatriations in those days, however the War Graves Commission, I understand, continues to maintain the places where our fallen military personnel are buried. A tribute to this organisation is well deserved. The morale took a bit of a dent and it was difficult for us not to be affected by reason of our close working relationship with the front line army units. It was early one morning about a couple of weeks later we heard the sound of Scottish bagpipes from the hills of "Rim rock" around Crater, followed by news on BFBS, that Crater (the town in the centre of an extinct volcano) had been retaken by the Argyle and Sutherland Highlanders led by Lt Col. Mitchell. We all knew him by his nickname of "Mad Mitch", and he was the kind of natural leader you always hoped to be near when the worst kicked off. He was a fearless and dedicated soldier who used his initiative and did not suffer fools gladly. From my own experiences of meeting him in the section he was highly regarded by his men and always ready to listen to a sound idea or opinion. He treated us with respect and gratitude for the standard of work we produced and we really did go the extra mile for any like him. I was sad to hear of the action taken against him later as a result of political influences. His book "On Being a Soldier" gives a fascinating account of the situation

Crater town viewed from "Rim Rock" vantage point

in Aden during 1967 and helps to understand the full picture of the situation. Up till the "Crater incident" we had been issued with the old short magazine Lee Enfield .303 rifles, a good powerful weapon with just five re-crimped rounds in the magazine. Re-crimped rounds were reconstituted rounds from old spent cartridges which were not quite up to the standard of nice new bullets, but they did make a big bang and came out of the end ... eventually!

Now the RAF woke up to the fact we were also right in the front line, so it was no surprise we were given a better weapon for what was likely to be some close quarter punch ups. We were issued with Stirling sub machine guns and two full magazines of ammo. We realised that this meant we were presumed to be in some kind of danger from being run over by a last minute attack from the emerging successful local "Liberation" party. All meals were doled out in the compound and I spent many hours photographing each departments CO handing over his little bit of history.

At least it helped to pass the time and the esprit de corps was actually rising to a new level as the final date of withdrawal rapidly approached. I also had an unusual perk. The C O had decided that all kit and equipment not being evacuated home would be taken to a remote part of the airfield and destroyed, buried or burned if possible. To this end I also became head taxi driver, ferrying the drivers of vehicle out to the dump and bringing them back to the compound. For this task I was given the ex C-in-C's Humber staff car, an absolute dream of a vehicle, with air conditioning and all mod cons. I was told to run it till the wheels fell off! We were all now assembled in the Motor Transport compound near the aircraft loading pan to be called on to load the evacuation aircraft as they swooped down almost every half hour of daylight hours. As it happened the locals did not invade the camp, any fool could see that an RAF chap with a sub machine gun was extremely dangerous, (to everyone on the planet), so they chickened out.

Hercules Transporter, affectionately known as "Fat Arthur"

On November 30th 1967, the last flight ("Chalk 67") Hercules C130 took off from Aden with yours truly on board. It was my dubious honour to be the last official military photographer to set foot off the place, and so ended 150 years of British presence in the Aden Protectorate. I ask myself this. Did it change anything dramatically for anyone in Great Britain? Did anyone (apart from the military) know where Aden was before the conflict kicked off in 1964? Does anyone remember it now, or know where it is? I think not. I came home a bit changed, wiser perhaps, more cynical perhaps, but grateful to be back in one piece and a wonderful family to welcome me home.

I do have to mention here a great tribute to the members of the CSE (Combined Service Entertainments) organisation who somehow managed to persuade a wonderful group of legendary entertainers to come over from the comfort and safety of the UK to perform in extreme heat and not a little amount of personal danger, for the benefit of the soldiers, sailors and airmen on active service in Aden. They included Hughie Green with Anthony Hancock and then followed some weeks later by Bob Monkhouse. Their punishing schedule won over the many audiences and created a special place in the hearts and minds of the troops.

I suppose this tour was the reality check I needed, to learn that we are a military force and whilst we mask our fears with humour and bravado, there are times when the grim reality hits you hard. Back home it had been difficult for my wife to have to see and hear the daily news coming out of Aden. As usual journalists always play up the sensational bits and even get the story wrong or even fabricate a bit of spice into the report to glam it up for effect. Even in those days there was information on details which journalists acquired which could have put lives in danger by compromising an operation. I was pleased that years later we included classes in PR work so that our own people could bring the facts to the public in a controlled secure manner. To this day I still have a problem trusting "news" from the press, but then I am just an old cynic.

Despite warnings for their safety, Hughie Green and Anthony Hancock came out with the first CSE show in 1967 at the height of the security situation.

Khormaksar aircraft pan protected by water filled oil drums

Bob Monkhouse in Khormaksar during the CSE show

He performed 3 shows within hours in temperatures exceeding 40°C!

"This is the first time I've been in a prisoner of war camp for our side!"

Chapter 18 - 1968 Return to Malta

After some disembarkation leave I was sent to JARIC at RAF Brampton and for a while I settled back into the old routine there. We had moved back to our home at Duncan Way in Huntingdon and Valerie had made a number of new friends from local people, which was a new and pleasant situation as we had always been accommodated on RAF bases with only families of military staff to socialise with. I was reunited with my old Warrant Officer Roy Elliott who was also back at JARIC and he kindly recommended me for a course on colour printing at the Kodak Centre at Hemel Hempstead. I was joined on the course with a colleague, Bob Weeks and we really enjoyed the course with their excellent tutors. We spent a good summer enjoying the local area but I soon found to my surprise that we were on PWR for a posting to sunny Malta once more, this time to the photo section at RAF Luqa.

We flew back to Malta in the September, being accommodated on the base at RAF Luqa. My boss at the photo centre was a wonderful man by the name of Squadron Leader "Chick" Evans, a true officer and gentleman. The work was a good mix of general photography and some not so nice work as one of the Canberra aircraft from 13 Squadron came to grief over the island after attempting a heavy load practice overshoot and stalled over an outlying district of Valletta, in St. Paulo cemetery. It was a bad scene with the bodies of the aircrew still in the location when we arrived. The officer in charge was having a tough time keeping away onlookers and "souvenir" hunters (I have never understood the morbid curiosity of people at disaster scenes). Every tiny item could hold some clue for the board of investigation and it was vital to photograph the wreckage in its precise location, which we were able to mark up on an aerial photograph of the area fortunately supplied by our photo section. One of my Maltese Air Force colleagues sent with me found it all bit too much and passed out when the flying boot he recovered turned out to contain the owners severed foot. It is not a job for the faint hearted as I also found out when the site commander wanted me to photograph the positions of hydraulic actuators in the very end of the conical shaped tail section which was perched on a steep slope. Having squeezed my body into the tiny tube section, holding my 35 mm camera and flash unit in front, I was taking shots of the unit when the whole section began to slide down the precarious slope with yours truly jammed inside like a sardine! I was aware of the jagged edges of the aircraft aluminium skin just inches from my torso, which threatened to take a neat slice or two from my protruding rear end if I fell the wrong way. I was also aware of the smell of aviation fuel which was obviously spilled around the area. One small spark or a carelessly thrown fag end from the onlookers would save the funeral directors having to bother with my remains! Strangely enough there was a second very similar incident within a month and by this time rumours about changing the unfortunate number of the Squadron (13) began to circulate. This second incident found us a lot better prepared as we had reviewed our procedures for just such an event and we were now finely tuned to deal with these situations. This one occurred as the aircraft (another Canberra of 13 Squadron) was passing over Hal Far (an old Royal Navy Fleet Air Arm base) near our own base at Luqa. I do vividly remember the chap from the Investigation Board signing for all the photographs we had produced using the name "Whittle" and I asked if he was any relation to the famous Sir Frank Whittle, inventor of the jet engine. He turned out to be his brother! I chalked that up to my collection of famous names to drop one day. It was around this time that I was called into the boss's office one day and he very graciously presented me with my General Service Medal (GSM) for service in "South Arabia" - Aden. The GSM was a very common award and simply meant that you spent more than 30 days in an "active service zone". The powers that be had decided many moons ago that this was a "fit all" medal which saved them re-striking a new medal for every little "brush fire" they would have to rush our forces into. The clasp worn over the blue and green ribbon stated which theatre of operations you took part in. Some of the old soldiers, like the RAF Regiment troopers and the many Army infantry regiments probably had GSM's with foot long ribbons to accommodate all the clasps! Like so many other service families, we had the pleasure of making many new friends wherever we went.

It is one aspect of service life that appeals to a lot of service members and you always feel a bit special as part of that large "family". True there were some not so nice people around in the forces, as in every walk of life, but more often than not, your neighbours were more than ready to be your friends and look after you when times turned sour for whatever reason. My son and daughter were educated by the forces education schools and to be fair, they were given every opportunity to succeed and achieve their highest ambitions. Some would say that moving around the world brings problems of continuity between schools, and they may have a valid point. Perhaps children can also benefit from knowledge and wider experiences of living with other nationals abroad. It was in the early weeks of 1969 that I was once again called to the boss's office, this time to be told I had been selected for promotion to Sergeant. This made a whole world of difference to me and my family as it meant a valuable increase in pay along with a rather cherished status of living standards. The Sergeants Mess had always been held in awe by me. There is a special atmosphere in the Sergeants Mess which only those who have experienced the life will understand, but best described as belonging to a most exclusive club. You can only become a member by achievement through many years of experience and hard work. It is quite difficult to reach the point where you can be considered for promotion, which is through a selection panel and only then by achieving annual assessments which are above many others in competition for a selective few positions available to those fortunate enough to be successful. It was a great comfort and honour for me that one of my most respected NCO's, Sgt Larry Magee, introduced me to the Sergeants Mess. He and his lovely wife Nan helped us to fit in with all the traditions and understand logic of the Mess rules. Larry was a great sub aqua diver of some considerable experience who was admired by all those who knew him.

Chapter 19 - Feb 1969 to Sep 1971 Cyprus

So with the promotion came the bonus of moving to Cyprus, which is a beautiful island with a fantastic climate year round. I was to become one of the staff members at the Air Reconnaissance Intelligence Centre (ARIC) at Episkopi on the southern coast and living in the outskirts of the town of Limassol in a very comfortable bungalow. Our neighbours were also in the RAF some based at Akrotiri, others like me, based in Episkopi. My boss there was a very dapper and elderly Flight Lieutenant Price who had a wonderful war record and had been a highly decorated Wing Commander who re-enlisted in the RAF some years after the war ended. He was a very clever engineer in his own right and was always coming up with wonderful schemes to improvise and improve things in general. Our social life was really very rewarding. The community spirit in the base and amongst our Greek neighbours was very family orientated. We attended a Greek wedding, invited by our neighbours who lived opposite and it turned out to be a fantastic revelation into the magical customs of all things Greek.

It was during one "winter" period we had a very frightening storm which produced several small tornados and created a great deal of damage along the southern coast of the island. I was driving our car with a load of children going to a birthday party when it hit and the hailstones made a terrible noise and were really huge, the size of golf balls (I do not exaggerate at all!). I expected to see the car roof hammered into a million dents but they were obviously well spent by the time they hit the car roof. I saw what appeared to be sheets of paper falling from the sky, only to suddenly realise they were sheets of steel roof cladding when they crashed into the ground around us. One of our colleagues living a few streets away found his car, upright in the back garden, not too far from where he had parked it, in the front of the house! There were many tales of lucky escapes and strange sights, like a waterfall going up into the sky instead of down over the coastal cliffs. We spent hours photographing damage to aircraft and helicopters overturned like children's toys around the airfield at Akrotiri. Happily this was an isolated incident during our time there. I became a member of the "Griffins Rugby Club" and had some great times both watching and very rarely being selected to play (being a bit small and not too fast I was lucky not to be flattened more times than happened!). Paul Jarrell, who worked with us at ARIC as a photo interpreter, came from

South Africa and was built like tank. At one game when he took off with the ball with several opposition players from the Akrotiri "Flamingo's" team hanging from his shirt (now in shreds) being dragged the length of the pitch until he crashed onto a touch down. I swear the ground positively shook with every pounding beat of his feet! We had a small litho printing department (as well as the general photo section) and I was able to learn a great deal from a very skilled printer Corporal Frank Riddle. This was to stand me in very good stead many years later when I started up my own small jobbing printing business as a lucrative sideline. So forty years later, thanks Frank, you were a great instructor. My Warrant Officer at this time was a chap called Sid Hope who was actually a cousin of the world famous Bob Hope (who was of course British born) and truly, his features were remarkably like the famous ski nose of Bob Hope. He and his wonderful wife Barbara were very supportive to all the families and he knew just how to get the best out of everyone. From time to time the powers that be held exercises designed to test our ability to defend the unit in the event of an attack, from whom remained a mystery to most of us, but then our not to question why etc. So we were briefed and prepared defensive lines of armed staff fully loaded with blank ammunition and stuck in pathetic bunkers made up best we could and trying to take the whole thing seriously, which was really quite impossible. We had an Army officer Captain Frank Clark from the Intelligence Corps (known as the "green slime" to the rest of the army). He did his best to create a sense of realism but then we came up with our own innovation and set up a system of Metz photo flash guns which could be fired off to temporary blind any successful intruders. It worked a treat when the "invaders" came at us with the usual prelude of loud bangs from thunder flash "grenades" to be met by blinding salvoes from half a dozen Metz flash units from our chaps lying in wait. The opposition complained bitterly that we were not fighting fairly and we were all technically dead from the "grenades" thrown over the fence.

The whole episode degenerated into a farce as far as I was concerned and proved sod all to anyone with half a brain, but then that's what you got from chair borne office jockeys. Cyprus was a wonderful period in my life especially from a social point of view, the climate was wonderful, warm all year round with winter only dropping to a mild 68 -75 degrees. We worked an early start and finished at 1 pm (or 13.00 hours in military speak, are there really 13 hundred hours in any day?). We would take a light lunch and zip down to Lady's Mile beach which extended from the edges of Akrotiri across towards Limassol. Most evenings we could spend at home or with friends and often going to the Britannia kebab house or other restaurants for a lovely cheap meal and a night with friends. It was probably the best place anyone could have lived with at that time. Of course this was all way before the developers invaded and turned the coastline into a hotel jungle of timeshare and tourist traps. Paphos was a sleepy fishing village with just one little bar on the shoreline. They used to have a moped parked outside on which was sat a very large pelican who would beg bits from anyone daft enough to feed him and as far as I know he returned every year to the same spot (that is if he actually felt the need to go anywhere else!). We organised a weekend picnic for all the staff, their families and friends on the beach at Famagusta (pre Turks invasion days). We borrowed several large 3 ton trucks from the army along with a dozen or so tents and set up a "holiday" camp on the beach. The advance party went up on the night before and did all the hard work, followed by the families and guests the next day. It must have been a long weekend, because we were there for all of the Saturday and Sunday, returning on the Monday morning after "striking" camp. I have to say most of the work was done by the unmarried ("singlies") lads and lassies, who were always in the forefront of volunteering to work hard for the benefit of families and especially children. There were a number of social events and sports days held at "Happy Valley", a special area within the Sovereign Base of Epskopi. My good friend Tom Donnelly was a very keen sportsman and was the key organiser of most of these days. He worked as the Chief maintenance operator supporting all our equipment within the HQ. My photo colleagues included George Marshall and Mick Harris who we kept in touch with for many years. These were definitely the happiest and best years of my service career.

Chapter 20 - Sep 1971 RAF Lindholme

Returning to the UK after such a wonderful "tour" was not something I was looking forward to, as the weather is never as good as being abroad and I have always been a devoted sun worshiper. On the plus side we had our own house to return to. All those months abroad had put rent from our American tenants into the bank which alleviated our mortgage very nicely. True we had one tenant who gave us a problem but the rest were very good and one chap even laid a grass lawn, put in a telephone and would not accept anything for doing so. He was just grateful we had allowed him to do so for his family's convenience and comfort. You always have a balance of good and not so good, with any group of people and my experience has underlined that so many times, no matter where we have lived. Shortly after we returned we saw a wonderful little bungalow for sale in Desborough Road, Hartford. It was not far from where we were in Duncan Way and it came on the market because the farmer who originally owned it had always rented it out but did not want to keep it any longer. The market prices were beginning to rise at the time and I expect he saw a good opportunity to make a bit more out of his investment. We made him and offer which he accepted and we then had to put our house on the market. As it happened there was a general appreciation of the lower prices in our area which was just about inside commuting distance for Stanstead airport. Their local prices of course were much higher and so we found a buyer who worked at the airport and wanted to move his family to Huntingdon, making quite a bit of money in the process, very wise, and very fortunate for us.

Having sold our house we moved into the bungalow and started work on bringing it up to a good standard. We had the advantage of a large area of grass leading to the road, owned by the council and this gave us a useful space so we could park a caravan or second car. Our neighbours were a wonderful retired couple, Mr and Mrs Webb, who we spent many happy hours talking to and he found a collection of aerial photos from WW1 in his loft left to him by some distant relative. They were very good and we sent them to the RAF School of Photography at Cosford for their Museum. Directly opposite I met a chap who turned out to be a sports newsreader for Anglia TV. We became very good friends and he eventually became a famous face on National TV reporting major sports events. Sadly I lost touch with him after a few years but he was an authority on all things sport.

During this time I was based rather inconveniently at RAF Lindholme, which was up near Doncaster so I needed to commute at weekends which did put a strain on our plans to refurbish the home. RAF Lindholme was a training base for Navigators and they used ancient Handly Page Hasting aircraft as flying classrooms. Unfortunately for me as a Sergeant, there was very little to administer as the photo section was only required to process the 16 mm radar films used to record the radar screens aboard the Hastings aircraft, apart from the usual medical or accident photography. However, one special event was held every year. The station hosted a special sports competition for the organisation known as BLESMA (The British Limbless Ex Service Members Association). All the personnel at the station turned up to provide support and assistance to the organisers and it was a remarkable affair which stayed with me for many years. To see the tenacity and determination of these young people (often struck down at the prime of their young lives by some dreadful accident or illness), was a very humbling experience. I am so pleased to find that modern Olympics are now moving towards greater inclusion of the Paralympics.

Chapter 21- "Lindholme Willie"

RAF Lindholme was an old wartime station with a history of a Wellington Bomber squadron. I found myself as the Orderly Sergeant one freezing cold winters night. (Orderly Sergeant is an additional duty). As part of my routine security checks I was walking around the hangers to be sure no one had broken in and stolen one of the four engined Hastings aircraft. It was quite normal for some overzealous young navigator student or aircrew to be working or leaving late so when a young scruffy looking aircrew chap came out of the side of the hanger, I shouted to him "All secure young sir, is it?" knowing full well I would have to go over and check the door where I thought he had just come out of. He just threw me a sort of wave in the distance and waddled off into the descending mist towards the Officers Mess. The only problem was there was no door I could find, not any where along the wall of the hanger he just "come out of". Now I know he was a fair distance away but I did see him exit the hanger and had it pretty well fixed in my mind where the door should have been, but it wasn't, nor had there ever been when I carefully looked up and down the long steel wall of the hanger. Of course, I told myself, he just stopped for a pee, that is why he didn't answer, I probably made him jump and he was a bit embarrassed to be caught having a pee in the open.

I never mentioned it to anyone that night but a few days later one of my fellow Sergeants was in his cups in the Mess bar and was relating the story of "Lindholme Willie" the ghost who prowls around the hangers on the anniversary of the day his aircraft crashed landed into the bog just down the road and the injured crew tragically drowned before anyone could get to them to assist. Yes you guessed it, the night I had seen the young man "walking through the hanger wall" was the anniversary of this tragic event. Now you can think of a hundred good explanations I'm sure and I wish I could, but I know what I saw and I promise you I was not mistaken in what I saw. So make of that what you will. It was during this time that the RAF had reorganised the photographic trade and I was required to attend a six month long photographic processing analyst course at RAF Cosford, near Wolverhampton. My Corporal was expected to hold the fort during this time and I have to say he did a very good job. He was faced with a particularly awkward problem because the RAF in their wisdom had recruited hundreds of trade assistant general dogsbodies who were waiting to select a proper trade when a suitable vacancy occurred and he was obliged to take a large number of them under his wing and try to keep them occupied until the RAF sorted out the problem. Dave Males was very shrewd in sending them off to join many adventure training courses run by the RAF's physical training centres around the country, which they thoroughly enjoyed and consequently did not lose their enthusiasm for the RAF. I thought it was a good example of motivation and man management so when I returned I sent a favourable report to our senior commander about it. Some years later I met him again as a young newly promoted Flight Sergeant at the RAF School of Photography, and eventually he made Warrant Officer in record time and well deserved it was I'm sure. RAF Lindholme was deemed no longer necessary to the MOD and they decided it was due to close down. You would have expected a certain amount of apathy amongst the station, but it was quite the opposite, being a very happy station for me, all the staff and locals were pleasant, helpful and nothing was too much trouble. The C.O. (commanding officer) had decreed that everyone should try to keep busy before we closed and encouraged all the mechanics, engineers and everyone to service their own cars, lawn mowers or any activity to keep them busy rather than lounge about.

It almost became the RAF version of that American series of Bilko's Army, where you could get anything repaired or fixed or even made. These days they would have just made us all redundant! I believe it is now part of H.M Prison system, so I don't know if any of the Prison officers see a strange young man in flying clothes walking about, but if anyone does, don't worry he is a very friendly ghost, just give him a wave and he will probably wave back. The RAF base was the training centre for Navigators who would be responsible for guiding the V bombers to their targets and to this end their flying classrooms were ancient Handley Page Hasting aircraft converted for this task, hence the Squadron number being 1066. We could often scrounge a lift up to Scotland or other interesting locations for a joyride as they were always moving around key bases to test the reactions of the units during exercises. We would play the part by donning Russian style headgear and talking garbage claiming to be seeking asylum! It did not fool many for long but it helped to pass the time and we enjoyed the change of scenery.

Chapter 22 - Head Banging at JSOP

My career plan necessitated a training course at the School of Photography at RAF Cosford. Our trade was now to consist of three divisions: Air Camera Fitters (ACF), Photo Processing Analysts (PPA) and Ground Photographers (Photo G). Air Camera Fitters were to look after the hardware to a serious depth of electronics and other engineering skills. The Photo Processing Analyst was to monitor all things connected with producing photographic images to perfection and the management of quality control (the new buzzword of industry). The Ground Photographer was to continue fulfilling the needs of technical, medical and public relations photography for the RAF. The two former groups (ACF and PPA volunteers) had to attend a mind blowing six month course at Cosford with the benefit of reaching the rank of Warrant Officer at some time in the distant future. The Photo G was to be considered already qualified but the disadvantage was to be a ceiling of promotion to Sergeant only. In all fairness this situation suited many of the General Photographers because they were not to be separated from their families whilst attending a six month head banging course and of course no threat of ignominious failure during the many exam points of such a course yet still being able to reach the dizzy heights of the Sergeants Mess without any further encumbrance. So off I went in the depths of winter to suffer the slings and arrows of Critical Path analysis, Sensitometry for photographers, Factors Affecting (the quality of air photography imagery) and many other obscure subjects.

The CO of the school at this time was Squadron Leader Gordon Ashman, a no nonsense architect of continuing high standards. Jack Eggleston was our Sensitometry instructor and he had a long history of wartime service and as an Instructor at the school. There were times when I considered his pedantic adhesion to minute detail of practice was excessive. For example we were expected to choose the scale and size of the graphs drawn up with a laborious hand drawn procedure for each of the tests and exercises undertaken. It would have saved hours of precious training time to have pre-printed pages with the axis already printed on the graph. I had a great respect for Jack as his knowledge was very deep. He had produced a text book on Sensitometry which had been adopted as our training manual on the subject. To his great credit it won him awards and International recognition. Our every evening was consumed in burning of the midnight oil for forthcoming slip tests and nail biting stress awaiting the many phase exam results. We lost a couple of good men along the way and I was saddened to say farewell as they had worked so hard but there seemed to be no quarter given regardless of your rank or determination, a failure of a key exam meant end of the line and back to your unit. Some of it seemed as useful as a chocolate fireguard, for example the flight planning sessions took a great deal of time on the course but apart from estimating the amount of film required for the sortie, I doubt any self-respecting pilot worth his salt would depend on a photographer to guide him to his target and bring him safely home. In the wisdom of hindsight, much of the course content seemed to have been included for the benefit of creating a difficulty filter factor and it was many years later before some of it proved worthwhile, albeit in a totally unrelated capacity! The motto prevailing at the time seemed to be "Don't argue – just give them what they want and get out of there". It was not until much later when I became an Instructor, I was able to ensure the relevance of content as paramount in course design. But that's a later chapter in the story! The "espirit de corps" carried us through to the final days and we did enjoy the physical sports as sweet relief. One day, we were playing five a side against the PTI's (Physical Training Instructors) and Dick Few came an awful cropper, dislocating his shoulder. He was a tough guy though and was determined to soldier on albeit with the handicap of his arm in a sling; not so clever when you are doing practical exercises.

Some of the most intriguing machines were the electronic printers such as the Milligan 105 contact printer and the SP 1070 continuous strip printer, both of which could "dodge" and shade in the detail on a negative of a ground area which had cloud shadow spoiling the contrast. It used a "flying spot" of illumination from a CRT (cathode ray tube) which scanned the picture format and automatically adjusted the exposure required on these specific areas. Despite my misgivings as to how the course could have been better designed, it proved a great asset in my later years and I am ever grateful to the Instructors at that time who gave us every encouragement. Some of their names will always live on with me. Names I can recall were Flight Sergeant Al Cox; Gerry Paine; Flight Lieutenant George Parry; Mr Dave Jenkins; Doug Pailin. The final days drew close and we successfully accomplished what seemed a mountain to climb. Our achievements were also later recognised by the British Institute of Professional Photography, a notable first for the military training of photography. On the way home I gave a lift to a colleague from the course (Reg Grindly) who also lived in our area and we were not far from Huntingdon when a large lorry came down towards us at high speed and well over the crown of the road. Fortunately my reactions were up to the mark and we managed to get out of the way, avoiding a disastrous head on collision. Sadly for the guy following us he was unable to stop in time to avoid our rear end and came to a violent stop. The damage to my car was not serious, just annoyingly avoidable, but my sympathies went out to the other driver's little van which was firmly planted in my boot. When we saw the state of the inside of his cab, he was sat among a pile of devastated wedding cake, along with the little bride and groom now sat on the dashboard! The look on his face said it all but he added "Oh God, I only started this job today!" Fortunately for all of us, a chap following the loony lorry driver had chased after him and got his number. He came back to see if we were all okay and kindly let us have his details as a witness. I was able to sort it all out some time later and phoned the boss of the wedding cake shop to explain the situation and happily his driver did not lose his job. My return to the base at RAF Lindholme was to be short lived, as by then the wheels had turned and decisions made for the final closing down. Our boss Squadron Leader Bennett, from the HQ explained we were to be given choices of new postings. So naturally I opted for RAF Wyton or RAF Brampton near our home in Huntingdon. A while later my posting to RAF Wyton came through and we spent the following few weeks closing down our little empire above the armoury, which being quite small did not take long. I did feel sadness as we always do when recalling the happier memories but the long weekend haul to and from the camp to Huntingdon was not something I would miss and life in a barrack block, even for a few days during the week can be tiresome and boring. I have to say that Dave Males and the lads included me in some of their "sorties" into Doncaster, where the local hop and a good number of young ladies brightened up the scene. I also have to say how friendly and welcoming the locals were, always very hospitable. I would like to think we returned the compliment by joining in the community activities and supporting them in return.

There is a good story which Dave Males related to me. He was driving over to his family home in Doncaster and when he arrived he noticed that one of the wheel hubs on the car was missing. He was certain he had started off with all four intact but he resigned himself to the loss and spent the rest of the day with his parents. On the following day a local friend of his parents came to visit and during the conversation commented on a peculiar incident which had happened the previous day. He was in his front garden mowing his lawn when, apparently out of nowhere, a chrome wheel hub came rolling along a plonked itself in the grass box of the lawn mower. It looked in new condition so he thought best to hang on to it as the luckless owner may have been a local neighbour. Dave Males asked his Dads friend if he could see the hub as he had just lost one adding that the chances are unlikely as they lived a long way apart. They were all astonished to find that it was in fact an exact match including a mark on the inside which Dave must have put on at some time so that the tyre valve lined up correctly! The base is now part of HM Prisons and I hope the staff and inmates can find the same kind of tolerance and understanding enjoyed by the RAF for so many long years.

Chapter 23 - RAF Wyton - "The Factory"

AF Wyton is a well-established base, just outside of the town of Huntingdon It is located close to another base less known (by design) but recently closed down; the Joint Air Reconnaissance Intelligence Centre at RAF Brampton on the other side of the town. The primary role for the photographers there was the processing of many miles of air reconnaissance film produced by the two main reconnaissance aircraft; the Victor and the Canberra PR9. They could both carry a massive amount of film and processing this was undertaken at a special building known as "The Factory". This building was located on the other side of the main road adjoining the base and set back away from public view. It was here that I was to meet up with some former colleagues (quite normal in our smaller trade group) among these was Warrant Officer Ron Commons (last seen in Aden) and Flight Lieutenant Terry Weaver whom I had known for many years before he was commissioned. The processing machines were designed for high speed production of the wide film format (9½" wide film up to 1,000feet in length) and the narrower 70mm film which varied from short lengths of around 50 feet to 500 feet.

These machines were designed and built by Clydesdale Engineering and could process the films from a dry input state to a dry output state at a rate of 120 feet per minute for the 70mm wide films and 40 feet per minute for the wide films. The magazines containing these films were down loaded from the aircraft and brought over from the Squadron dispersal points where we unloaded them into special light tight cassettes for attaching to the end of the processor machines. Some of these magazines were extremely heavy, but each had one young well-built lad called "Chunky" Walcott who could handle one of these magazines under each arm without difficulty, an amazing feat of sheer strength for a young 'un. This young lad I well remember because he was subjected to a bit of teasing about his weight on the main camp (which was slightly over the norm). Being a young lad he was eager to fit in and felt he needed to do something about it. He also liked the game of rugby so he went along to the rugby training group on a regular basis to lose some weight and hopefully join the team. Apparently he had finished a fairly hectic session of training on the field and went across to the NAAFI where he drank a pint of cold milk. His heart must have reacted because he was downed in a second and despite valiant efforts by John MacDonald and other colleagues, there was nothing anyone could do to revive him. We were all devastated at his loss. We particularly admired his convivial nature and willingness to go the extra mile whatever task was set for him. I was also made very conscious of how easily anyone can unwittingly be the instigator of a bit of mickey taking without due thought to possible consequences. The men and women I worked with at "The Factory" were in no way guilty of any part of this tragic incident, they were quite the opposite being the very best of comrades to each other at all times. It has always been my experience that the photographers considered themselves a special and unique team who worked and played hard wherever they were. It was during one otherwise uneventful day we were warned about an imminent set of films which were about to be brought in. These films required special processing as they were infra-red false colour material which had to be processed on the Kodak Versamat colour processor, a somewhat slower machine than the type 11 and 12. The team we selected for their experience in operating the Versamat and the quality controls necessary to ensure perfect reproduction. At the time the target content was not divulged and the processing was completed without incident. We were of course aware of the number of people around who had been granted access and observation of the procedure (mostly in suits and looking rather officious). It was some time later we learned that the films were used in evidence at the trials of the infamous child murderers, Ian Brady and Myra Hindley. Infra-red false colour is a concept of altering the visible spectrum (colours of the rainbow) up the scale and into the infra-red spectrum, rather like a piano player can move up a scale on the keys. An infra-red filter is placed over the lens of the camera (it looks to be totally black) and the wavelengths of vegetation which would normally appear green on the colour film appear a crimson colour, except where the vegetation is dead (for example in trees affected by Dutch Elm disease or man-made camouflage). This sort of vegetation records as a near black patch and the same effect occurs when ground is disturbed by turning over the surface vegetation as in burying something below ground.

It is now public knowledge that many of the victims' burial sites were clearly identified from these films, the locations were examined and carefully recorded for the trial. I recall many years later that Myra Hindley persuaded the authorities to allow her to visit Saddleworth Moor when she claimed to know where little Keith Bennett's remains were buried. She was unable to identify the location as it turned out but she enjoyed the notoriety and freedom from her prison and the focus of the media interest once again. Myra Hindley subsequently died without revealing the site in question and the cruellest vindictive act was placed on Keith Bennett's long suffering mother who sadly passed away without ever being granted closure for her son. To me personally it was one of the cruellest acts of the most disturbed and evil minds ever to be given the benefit of our legal system. I only hope that Lord Longford and his like-minded defenders of these vile people will be remembered in history for their naivety and self-seeking posturing. May God forgive them all, for I cannot find it in my soul to do so.

The huge Victor reconnaissance aircraft showing the "fan" of 8 F96 cameras installed in the adapted bomb bay

Eight of the F 96 cameras being unloaded from the camera bay

Inside the PR 9 Back hatch

One of the most interesting detachments (an exercise to another overseas air base), I was privileged to be part of was to the beautiful country of Norway. The Canberra reconnaissance squadron (No 39) was to exercise at a place called Brekstad not far from Trondheim. We were flown into the base aboard the Hercules cargo planes which we had spent months working with to carry our mobile photographic support cabins. These units were made up of structures looking like "Portacabins", except they were very cleverly designed to be raised up on legs if necessary so a lorry could pass underneath and then the cabin could be lowered on to its back. These cabins could also have their own "castoring" wheels at each corner so they could be manoeuvred at ground level or inside aircraft for stowing securely. Each processing cabin had independent air conditioning and each end was fitted with a tunnel structure so it could be docked onto another and build a wonderful complex which was set up very quickly and totally independent of the usual services such as drains and power, having its own generator units to boot.

The concept was quite brilliant in its day and proved the backbone to the highly successful mobile photo support units throughout Europe. Shortly after landing we managed to set up shop just in time for the first Canberra aircraft to land with films from his first sortie. One of my airmen had the knack of transferring the 70mm roll of film from each magazine into the processing cassette in total darkness in less than 30 seconds flat. I never did discover how the hell he managed it but perhaps it was best I did not!

An ATREL cabin being maneuvered on its running gear

A typical MAREL complex (RAF Laarbruch)
Note the ATREL cabins docked into the main structure

Whatever, the results were an astounding performance of rapid film processing which no other military reconnaissance organisation was ever able to match. The cassettes were in .position and the film sped through the developer tanks (containing May and Baker Exprol A developer) at 120 feet per minute to be collected and spooled by the operators in just about a minute or so. The Norwegian observers were astounded and likewise the Americans who were still struggling to improve their 17 feet per minute Versamat processors by placing two films alongside each other, achieving at best, a 34 feet speed production. We almost became too good for our own photo interpreters as they had some difficulty keeping up with the amount of targets and material we continually stacked on the end of their Vinten 5 strand viewing benches. It may appear to sound conceited but I can assure the reader that the RAF reconnaissance teams at this time were sweeping the board on every NATO exercise and competition thrown into the mixing bowl. It was in no small part a real credit to the training, enthusiasm and endeavours of every team member and I do include our much taunted PI's (photo interpreters) with whom we always had a terrific banter and camaraderie.

Flushed with success, (please pardon the "in joke" as some of these exercises were titled "Royal Flush") we were able to relax and enjoy the benefits of fishing for cod in the middle of the night in broad daylight! Terry Weaver and I had one evening fishing session when we caught a sizeable cod each, only to see two young lads in a small boat out in the Fjiord struggling to lift their catch of a three foot long cod weighing as much as they did. We were suitably humbled and took our meagre fish home to grill on the BBQ. The air in Norway is so good you could eat it and despite filling ourselves with all they could offer at the breakfast table we actually did not put on any weight. I am sure it was down to the diet of their food, some of it being raw fish and their very active lifestyle where sport is king. The young Norwegian Air Force Sergeant, who was our liaison man, lived in his own house on a farm near the base. This was not unusual as most of the volunteer service men lived in their own homes near to their base by choice. We were also surprised to meet the pilots of the Norwegian Air force fighter aircraft, some of whom wore long hair (well long by our standard short back n'sides) and many of them were Sergeant pilots, unlike our RAF Canberra aircrew who were all Commissioned Officers. We were also intrigued by the forward thinking in local planning and lifestyle. Many of the main roads running through the flatter parts of the country were constructed as emergency wartime runways with the garages also set up to accommodate aviation fuel storage tanks.

39 Sqdn Canberra PR 9

Local houses were constructed of wood in the most part but had an excavated base with a concrete walled cellar which housed their emergency winter storage supplies and acted, if needed, as a shelter in a time of war. This was at a time when the Soviet Empire was just over the northern border and posturing continually as highly mobile war machine. When a young Norwegian couple came to be married they could choose their home from a range of kit formed structures which were placed on top of these pre formed cellar foundations. All the water pipes, heating ducts and electrical looms were trunked up from the centre of the home alongside the central open fire place which helped prevent winter climate damage. The windows were all triple glazed and supplemented by fitted wooden shutters to provide added protection in severe cold. All this of course in the 1970's when we were just about discovering the benefits of double glazing.

We were rather taken aback by the cost of living there when we found that a bottle of whiskey would set you back more than £20 equivalent and beer was a stunning £3 a pint, not a lot by current standard but this was 30 years ago and our wage packets were certainly not up to that kind of expenditure. Life at home in the UK had not gone well for my family, my wife and children were all taken down with measles and they were in a desperate situation. My good friend Flight Sergeant Pete Wilkins and his wife had stepped in to help out. Pete was an absolute star at this time and I will always remember him and his lovely wife for their caring diligence typical of the "family" unity which existed within our team.

Front View of the Canberra PR 9 showing navigator's access

The Canberra PR 9 back hatch to the camera

Chapter 24 - Rheindahlen 1974

As I had been in the UK for some time it was rotation time for me once more and a vacancy had arisen in Germany at the Photo Reproduction Unit at RAF Rheindahlen, also home to the 2nd Allied Tactical Air Force HQ, otherwise known as "The Big House". Once more we stacked and packed our most treasured belongings into storage and shipping crates for those we chose to take with us. By this time we were living in a very nice bungalow in Hartford, Huntingdon and it was hard for my wife to break links with both her friends and the part time work she had taken up. I know there were lots of benefits in living abroad and the children had a good education from the service schools at the various bases, but it had begun to take its toll on our marriage. I was choosing not to focus on this, as the benefits of the social high life and adventures travelling around the wonderful countryside and down to Switzerland seemed to outweigh the downside. At the HQ we processed films from the clandestine cameras fitted to the Pembroke aircraft of 60 Squadron. These aircraft flew up and down the Berlin Corridor transporting various personnel to and from Berlin and at the same time took the opportunity to collect aerial images of anything interesting which the East German and Russian military were doing.

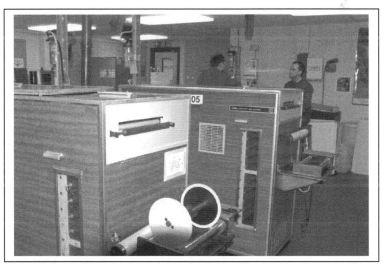

The Kodak Versamat film processor

. Our film processing machinery was the Type 12 and the usual selection of hand and machine printers. I was very dubious that we could get the best results from the Type 12 as it relied on an adjustable friction clutch for transmission. This was not the most accurate method as the engineering was subject to wear on resin fabric clutch plates and the simple pressure of a tensioning spring. The Versamat processor in this instance would have been a much better prospect albeit much slower, I felt too much emphasis was laid on the speed of production, which in normal tactical reconnaissance was essential, but not in this instance where quality of image was paramount and there was not the pressure of mission reporting turnaround time. Perhaps I was being naïve and there will be many who will argue the opposite but I stand by the fundamental principle of better to wait an extra few minutes than lose imagery from vital films due to malfunctioning equipment. To me the Type 12 was a step too far, for wide film processing. Its brother model the Type 11 was ideal and fantastic for the 70 mm film of tactical reconnaissance. I am sure the arguments could linger on but the death knell of our wet film processing for reconnaissance was looming on the distant horizon.

There was an organisation called BRIXMIS. This was an organisation formed as the result of an International agreement between the powers occupying the Berlin area. The title BRIXMIS, stood for the British Military Mission which was allowed passage through the Berlin corridor and there was a similar set up called SOXMIS (the Soviet Military Mission). The vehicles used to transport "observers" were specially adapted (by both organisations). This was a military vehicle (usually a high powered Opel Kapitan or similar) which travelled up and down the Berlin corridor. It usually contained a crew of Intelligence Corps personnel and RAF photographers. The idea was again to observe and record any opportune targets which presented themselves   We also had a large workload for colour slide production (in the days before PowerPoint presentations with computers) for briefings by senior staff officers, especially our head man who was Air Marshall Sir Michael Beetham. He was a stickler for absolute professionalism (and why not) with every slide being given a special background and colour. I do recall Corporal Dougie Taubman and his team working many long hours to keep up with the deadlines. My other Corporal at the time was Harry Carmichael who was a very competent photographer and my being essentially an aerial reconnaissance man; I picked up a lot of useful guidelines from him in the field of general photography. I have always held the view that photography is a never ending learning process and thanks to many of my senior and junior colleagues in the trade I felt confident to talk with some degree of experience and knowledge later in life. I was also very fortunate to have a great friend in my old Sergeant from Aden days, now Flight Sergeant Ted Taylor. Ted was a really skilled manager of people under his supervision and was always able to bridge the gap when conflict flared up. I do confess to being very hard on one Corporal Tony Ray, who had tried to remedy a situation albeit without consulting my expertise and the result was a bit of a disaster. I was extremely cross and blew up without listening to all the facts (as sometimes happens under stress) but I should have known better and Ted came to the rescue pouring oil on troubled waters. I have to say that subsequently this Tony Ray and I got on very well and he was a great help to me when I had a bad road accident returning from a trip to Switzerland. Fortunately the only injuries were my pride and the car which was written off. He went out of his way to ferry me around until we got it all sorted, for which I was and am ever grateful. Flight Lieutenant Colin Debenham was our Flight Commander and the Warrant Officer was Frank Geddes, Ted Taylor was eventually posted home and replaced by "Whiskey" Walker whom I had a great deal of respect for albeit a number of "discussions" as to the best machines and processing as previously mentioned. Not to forget my fellow Sergeant at this time was a young ginger haired chap, name of Vic Kinnin. We were to meet up again many years later, he as the CO of the School of photography and I as one of the Instructors.

My family were living in a very spacious apartment in Mönchen Gladbach and we had an excellent social life courtesy of the Sergeants Mess. We later moved into a home on the base itself and enjoyed the convenience of all the sports and social facilities on our doorstep. I also fell into a trap of trying to be too helpful when my wife wanted us to attend an amateur theatre production at the Rhine Army Theatre Club. After the show we were invited back stage and I was asked if I would help out in the next production by reading in a part during casting as they were short of a couple of people on the night in question. As it was supposed to be just a helping voice to fill the gap until the other actors came back from holidays, I took up the script and read the bits they needed. The Director was a wild looking hawk faced character complete with long hair and beard, called Mike Luckins who taught drama at the local Forces Education School. After the reading session we went home and that was the end of that, so I thought. A bit later on Mike Luckins contacted me again and asked if I would repeat the exercise as they were still having difficulty getting someone for the part. He was that sort of character who would sell ice cream to Eskimos and I was slowly sucked in to the web of amateur dramatics. Now I have to tell you my memory for that sort of thing is rubbish and there was no way I was going to be able to learn more than a couple of lines for a walk on bit part at best. My worst nightmare began when he decided for reasons best known to himself that I was the man for the lead role and the production was an amateur premier of a play called "Saturday, Sunday Monday" by Eduardo De Fillipo (since made into a famous West End play starring Frank Findlay in the role I was nailed for!). Additional pressure came by way of being entered for the Joint Services amateur competition for the whole of Germany, no sweat then, just a walk in the park! I spent the next few months muttering pages of script frantically trying to get my head round the fact that somehow I really had to remember over 100 pages of script, cues and stage directions to boot. How I managed it I really do not know to this day and I will never ever go near any amateur theatre group again, but I did and it was a great success thanks to the diligence and patience of Mike Luckins and all the other actors. Mike, I believe went on to great things in the teaching of drama and as far as I know was last heard of working in Bilston, in the West Midlands at one of the Colleges of drama. I am so grateful for the experience of facing a 400 strong audience and being able to think on my feet when things went horribly wrong (according to the script anyway!) but the practice of pacing speech and clear projection gave me the confidence when I was called on to do TV documentaries at the photo museum later in life.

I have to mention here about an incident which shocked and appalled us all at Rheindahlen although it occurred many miles away at the Senelarger ranges where the RAF exercised with Harrier Tactical Reconnaissance force. The mobile photo labs were deployed out to that area at a time when there had been a serious drought for some time during a very hot summer. There had been numerous warnings about lighting fires in forest areas because of this situation. The Mobile photo support unit was set up deep in the woods of the area and the cabins formed into a sort of loose square facing each other. The CO of the unit had organised the usual perimeter defences as it was expected that army units would attempt to infiltrate at some time during the exercise, probably at night under cover of darkness. To this end the team had strung together some tin lids from used film containers to act as jangling audible warnings should the "enemy" barge into them. All seemed fine and set for the night but a decision was made that they were too visible (being painted white) and they would need to "toned down". There was no matt black paint readily available so it was decided to use the methylated spirit from the processing machines to make a small pan of fire to blacken them with soot, well that was the theory. What happened soon afterwards will live in the memory of all those concerned for a very long time. The person pouring the methylated spirits from a large 25 litre container came too close to the ignited small pan of methylated spirit and the ensuing fireball was estimated have been around 80 feet in diameter. The chap holding the container felt it volley from under his arm like a rocket propelled missile, which in effect it probably was. He was fortunate as the explosion was well away from him when it occurred. Sergeant George Marshall was not so lucky, he had just opened the door to the cabin and stepped out onto the metal staircase descending to ground level, and fortunately for those inside the cabin door had closed behind him. He met the full force of the fireball which burned every part of his exposed body, his face, arms and even down inside his boots to around his ankles. George was a very fit man and an accomplished choir singer. He vocal chords were damaged badly and affected his voice. His face needed plastic surgery and his hands were the same. The military hospital performed some repairs which to me appeared nothing short of miraculous, saving a great deal of tissue by immersing his hand in bags of special ointments and though his face was badly scarred he recovered remarkably well. He grew a beard for many years to protect his skin from exposure. The medical authorities were very surprised he survived at all and even more surprised at his rapid healing and progress to as near a full recovery as you could reasonably have hoped for. He ended his career still serving in the RAF as a photo processing analyst and held the rank of Flight Sergeant on his retirement. That much abused expression "lessons to be learned" is often expressed as some sort of panacea, but flying in the face of the nationally declared fire hazard situation and the sheer danger of the intended activity was there for all to see. The overenthusiastic actions to provide solutions became a near lethal one. The only saving grace was that the whole incident could so easily have become a devastating catastrophe resulting in multiple deaths and casualties, but for the diligence of the main victim closing a cabin door behind him.

We still meet George and his lovely wife Margaret from time to time and happy to say they have successfully left the near fatal tragedy well behind them, but then so many of the people I have had the great privilege of working with are of similar fortitude, a great credit to them all. My wife had the good fortune to be employed in the "Big House" under the Army Intelligence Department as an illustrator for their graphics department. She did very well there and enjoyed the work. The department management were a very good bunch of people and looked after their workers with a deal of respect. It was shortly after the major accident with our car that we found a special offer being made from Volvo cars and the NAAFI retailers on the base. Because of some distribution problems their latest model was now on offer but they had a stock of the earlier models as yet still unsold. It was one of these models which we managed to do a deal on for a huge 50% reduction of the regular price. It was an offer too good to miss and we went ahead with the order. Because we were paid at a special fixed forces exchange rate in local currency , there was also a sizeable discount in our favour, if we paid in cash with Swedish kroner, again too good to miss. We had a limited choice on colours but the bright yellow we were offered as readily available also attracted a sizeable discount from the insurers because of its high visibility. It was known as the "two ton budgie" from then on, much to amusement of my colleagues who did not miss an opportunity to leave bird seed and cuttle fish around my desk and anywhere they thought I would be liable to frequent in the workplace. The car was a dream machine, fully automatic with tinted windows and drove beautifully. I have to say it gave us excellent service for over 12 years, which is the longest time I have ever kept any vehicle. Like all good things which have to come to an end my tourex (tour expiry) date came round and we made preparations to return home. All in all it had been a very good time and I had managed to broaden my experience and skills. I was however a bit surprised when my place of posting came through as RAF Wittering, not as I was expecting another tour at JARIC or RAF Wyton. But then the RAF can be an unpredictable animal whenever you think you have it sussed out! So it was onwards and upwards... literally, as RAF Wittering was then the home base of the Harrier jump jet training unit and operational base of No 1 Squadron its fledgling operational unit.

Chapter 25 -1976 RAF Wittering - Arctic

Surrounded in mist and fog, the Airfield at RAF Wittering was invisible apart from the main gates at the edge of the A1 main road when I arrived early on my first morning. Because of the distance to Huntingdon we had decided that it would be easier if I stayed on base during the week and commuted at weekends. This was now becoming common practice among many service homeowners as the property market potential began to make the prospect of home investment an attractive proposition to many service members. After the usual arrival procedure (a tedious and time wasting exercise which took up most of the day passing from one office and department to another) I settled in my offices at the RIC (Reconnaissance Intelligence Centre). This is a group of semi-permanent but portable buildings called the MAREL (Moveable Air Reconnaissance Evaluation Laboratory) which is has internal docking facilities for the ATREL cabins (Air Transportable Reconnaissance Evaluation Laboratory). My God, I hear you cry "who the hell dreamed up all these "alphabetty speak" long names and initials"? Well yes, I have often wondered what sycophantic prune copied the boys across the pond, who wallow in such phrases. I am sure they are solely designed to flummox and convince the long suffering tax payer in to believing they really know what they are doing. Q E D, it must be good if it has a very long name! There I've done it again. "Alphabetty speak" is taking over our commerce and the English language, I swear. So we had a really clever system of being able to deploy (set off) in support of the jumping jets to any part of the world at a moments notice, subject of course to the supplies and materials being readily available.

My first experience of watching these fantastic aircraft was indeed a revelation. They could, it seemed literally fly backwards as well as nearly straight up from lift off (and I do mean lift off). They were the answer to many prayers and their subsequent success in many theatres of operation proved their worth tenfold. They really must have been good because the US Marine Corps bought a ton of them. now that's what I call hands across the sea! The mainstay of our side for the Squadron was reconnaissance and to this end there was a pod shape which fitted under the aircrafts belly and contained a selection of cameras ranging from the 70 mm film carrying F 95's to the wide film F 126 camera. The Harrier also had an F 95 camera fitted to the port side (left) of the pilot in the nose of the aircraft. Our main production throughput was the 70 mm films from the F 95 cameras and to this end we had acquired a great deal of experience. My WO in charge of the RIC was Ted Fordham and his deputies were a couple of wonderful NICO's, Flight Sergeants Bruce Smith and Colin Beatty. My partner in the team was Sgt Sid Jeffries, a guy with a great sense of humour and knew exactly how to motivate his men. We had a very good team spirit and there were some of the most capable operators it has been my pleasure to work with. After a useful length of time for me to cut my teeth on a number of operational exercises on the base we received word that the Harriers were to go on exercise up into the Arctic Circle at a place called Tromso in Northern Norway. It was the first time they had been subjected to the extremes of climate at this level so it was a very useful exercise (as later events in the Falklands were to prove). Surviving in Arctic conditions was a whole new ball game to most of us and we received a number of interesting scenarios and talks on the "what and what not to do". Before we departed we were issued with arctic special clothing, a very comprehensive set of fur lined anoraks, "mukluk socks" for our special winter boots, gloves etc. everything Captain Scott would have given his eye teeth for. We were also left in no uncertain terms as to the cost of replacing any or all of the kit, just in case we managed to lose it somewhere! As a run up to the big day when we left we managed to practice assembling and setting up the RIC, just to ensure everyone had a specific role and understood the needs and priorities. The big day came with the Hercules aircraft rumbling in like giant hippos, swallowing up the tons of support gear and supplies for the detachment. The ATREL cabins were lined up and moved on board including the ATGU (Air Transportable Generating Unit). It was a gigantic portable power supply for the whole of the RIC and held to large generators which could supply the 3 phase power required by our volt hungry processors in the cabins. We really must have looked more like a flying circus to the outsider and I suppose this would be a reasonable similarity in term of organisation and planning. One of the great things about being part of this team was a twofold sense of doing something really useful and belonging to the support of one of the foremost Squadrons in the RAF at the time.

The flight to Norway was noisy and not exactly comfortable; being a military cargo aircraft, the "passengers" seats were simple fold down frames with nylon webbing to form the "seat". I managed to get a visit to the flight deck and watch the world from a bird's eye view as is slowly slid by underneath. It is a fascinating sight, even for my flight experienced soul. The aircraft handles beautifully with ease and precision, despite its massive bulk. (I managed a short spell of handling the controls thanks to a very obliging skipper). We arrived at Tromso in clear weather and no sign of a snow flake anywhere, almost like a spring day in the UK. The cargo was expertly unloaded in a very short space of time and we were kept busy for the next few hours siting the cabins in the required layout and docking the units to form our completed RIC. It all went very smoothly and we were ready for the first pair of Harriers incoming from the UK base with some practice films just to keep everyone in the spirit of the exercise. It all passed off without a hitch, Mick Horne doing his magic in rapid transfer of film from magazines to processing cassettes in record time. At the close of the day we received warnings that a "polar wind" was forecast and we could expect a big dump of snow the next day. After a trip to the mess halls we all turned in for an early start to the next day. Our accommodation was made up of long wooden huts interconnected to the usual facilities with triple glazing fitted to all windows and doors which had double labyrinths to retain room temperatures. They really know how to build effectively in Norway, as you would expect. We awoke the following morning with the sun glowing through the windows, but I had the weirdest sensation in my head that I had gone deaf as the silence all around was almost oppressive. True to form the forecast was spot on and the silence was due to the two metres of snow nature had dropped on our home. We could hear the sound of "lawn mowers" outside. The "lawn mowers" turned out to be hand held mini snow ploughs which the Norwegians use to cut a path through the snow to doorways etc.

They really had it all worked out from a lifetime of experience in this climate. Even the crew bus which turned up to transport us across to the airfield had ice tyres with studs to grip the ice on the roads now covered with a compressed layer of snow. Our driver explained that in Norway every truck has a built on snow plough attachment frame so that the first one out after a snow fall, fits a plough to the front and sets off clearing his own path as he goes. Now that's what I call forward planning. Suitably attired in our weather proof kit we soon realised that living in arctic conditions was a whole new experience and serious attention needed to be paid to the survival tips as briefed when the snow began to fall again we were very aware of the "white out" conditions which could easily lead to disaster. The Norwegians had placed metal spikes along the pathways to form an "avenue" The spikes had a loop at the top end, at waist height through which a wire hawser had been threaded. We were wearing belts with a sort of dog lead and clip attached. This clip was placed onto the wire so we would not lose our way if we strayed from the path in the white out conditions. It was quite possible to lose your sense of direction without this clever device and if you did get lost and wander off, there was a time limit before the intense cold would claim you as a victim, at least from frostbite if not worse. It was a sobering thought. A short while after the snow had cleared from the skies we watched the landing of twin engined a light aircraft. It turned out to be the local "school bus" which carried a number of children to the base from remote areas. This day was a special day off for them to see the RAF planes and they were all gathered at the windows of the tiny airport, peering out at the line of Harriers on the nearby apron. The CO had decided to combine a bit of PR along with the some exercises planned for the day so our display pilot climbed aboard and started up the engines. I am not quite sure if the children had any inkling of what was they were about to see, but along with many others, few had actually seen the Harrier strut its stuff outside of the UK at that time. The first display was a straightforward short take off, and I do mean short! Once airborne the pilot returned in front of the audience of goggle eyed children and just hung there hovering, to their astonishment and awe. Not to put it mildly but the next set of manoeuvres were awesome as he flew backwards, sideways and completed the ballet with a curtsy to the children! I am not sure if they really could believe their little eyes but their faces said it all. Most service men and women are really a soft touch when it comes to children and these were no exception. After the pilot landed he came over to the children inside the airport lounge and spent the next half hour signing his name on schoolbooks satchels, lunch boxes and just about anything they proffered. It was a great start to our programme and one I shall not forget. We managed to produce copies of the squadron badge and handed them around for souvenirs. The rest of the exercise was a solid endorsement of the Harrier and its capabilities, both as a unique fighter and a reconnaissance platform.

They say copying is the greatest form of flattery and the US Marine Corps did precisely that, acquiring the Harrier into their formidable arsenal. It is a tribute to our aircraft industry that many of their productions serve a very long time with the UK Forces, outliving by far the machinations of transient government ministers and leadership! The role of the Harrier came to the fore during the Falklands war and I was sad to hear of its recent demise. Whilst sentiment is a precious commodity, on this however it can be over rated, when time and tide wait for no one as there are always bigger, better and more efficient tools in the pipeline waiting to win their spurs. My personal life was also in need of some reviewing, being 38 years old, I was past my sell by date for youthful exploits and my family needed better attention so I made the decision to try to get away from operational stuff to be closer to the home. Flight Sergeant Colin Beattie was one of my mentors and a close friend at the time. He suggested applying for a posting to the training school at RAF Cosford, this would bring our families and relatives within easier reach (all being from the Midlands) and my wife was keen to return to more settled existence having moved "home" 22 times in

22 years! So I applied for a post at the Joint School of Photography, went along for an interview and was found "fit for purpose" to join the team. Little did I know then it was to be the best decision I could ever have made.

Chapter 26 – An Education in Training

It was September 1978 when I drove through the gates of RAF Cosford once again and not without a little trepidation. This was a training camp with all the trappings of discipline and order I was not always too keen on, having enjoyed the "can do" of squadron life and acting on my own initiative as needed to get the job done. My Warrant Officer was a chap I knew well having the same name as mine, Peter Humphrey, up to this time, was the only person I had ever met with the same surname. The photographic trade was a small group of people compared with other trade groups. Many of the staff were old friends and colleagues I knew from past experience so it was not a socially dramatic change. I was assigned to the training of Air Photography Operators (APOP) at a phase of their training which required them to fit and test the cameras onto the aircraft, along with before and after flight inspections. This was undertaken at the airfield site in No 521 hanger. My colleagues on the team were Sgt Al Barrett, "Curly" Goeghan, Ron Graham and Mr Al Cousins (an ex RAF Corporal Instructor at Wellesbourne Mountford). We had a great guy overseeing us at the airfield Warrant Officer Hunt, who left us to our own devices but always ensured we were looked after and cared for. One of the other chaps I recall was a Flight Sergeant Pete Rosebury (also from the airfield engineering staff and continued to share his experience later in life at the RAF Museum refurbishment centre).

The Phantom aircraft with the under-slung camera "pod".

The full length of the "pod" showing the many compartments opened
up, including the infra-red line-scan camera

We used the photo reconnaissance pod of the Phantom aircraft and the
Canberra PR 9 for practical exercises and managed to provide as realistic
scenario as we could. My only gripe being the tunnel visioned attitude of
the camp administrators who insisted that students marched to and fro from
the domestic site to the airfield. In inclement weather this proved to be
disastrous as the students arrived soaked through and spent the rest of the
day in shivering overalls and underwear whilst their uniforms steamed
away in the boiler room. The classrooms were not exactly warm during
winter and we lost many precious hours of students training time because of
ill health and time off for sick parade, a totally counterproductive way of
"training". They were also ordered to march in columns of three abreast,
normally okay on the base but they were passing along public roads over
the narrow bridge by the railway. There were many incidents of near
calamity when drivers unaware of their possible presence narrowly avoided
mowing down the file of marchers. They did have a hand torch to hold at
the front and rear of the column but this was often about as effective as a
candle, especially in foggy conditions. It took a long time before I
convinced the authorities that a compromise of reducing the columns of

three to two would lessen the risk. Happily, the authorities relented and even provided buses for transportation of all personnel to and from the site. We had managed to sell our home in Huntingdon and bought a bungalow in Shifnal which was very suitable for our needs being close to the base and to our families. I have to admit that I fell in love with Shropshire as a county and have never felt otherwise since. All in all it was the start of a very good career move. My flight commander turned out to be Flight Lieutenant Peter Stafferton, a man whom I held in high regard from days at the PRU in Rheindahlen. He was always eager to listen to ideas and suggestions with encouragement and support. His wife Sandy was a great friend and support to all who knew her and she had a perceptive insight as to what was needed from the point of view of the families of the servicemen and women. I was to learn a great deal during those initial years, despite my own experiences I was astonished to find how much I needed to know to be able to teach with confidence and credibility worthy of the position. It was a very steep learning curve in many ways, not just with photographic technicalities. Thankfully my fellow instructors were willing to share their methods and experiences in the teaching techniques and I became confident enough to share what little I had to offer with them. I do recall I had never been confident with the Sensitometry parts of my PPA course so I grabbed the opportunity to dig deeper and thankfully I gleaned enough to enlighten the dark holes in my knowledge. My wife had managed to secure a position in the drawing office of the local offices of the Brown Boveri Corporation. We seemed to have found the solution to our immediate marital problems and life began to seem more settled on the marital front.

Chapter 27 – Toxteth Riots - Liverpool

Like many of us during our service lives we focus on the career and put up with the usual trials and tribulations of service life to ensure we keep a clean sheet and don't "rock the boat" to safeguard our future. Whilst this is common sense to a degree we can assume too often, that what we want goes for our partner too. This is definitely not always the case. Sometimes the continual moving around, changing homes, making new friends and fitting in to the local social circles may become the straw that breaks the camels back. I was ready to face a new phase in my career and go for a commission, thanks to the support and encouragement of my boss Flight Lieutenant Pete Stafferton. Pete was a very good officer and a true gentleman, his understanding and appreciation of his men went a long way to creating a great team. I learned a great deal from him and always felt I owed him for that. It was only when I began to firm up my plans and discussed the prospect with my wife that I was to realise that she was in no way in accord with my ambitions. In fact she was opposed to any future prospect of further moves with the RAF. Truthfully it was not really a shock as she had made several comments over past times on how insecure she felt and now wanted to make a break from service life. Over the next few weeks it became clear that I would be on my own if I pursued my ambitions. So rather reluctantly I decided to take a hard look at what else could be on offer.

Like many others, I had little or no idea what would best suit any of my skills and whilst I was a capable instructor, I was not confident that there would be anything available to suit. I did attend an interview at British Aerospace but they were only interested in people willing to live in Saudi Arabia on contract of a few years, admittedly renewable, and at a reasonable salary, but this I thought was not solving any of my problems in keeping our marriage intact. I placed my details in the Professional and Executive Recruitment journal, prepared my CV and waited for any responses. I had several but the only one I found came close to solving my situation was with a chap setting up his business in Liverpool. Alan Dickey was a young high flier who was working with J Walter Thomson, a well known advertising agency. Since his father had passed away he inherited his father's business in Chapel Street, Liverpool. D.O. Photographic, as the business was called, specialised in graphic reproductions of a wide range of items, including rescaling drawings and giant enlargements. He needed a manager to run the technical side of the production and train up a team of operators with a view to eventual partnership as the business grew. I could commute there from Monday to Friday, renting a small apartment in Southport during the week and a company car was thrown in. Salary was not exactly equal to the RAF but then I would be receiving an RAF pension so it was a strong possibility and a bit of a challenge to boot. At least I thought it was a start as there was not much else on offer at the time. The premises in Liverpool were located in the basement of an office block. The equipment was a bit old fashioned but it was at least reliable and fairly easy to maintain. The photo processor was a 54" wide automatic print developer which completed the throughput in around 10 minutes from dry input to output. We used specialised waterproof paper and translucent film. The copy camera / enlarger was an old "blow back" machine mounted on rails similar in principle to the large copy cameras I was conversant with in the RAF. Some of the work included the plans for the new by pass around the Muslim Holy City of Mecca and had to be approved by some very high officials. The Lebanese company handling the project was headed up by a tough Australian civil engineer who demanded perfection as standard and rightly so under the circumstances! The other memorable task came from the Mersey Docks and Harbour Board for the organisers of the "Zussman Project", which blossomed into the fantastic Albert Dock refurbishment and was the forerunner of the redevelopment of the Liverpool Docks. Several exacting tasks came our way from this contract; the first challenged my fear of heights. We had to photograph the entire face of the famous Liver Building in minute sections to create a massive mosaic. They used this set of pictures to assess the restoration and cleaning of the whole structure. I spent many hours on top of a very high gantry using hired cameras to accurately record each area in scale for assessment.

We also won a contract to copy hundreds of old historical photos depicting the history of Liverpool and enlarge them up to exhibition standard for the Maritime Museum. I have to say I was fascinated with the quality and detail of many of these wonderful pictures. It was a total pleasure as I had listened to my father's stories of the city history when we visited my Grannie in Alverstone Road, just round the corner from Penny Lane. On many occasions, we worked till late hours to meet deadlines and being too tired to sleep, I spent happy hours in local taverns with Alan listening to the wonderful humour and sheer hospitality of the people of Liverpool. I do recall one day there was a local bye election in Southport and I had wandered over to the Blundell Sands Hotel near my apartment to be confronted by Shirley Williams who was the local candidate (before she was a Liberal MP?). After we talked about local issues for a couple of minutes, she was keen to know all about the RAF and my career. I was reluctant to go into any detail and kept it to the general photographer aspects. She was a fascinating person and so knowledgeable on many subjects. I was particularly struck by her sincerity, despite my instinctive mistrust of all political people. I rightly guessed then, that she was destined for a high profile in her political future. It was about this time that a certain Derek Hatton became a vociferous noise on the streets of Liverpool, urging the down trodden workers to unite and rise up against the establishments and their leaders. Admittedly things were glum in the city and suburban areas. Unemployment, closed shops and derelict housing sites were increasingly apparent. The mood of the city was beginning to feel hostile to authority, sadly not without some justification. The ordinary people felt let down and action was desperately needed to remedy the causes. The situation boiled over one weekend when the riots began in Toxteth, my father's birthplace. The situation got out of hand very quickly, which indicated some serious organisation, and the police response was hard and determined, with riot police in full gear stretched across roads and blocking the waves of young violent protestors. Alan and I were driving to work from Hope Street when we turned towards the Westminster drive-in bank and saw it in flames with smoke also pouring out of the Rackets Club centre.

Unwittingly we had driven straight into "no mans land" between a line of riot police and a group of rioters making a deal of noise and threats. For a short while we were both astounded and petrified until a tap on the window at my right drew my attention to a young lad with a sawn of shot gun pointing at my head! He was shouting at us to get out and hand over money, whilst a few of his mates were just a few feet away. Stupidly I wound down the window, and then gave him my wallet and a cheap watch. He seemed a bit placated then demanded Alan's wallet as well. As I smelled the oil on the end of the shotgun I encouraged Alan to do likewise if he really needs a technical manager to continue in his employ with a head on his shoulders! Because the police were by this time beginning to take an interest in the proceedings the guy with the gun must have thought discretion was the better part of valour and disappeared into the bunch of youths on the pavement. I decided we should also get the hell out of there and encouraged Alan to reverse as fast as he could, away from the potential confrontation. Thankfully my forceful commanding voice got through his momentary paralysis and we got out safely, albeit backwards and all over the road in a crazy swerving manoeuvre. This also fortunately scattered the guys who had begun to approach from behind, well out of the way and we were clear free! We turned into the only roads we knew were still clear, taking the long way round to Chapel Street. On the way we came across a group of riot police on standby near their vehicles. Alan jumped out and ran over to them explaining what had just happened. A very burley policeman listened for about ten seconds and suggested his luck was off, or something similar sounding and Alan returned to the car looking very sheepish. It was like being back on active service again for me. At least my wallet only had £2 in it and nothing else, my watch was a cheapo because of working with chemicals, so the robber boy got nowt worth having from me. Alan unfortunately was £50 lighter and his Seiko was a bit more expensive than mine! In the next few days things went from bad to worse as our other processing lab nearer the drive-in bank had also been torched, no particular reason, it was just a handy target. I was soon to learn that poor Alan had insufficient insurance cover on that one and as a result the bank did a nasty and repossessed his home against the loan for the other premises. So after two fascinating years in my new civilian career I was out of a job and looking for something to do again.

Chapter 28 - 1982 A Career in Training

As good fortune would have it, I was not long out of work, thanks to being given a "heads up" by Dave Males, my colleague from Lindholme days. He was at Cosford at the School of Photography on the staff as an Instructor. I would have to apply for one of two vacant posts for Instructional Officers and hope I was included on the short list for an interview. To my eternal gratitude I was asked to attend with a sample lesson ready to display my talents should I pass the initial interview and examination paper. It was not a foregone conclusion at all and the paper asked some very deep searching questions on my knowledge of the appropriate skills required. The lesson presentation was also an intense episode where nerves and ability were tested. I was successful along with another old colleague, Roger Williams and so began my second career which was to last for 24 years.

I was obliged to attend the Instructor Training School at RAF Newton, Nottingham, despite having completed this same course just four years previously (I was informed that this did not count as I was now to be employed by the Civil Service). In fact it was to my benefit as I managed to achieve a grade A2 on completion, (the highest being A1 which can only be awarded post graduate). The staff at RAF Newton were selected from the best of the best in terms of skill and experience. The "no nonsense" techniques implemented there would be of distinct advantage to many other forms of education, especially in regards to secondary education. The motivation of children in preparation for the real world of responsibility and competitive application would benefit form the skills taught by the RAF Educators at Newton. All this gave me the confidence to launch my second career as I meant to continue. I have to add that most of the "civilian" instructors at this time were ex service due to the fact that we had to have sufficient knowledge and experience to teach skills across the board of aerial and general photography. There were few people from external theatres with the required experience or knowledge at this level. I do have to mention some exceptions to this norm and Peter Davies was one such person who had a very deep scientific knowledge. I had the privilege of working with a number of very talented Instructors who were very helpful and totally professional in sharing skills and knowledge with those of less experience with the techniques of instruction. My students were usually young men fresh from training and as such were still under the influences of the strict discipline applied at the "boot camp" (basic military training). Without eroding this in built respect for authority I needed to ensure that their chosen career path was going to hold their interest and be of mutual benefit to all. I was also quite surprised to discover a lack of certain basic skills in the areas of numeracy and literacy, especially since the politicians of the day had all emphasised the need for education and raising standards in our schools. The problem became obvious when the objectives covered the preparation of processing chemicals. Few of the students really understood what "percentage" or "ratios" meant in practical terms of preparing solutions and little or no mental arithmetic was forthcoming without the aid of a calculator. So it became necessary to back track and establish the fundamentals before we could proceed. The students were also encouraged to supplement their lesson handouts by making notes during the lesson and creating a useful reference for their revision before the periodical exams. I monitored the accuracy of their notes from time to time and noticed that some students had poor skills at recording handwritten notes with little regard to spelling or grammar. I was lucky to have experienced a grammar school education in the early 50's, but it did come as a bit of a shock to find modern education had failed to equip these students properly for life in the real world, where basic maths and English would be expected to be available from them. Sadly this exercise had to be repeated for many years and I still find many young people are unable to apply these basic skills in retail and other walks of life.

I continue to hear the need to retrain students, after leaving state school education, before they are deemed "fit for purpose" as employable. To their great credit I also know they catch on quickly once shown the relevance and true need for absorbing the necessary skills. I have been flattered by the number of my

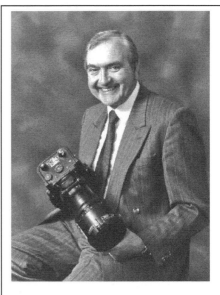

Dave with an F134 camera 1994

old students I have since met who went on in later years to become self-employed in a successful business venture. They always made a point of referring back to our early days of retraining their basic skills and I do feel better for that. Our key mantra in teaching techniques was always: "keep it simple" and take one step at a time. "Student see and student do" was a critical timing of duration to maintain attention, interest and prevent boredom setting in, which is more likely to happen with adult students. As an Instructor it amazed me how much I was to learn from the many questions thrown up and how little I really knew in the early days. I am ever grateful that my attempts to motivate students were unwittingly reciprocated by their curiosity and interest for me to ensure I had available resources to answer their questions. I know it has kept my mind active to the point of exhaustion at times but it also had the enormous benefit of keeping my attitude in tune with young people and some of it rubbed off staying with me into my elder years. As often happened with military equipment we tended to be a way behind the "curve ball" of current technology as most of our kit was designed for rugged duration and echoed this in terms of cost. As the years progressed into the 80's and 90's we began to acquire more and more "off the shelf" equipment and consequently this was a fortunate dovetailing for being commercially aware of products and available technology which heralded the forthcoming digital revolution. My initial years as an instructor demanded that lesson preparation was branded with your own make up, whilst retaining the sequence and limitations of the objectives of the course curriculum. There was a lot for me to learn as this was a whole new world of training jargonese and methods, some of which I knew were overdue for a detailed revision. I was also becoming aware of the drift from these parameters that occurred in some of the areas of training. It was a difficult balancing act to expound your ideas of what was thought to be needed without upsetting those of greater experience and somewhat set their ways from a comfort zone. I did get into trouble unwittingly from time to time as enthusiasm and impatience can override tact and diplomacy. I was also acutely aware of my enthusiasm causing me to overstate my case to a point of being dismissed as talking too much and too long with those I needed to get onside. I can hear the mirth echoing in my ears even now as they may be reading my "confession" of my shortcomings. I have always felt it necessary to be realistically honest with your own faults as well as standing firm when you believe you are right. Sometimes this is not conducive to others "political" ambitions and I paid the price, quite rightly so.

The Long Walk
It was around this time in the mid eighties that I learned of my friends association with the SAS during WW2. I met him many years before as a friend of the family on my wife's side. Horace Stokes was a manager of a pub on the Tyburn Road in Birmingham and had a very distinguished

career training commandos in Scotland and took part in a number of raids by the fledgling SAS in Sicily and Sardinia.* He was now suffering from cancer and was not expected to survive more than a few weeks.
Available from Amazon Books: "No Ordinary Life" by Peter Stokes

I spoke to him about his situation and true to form he wanted no fuss but asked if I could help raise funds for some driver syringes for the Macmillan organisation that were looking after him. These syringes allowed him to continue as normal as possible without the effects of large doses of morphine being administered in one application. This worked by metering specific smaller doses at the optimum rate allowing the patient better mobility and lifestyle. We thought about an appropriate fund raising scheme and I came up with the idea of a sponsored non-stop walk from Birmingham to London. I felt this would follow in the footsteps of the legendary endurance of the wartime soldiers under his command. Like a complete idiot I volunteered to do the walk myself. Now I have to say I was reasonably fit as I played badminton every lunchtime at Cosford but I knew in my soul that this would require a serious regime of fitness and organisation to be able to complete such a task. As a member of our local Lions International group in Shifnal, I put the idea forward and they agreed to help in any way they could. I gave myself a nine month work up to the standard of the fitness needed. The RAF physical training Instructors at Cosford became my mentors and advisors throughout this time for which I am eternally grateful. I began by walking to work everyday and increasing the load in the back pack I carried. I also began long walks to Birmingham and back in the early hours of Sunday mornings. The Lions club members volunteered to act as my pace makers on the training walks which had by now increased to more than 20 miles per day at weekends. We had decided that the best and safest route would be to start at the Pebble Mill TV Studios in Birmingham and take the A41 almost directly down to the Shepherds Bush Studios in London. I needed to experience each part of the route with the rise and fall of various hills to understand the pace needed and the time each part would take. We managed to complete this well before D Day and then set about preparing the escort vans and the members who would be available for the big day which included support drivers, forward lookouts and pacemakers. By this time I had completed around 1,400 miles in training so I was about as ready as I could have hoped for. A very kind professor at Aston University (who was an experienced Fell runner) gave me some very useful tips on what would be easily digested on route before fatigue prevented the digestive system accommodating food and subsequently depleting my energy levels. It was very sound advice and worked extremely well throughout.

The big day came and after a useful interview on air with the local Radio station we set off around 9 am. Most of the day went well with a dry day and a good pace within our target aims. Towards the evening however the rain came down which kept me fresh and cool, but I began to find the nighttime and early hours very taxing as the body demanded rest and sleep. The Lions pacemakers and escorts stuck by me and they really were terrific, continually spurring me on, with humorous banter and essential foods supplies right on schedule. It must be said they were absolutely fantastic and they must have felt very tired and fed up with the monotony and the bad weather. Came the dawn and the sun broke through the clouds to help dry us out. It was very welcome and allowed me to take stock of my blisters which had now become more than a bit painful, despite all my precautions and practice, the wet weather had played havoc with the footwear. I decided to take drastic action as I was determined we had to complete the walk with so many people cheering us on and donating buckets full of money ion route. I took out a sterilised scalpel and cut them open to get rid of the fluid which was bulging out my footwear and causing the pain. The delay was only about 5 to 10 minutes so I considered that fair game in the greater scheme of things. There was this nightmare hill in front of me just before Tring in Ayelsbury, which I knew about thanks to my practice walks. It was the sort of hill which is very deceptive. Just when you think you are coming to the top, a new hill appears to climb up from its summit and off you go again. This happened three times and covered several miles. I was on the top looking down and began the decent, which any experienced walker will tell you are worse than going up because the hip joints and knee joints get a real pounding with the steeper inclines. Fortunately I was totally distracted by the wonderful people who had turned out to greet us, including their local Lions club members who had organised the reception committee. The cheering and clapping lifted my spirits into the heavens and my legs became power houses of energy again. I really do understand how this effect helps many athletes who compete at International events. It is quite euphoric and gives you energy and power you never thought you could muster! As we approached London suburbs we were greeted by many people who needed to know what we were doing and why and there were times when I really need to crack on and save my breath for the task ahead, but you have to respect that their donations are the reason you are doing it. We finally approached the TV Studios at Shepherds Bush and I really need some final support on this last mile or so as my legs were in a state of near collapse, so with a little physical support under each arm I staggered to the finish line to be greeted by the Macmillan officials from their local office.

To be absolutely honest I do not remember the final mile very much. It was only when I sort of surfaced into consciousness in the vehicle on the way home that I realised I had actually done it. I had walked non-stop for 136 miles in 24 hours. I don't know if I broke any records, frankly I didn't care. What I had managed to achieve, with the wonderful support from the Shifnal Lions club, the RAF PTIs and many other sponsors, was to raise over £3,000 to buy ten driver syringes for use by the Macmillan organisation in the West Midlands. I do recall that one company was Brintons the famous carpet manufacturer, based in Halesfield near Telford at the time, who donated a very large amount and I have always held them in the highest regard ever since. I continue to hold cherished memories of all those wonderful people in Shifnal who supported our Lions club and the many endeavours they undertook to improve the lot of those less fortunate. It was my honour and privilege to be associated with them all.

Meanwhile back at the training school, I learned a number of quite amazing techniques with visual aids and the problem solving training techniques advocated. In the early days of course it was all done with cumbersome OHP (overhead projector) slides, magnetic strips and cardboard cut outs. This all took many hours which had to be completed in your own time as the cycle of the training programme gave very little available time to lesson preparation. This was something all the instructors felt was missing from the appreciation of the management of training in general. We had a very wide range of courses available (and continued to do so for many years) up to around 36 at one count. I had an idea at this time to alleviate the problem of "recruiting" current serving members to volunteer for instructor duties. Many Sergeants were reluctant to take on this role for personal reasons. I remembered that many years ago, when the school was located at Wellesbourne- Mountford, there were a number of Corporal instructors on the staff. So I suggested that this be re-introduced to help fill the vacancies to see how it would fare. The bosses agreed and several Corporals were taken on, which to their great credit, they proved to be excellent trainers and eventually achieved promotion to Sergeant whilst still at the school. One such Corporal was Tim Robinson who returned to the school after his service career ended and is currently at the school after many years as a Civil Servant on the Instructional staff. The great benefit for me was the ability to sit in on some occasions to watch my colleagues and learn a great deal from their knowledge of the subjects and their techniques of instruction.

My personal life was beginning to show signs of strain. My past service life and the amount of hours I needed to spend with the new career began to pour salt on old wounds and it was not long before our relationship had reached new low ebb. Unknown to me my wife had found the kind of attention she needed from another and I should have opened my eyes and avoided prolonging the inevitable. In the wisdom of hindsight it would have been the better option and less painful for all concerned. I was left in no uncertain terms one morning when I found the ultimate "Dear John" letter in a pink envelope on the table. It was over after 30 years and the finality gave me very mixed feelings of relief and sadness, relief from the stress of the oppressive atmosphere of tension when we were together in the home, sadness that I had wasted so much time on trying to repair a doomed relationship. I wished that we had been more honest about our feelings and perhaps we could have made it easier for us to come to the same conclusion earlier. I was conscious that monetary priorities were some of the cause. My full service pension was due at the same time of the hearing and played a major role in the settlement calculations. As the barrister explained, my pension was deemed "sacrosanct" but a clean break settlement was a negotiable deal. Despite my wife's assets and earnings, I was at best going to receive half of the residue from the sale of the family home. Despite her assurances that she would be living on her own her partner was already in co habitation and financially more secure than I was about to become, little did I know! At the same time my old colleague and fellow instructor, John MacDonald had left the RAF and gone to live in the Algarve, Portugal with his wife. I happened to be in touch and he suggested I come over for a break. I accepted his kind offer and spent time in the sun with his friends and the local Portuguese. I was driving through a local town near John's place when I saw a row of newly built apartments for sale very cheap compared to UK costs. We went along to the agents and I decided that the Algarve could be my future home. It was all done on the spur of the moment but when I returned to the UK I was expecting to be able to fund most of the apartment from my half of the residue from the sale of the family home. Big mistake no 2, in divorce always expect the unexpected! After the nausea of solicitors cranking up the "taxi fare" whilst stringing out procedures (barristers cost £500 per hour), it came down to the money as always and the rest was history as they say. Because of the clean break settlement, all funds from the sale of the family home were paid to her, which also left me in debt to the solicitors. I needed to take some leave to get my thoughts together and sort out a plan for financial survival.

My wife's best friend Carole came round during all this turmoil and asked me what I had planned. I told her I was trying to arrange for a mortgage to buy a house locally but she came up with a suggestion which made better practical sense. She had lost her husband (just 49 years old) to a tragic brain tumour a few years before and was trying to fund the cost of keeping their large home. She proposed that I could rent half of her home until my problems were resolved. It was two cottages converted to a single dwelling but had retained the divisions conveniently with the two staircases. My options were very limited as the buyers of our family home needed to move in and I had no home to go to. It turned out to be a very happy solution. Carole even came down with me to the solicitor's office and negotiated a bill settlement down to much less than the original "estimate". I was soon to discover that she was a top class negotiator in all things financial and she became my mentor in my recovery along the road to financial stability. I suppose it was inevitable that we would find such compatibility in each other and a few years later I proposed one weekend in Chester that she become my life partner, to my eternal delight she accepted. We were conscious that there could be some awkward situations from both sides of the families, due to her association with my ex wife, her own children and her late husbands in-laws.

On March 30th 1996, after a civil ceremony in Bridgnorth, we travelled to Speke airport which was being renamed as John Lennon airport. British Airways were also celebrating 25 years of service with Concorde and sent one to take passengers on a celebration flight. Carole had arranged for us to take part and we were given the VIP treatment. The Concorde took off after we had completed photos courtesy of our local RAF photographer. It was actually delayed for 20minutes because of us, but as it was a bit of a special occasion the crew were more than happy to oblige. At 10,000 feet, Padre Eddie Core from RAF Cosford conducted the blessing to the surprise and delight of the other passengers. He stated that he had to make a good job of it as his "Boss" was seriously close! The "Boss" must have been pretty close because from that moment on my life changed for the better in so many ways.

Carole Ludlow-Smith and the author about to board Concorde
at John Lennon Airport, 30th March 1996

There will be many readers who have been through similar personal experiences with a matrimonial relationship which breaks down. Sadly today it is not all that uncommon. I would like to place on record here that whilst it may seem like the end of all things dear to your heart, sometimes it is for the best and if you can turn the page, accept your own responsibility in such turmoil, there is light at the end of the tunnel. My personal feelings for what its worth, seem to have come around to the fact that in the end it all boils down to a point of view in which it takes two to tango. So avoid the blame game and save your money from paying the solicitor's holiday in Barbados. Carole's family and friends all had their own thoughts on the turn of events, especially her Father and Mother in law who had lost their son so tragically. I tried to understand and respect their feelings by letting the positives of our new relationship permeate through their misgivings. No one really likes change which can be somewhat uncomfortable to accept and it was a big ask for her daughter Louise and her son Phillip to feel otherwise. Needless to say everything takes time, but their acceptance of my role coming into their lives was received with grace and a lot of understanding. To their credit they were all generous with their support and hospitality and I will be ever grateful to them for this. My step son Phillip has been very successful in his career, despite the ups and downs of running your own business. He is now considered one of the leading lights in the nursery trade. Louise is my heroine, as an outstanding example of a modern mother raising three children and holding down a vocational career in helping people with learning disabilities. Her children are a shining example of what can be achieved with a true family spirit. Her husband Shaun is the epitome of a hard working, caring father with the most wonderful relationship with all his children. They are all grown up now and working into their own careers. In all the years I have known them I have never even heard a voice raised in anger or witnessed any conflict among them. Louise managed all this and achieved a BA honours degree into the bargain. I hold them up as a shining example of how it could and should be done.

Chapter 29 - The Millennium Approaches

One weekend morning I received a call that I had been awarded the Commander in Chief's commendation in the New Year's honours list. It was to be the start of some exciting times for us. I had taken on the responsibility as curator of the in-house Museum at the school and after a few years, my colleagues Dave Jenkins, Jack Eggleston and Gerry Paine had created a great improvement in the quality of the exhibits and provided a storyboard around the history of the progress since WW1.

I had managed to persuade the director of the RAF Museum at Cosford, Mr John Francis, that we had something worth putting on display for the general public. Up until this time the collection was housed within the school premises on the secured site, but the increasing training needs for the Army surveillance programme demanded more space and it ad to go somewhere. The general public were therefore excluded from viewing the collection unless they came as members of various camera clubs and photographic organisations during a pre-arranged visit. I would arrange a visit programme and some of the other instructors would help out by setting up suitable display of the more modern methods to help the evening go with a swing. It all worked very well but the training needs had to take priority and so my new plan was approved.

It was agreed that the inventory of the collection could be transferred to the RAF Museum and the director would refurbish the old parachute packing room into a display gallery for us to complete, furnish and prepare as a Millennium project. The existing cabinets were brought up to public safety standards by replacing the old glass and installing alarms where necessary. We managed to acquire funding sponsorship from Kodak, and a few others who donated, materials and a very large flat screen monitor courtesy of Calumet. It was the largest we had seen (at this time) and we made full use of it, creating a rolling PowerPoint display depicting the role of reconnaissance and others showing the Military Photo Competition pictures. We approached Lord Lichfield's secretary at his Oxford Garden studios and to our delight he graciously accepted our invitation to open the Gallery on 16th June 2000. He completed the project with a spectacular day's visit which also included a whole day at the school talking to students and staff. He was a delight in his rapport with all and related many of his now famous stories of events during his amazing career. It was a terrific start to the new home for the unique collection and continued to draw interest from photography enthusiasts, TV documentary producers and many members of the just curious public who came to visit, especially on Air Days (usually held in mid June). It had taken us six long months of working late nights, weekends and all the hours which could be spared. I can only say that without my fellow enthusiasts,

Photo: Dave Jenkins, Jack Eggleston, Dave Humphrey
Three generations of curators from the former JSOP Museum

director John Francis and Al McLain of the RAF Museum, Dave Jenkins, Jack Eggleston and Gerry Paine, my co-workers on the project, none of it would have been possible The material and equipment may well have been scrapped and lost forever (as happened when the Farnborough Science Museum was closed down). We were often called upon to be interviewed by a number of TV documentary producers and I do vividly recall a chap from Australia, Mr Jeff Watson. Jeff was originally from Birmingham and worked for the BBC before emigrating to Australia where he set up his own production company. He wanted to use some of the artefacts and the displays to illustrate his documentary on the legendary Wing Commander Sidney Cotton. We obliged and he kindly sent us a copy of his production entitled "Last plane out of Berlin". It was a brilliant production done on a shoe string with actors and aircraft similar to the Lockheed 12A flown by Cotton on his clandestine missions over the emerging Nazi Germany before the war broke out.

Lord Lichfield opens the Military Photography Gallery
in the RAF Museum, Cosford, June 2000

Photo: Dave Humphrey, John Francis, RAF Museum Director,
Group Captain Williams, OC RAF Cosford and Lord Lichfield

To me it was exactly the kind of human story we all love to hear, as Cotton was a controversial outspoken colonial wild man who bucked authority to the point when they could tolerate it no longer and sacked him in the middle of the war! To his enduring credit he actually understood what was needed with far greater clarity than those supposedly in control. And the fact that they continued to use every principle he laid down, proved him to be the wiser. There were other productions for the BBC and the "Discovery" channel in the USA which we were invited to support from our collections and this we did, time and again.

Chapter 30 - The Museum - "Cold War"

The year was 2003 and we had watched with interest the growing mammoth construction of the "cold war" exhibition project as the "big dig" laid the foundations for the modern architect design funded by the National Lottery. We were hoping to be invited to transfer or contribute some of our collection (we had a lot of material stored as the current Gallery was not large enough for all of it), but we heard nothing for many months as it grew into a spectacular angular shape which was to house many aircraft and much of the equipment and materials associated with the cold war. I received a call from John Francis on one occasion asking me to come over for a discussion. On arrival we went to the gallery to meet him but all we found was the RAF Museum staff frantically packing away all our months of hard work and displays of equipment into boxes. We protested as hard as we could but we were assured that this was a "temporary" storage problem as the architect wanted the building levelled and removed because it was spoiling the sight lines of his "Cold War" project from the main building. We were assured that there was a plan to re house the missile gallery exhibits among the existing aircraft layouts in the other hangers and we would then be able to reinstate our display at this location in the near future. It was a dreadful blow to the hard work and efforts put in by the team, not to mention that the items donated by Calumet had been relocated for the benefit of the audio visual display in the conference room, where commercial conferences were being hosted by Museum enterprises.

The No 6 site at RAF Stafford was the new home for all our materials and equipment. This was owned by the RAF Museum at Cosford and acted as a satellite storage cell. We went over to ensure the state of our material was to be properly cared for during this "temporary" period of storage and I have to say that the staff there were more than sympathetic, helpful and obliging in ensuring we were satisfied with the selected areas being heated and weatherproof etc. It was far from ideal and I was not in any mood to accept compromise until the problem was resolved. Some while after this, our empty building was occupied by the contactors constructing the "Cold War" project. On completion of the project this historical building (a wartime parachute packing hall) was demolished without any further consultation. I was then told that the project of moving the missile gallery had been delayed, without any particular reason but it would go ahead "soon". In the meantime I visited the missile gallery, assessing its size and potential. We made accurate measurements of the floor, door, window and power point locations. It took a while but eventually I came up with a suitable set of drawings and included a work office at the one end (as in the previous gallery). It was all looking a bit more promising as the light and access was liable to be more conducive to the traffic of the public instead of diverting into an individual building; so far it had some promise of an improved version of the other gallery. I was re-assured it would go ahead as soon as the heads of department gave it the approval. John Francis retired a short while later and advised me to seek some powerful sponsor who could bring pressure to bear on the project. Sadly a few years later I was to hear of the passing of Patrick Lichfield after suffering a heart attack. I could feel the impetus slipping slowly away and despite letters, e-mails and phone calls, there was a deafening silence in response. I am hoping that this will change in the near future and I ask all manner of interested parties to urge the re-instatement of a unique piece of military history which was presented gift wrapped to the RAF Museum and apparently removed on the whim of an architect (if that is to be believed). There is an old saying that to forget your history means you have no future. I hope this is not allowed to prevail in this case.

Update: As this book goes to print, the Museum is now to be reinstated at in its original home back in the training school at DSOP. Thanks to the intervention of the OC Jon Jarvis and a few good men: Tim Robinson, Flight Sergeant Andy Malthouse, Ian Dunning, John Freestone and Mal Price, along with yours truly as advisor. The team will co-ordinate the new installation and facilities to be completed in time for the DSOP Centenary celebrations in 2015.

Chapter 31 - 2004 Time to Call It a Day

At the age of 64, my physical ability to keep up with the troops of the light infantry and the young high flyers of the RAF began to show in my pulse rate and purple face! The rapid changes in computer technology were beginning to run away from my ability to keep up also. Geoff Sellars was kindness itself and gave me some really interesting areas to work on inside the Training Standards cell and ensuring that all examinations were constructed in a "realistic, relevant and valid" manner. It appealed to my instincts and questioning nature to ensure fairness for the student in terms of what and how they were given instruction. I had learned a lot more tact and diplomacy under his guidance and it worked so well in this new area. Surprisingly enough my contacts with the Army had only been at "shop floor" level but now I went to their training HQ at the old RAF base at Andover, to learn more about the how and how not to test what has been taught. It was a great revelation and my first contact was with an American officer from the US Army. After a few "whooahh's" and the usual macho yankie doodle stuff we got down to business and he was an extremely intelligent and astute young Major. I was very surprised and impressed by their methods, techniques and perceptions of what is and what is not needed in testing the lesson instruction. I was able to apply the whole gambit and make seriously useful changes to the way we had been using exam techniques. Most importantly it did the job of examination better, more efficiently and ensured that we did our job better. So there you have it, never judge a book by it's cover (it may be camouflaged anyway!) and keep an open mind until you see the content within.

I knew it was nearing big decision time for me as we were both beginning to understand that time really does not stand still and we had a lot of plans for our retirement. We wanted to spend more time at our home in Portugal and we wanted to travel more without the restrictions of "school holiday" time frames. We had been so lucky to date and visited many countries albeit on short visits. I made the decision to retire just one year early as it was a good opportunity for both of us to come down slowly into retirement and still stay active. So it was that in November 2004, we threw a nice party in the Sports pavilion at Cosford and had a wonderful evening among our many friends and colleagues. At Carole's suggestion we made up a trophy as my legacy to the school to be awarded by the CO to the "Best Instructor" on an annual basis. We had it made from a crystal block and it seems to have been put to good use since.

Chapter 32 - Living the Dream

" **A**ll work and no play makes Jack a dull boy" so the saying goes. Carole and I have managed to fulfil our dreams throughout my second marriage as a promise to ourselves that we would make the most of our time together. Every year of our relationship has been filled with an adventure in travel and achievement of a target, sometimes more than just one or two. Carole is a great believer in investing in yourself as the best investment you could possibly make. As I know only too well, ignoring the needs of your social life can be a disaster waiting to happen. We planned each year with a schedule of activity and thanks to Carole's life long friends, Ann and Harry we became a formidable quartet with a portfolio to excite the any travel agent. It all came about for me when Carole's tragic loss of her first husband had left a great gap in her life. Her enduring spirit of adventure and her close friends had continued to lift her from the awful depths of initial emptiness following her loss. To this end they had arranged a trip to the USA and when our relationship had begun to become more than friendship, Ann and Harry kindly welcomed me into their circle. It was the beginning of a very exiting period in our lives.

First Impressions of the USA - West Coast coach tour
Our first adventure together was a conducted coach tour of the American west coast which took in Los Angeles, San Diego, Phoenix, then across the Nevada desert to Sedona and onto Las Vegas. The coach supplied was very comfortable, very large and had everything on board to accommodate our needs, which was just as well as the distances were staggeringly long between locations. Our wonderful driver was a young lady who was not only a very skilful driver but had the knack of well honed people skills along with the ability to load and unload the tons of luggage with dexterity to shame the fittest of any of us on board. She also befriended an elderly English chap who was obviously a recent widower and seemed a little reserved and alone. She took it on herself to ensure he was included in her rapport and he certainly brightened up from her delightful attentions! Some mornings required really early starts at 5 am but it was rare for any complaints despite the age group of our fellow travellers.

The sheer size of everything and the distances we travelled were the greatest first impressions. Every one seemed to have so much more space available for homes, shopping areas and the huge cars seemed appropriately in scale somehow. There was also a very positive "can do" and "how can I help you" attitude prevailing throughout. It still impresses me greatly when you enter any "store" (as they call shops) to be greeted as if you are the only customer they have had all week. They have the knack and training to be so polite and helpful without walking into your space so you do feel special. Their manners and hospitality are almost embarrassing to the English reserve and staid unbending posture to new faces, a very endearing trait once you accept it as their norm. How refreshing it was from some of the grumpy reluctance to acknowledge your presence which sadly prevailed in many UK retail organisations at the time. Happily their mantra has now permeated in to the training of the UK retail and service industry. Of course there are difference, in their system of wages for instance, wages are very basic in the USA and rely on tipping for good service to make up the bonus for hard work and enthusiasm. Some merit does exist in this as it does promote this "can do" attitude and motivate those who perform better than others. Overall I was impressed by their positive outlook in all things born from encouraging entrepreneurs to promoting their ideas and facilities. I was also impressed by the American priority given to comfort and ease of working. Everything from hotels, retail stores, cars, public transport and furniture was designed to be spacious, effortless and oh so comfortable. The small touches of "luxury" were taken as standard and someone somewhere had a job to keep on top of everything. I became aware that each worker had a specific training, uniform and self respect. There was an air of confidence and efficiency which oiled the "machinery of living" so to speak. Perhaps this was a naive opinion on my first visit and to a small extent this may have been be true as we spread our visits further afield. However, essentially I have seen little to change this to any great degree since.

Among other wonderful experiences along this journey I must recall the visit to Los Angeles and Pier 39 in where we had meal of clam chowder (a kind of soup poured into a "bowl" of bread cut from a cottage loaf as we would describe it. In the bay nearby we watched a group of seals sun bathing on the floating wooden piers, oblivious to the entire goings on around them. In the evening we walked to the top of the famous Knob Hill where the Hotel Fairmont has a rotating bar on its roof overlooking a spectacular scene of he city below, especially at night with the sparkling lights of the city creating a carpet of luminance. This hotel was used in the making of the Film "Hotel", from the book written by Harold Robbins (of The Carpet Baggers fame). Shortly after, we arrived at San Diego, a wonderful city which was to become one of our favourite to visit in years to come. It is home to the US Navy Seals training centre and the Us Fleet. We were lucky to be there to watch the arrival of the US Navy ships on their return from the Gulf War. We passed on to Flagstaff and across huge wide

Behind the Lens |

open spaces on our transit to the Grand Canyon, truly one of the most awesome and spectacular sights I had seen to date. Because Ann and Carole wanted to see the Hoover Dam in preference to the flight in a light aircraft, they chose to stay with the coach tour. Harry and I had good seats up front for a birds eye view, made all the more special because it was piloted by a Vietnam veteran who flying skills and knowledge of the Grand Canyon made it a truly memorable occasion. We landed at Las Vegas and joined up with the rest of the coach party to enjoy the great hospitality of a town that is truly remarkable, even more so when we were informed it was now run by Mormon Church members and has been for some years since the Mafia gangs were rooted out. We thoroughly enjoyed the wide variety of free fare available everywhere and managed to resist the temptations of the serious gambling halls although the various casinos were incredibly spectacular. The bus tour took in all the homes of the rich and famous stars who have entertained here (including our own Tom Jones). No visit would be complete without a visit to the Liberace Museum, to see his spectacular Rolls Royce and the many outrageous costumes. It was all very glitzy and flash but nevertheless quite mesmerising. We flew home from Las Vegas via Chicago and Yew York which in itself was a revelation as to the vast size of the country. It also explains why they have so much space to live and how they use it so effectively to provide a degree of freedom and comfort, something which the UK could not emulate with its dense population per square mile. So that was it, my first and definitely not my last impression of the USA.

Orange Lake (and USA II)

Our second visit together was in the following year to Orange County in Florida. This time we travelled independently and hired a large car for the duration. We rented a substantial apartment inside a large club complex called Orange Lake. It had wonderful facilities for relaxing and entertainment. The cinema (on site) was showing the film "Apollo 13", a true story of the near disaster starring Tom Hanks, which had just been released. It was very appropriate as we planned a visit to the Kennedy Space Centre. The highlights for me on this tour were the usual points of Hollywood, Universal Studios, Sea World and the ultimate Disney World. All created from the skills of those illusionists from the film industry who construct the magical effects and spectacular impact for young and old. It becomes a competition in awe and surprise to tantalise the senses into believing the impossible is possible. My only regret, I would love to have experienced all this through the eyes and mind of a child.

Sidney Cotton's "Ghost"

It was during this vacation that I wanted to visit the NASA Executive Airfield at Titusville near Cape Kennedy. In my research on Sidney Cotton's life story, I had read that Graham Dinsdale (an ex RAF photographer) had traced the Lockheed 12A used by Sidney Cotton as being returned to the USA. Apparently it was slightly damaged in an air raid on No 1PDU at RAF Hendon back in 1939 and eventually it was crated up and shipped back to the USA. Shortly after we arrived at the airfield at Titusville I was introduced to an elderly man who had worked on the very Lockheed aircraft and he gave the details of the owner. It turned out that the aircraft had been fully refurbished, including the secret sliding panels which hid the on board spy cameras from the prying eyes of the German military authorities. It was alive and well flying tourists around on "Champagne Sunset" flights and had appeared in many films such as "Casa Blanca" with Humphrey Bogart, "Doc Pepper" with Michael Redford, and more well known in the American TV series "The A Team". It was apparently offered for sale more than once, some years after my trip, but no one in the UK seemed to be interested in its purchase, how sad is that.

Edward and Mrs Simpson - history repeating itself

I suppose I should call this part as USA III, It was also completed just a year after the last trip, so you may be forgiven for thinking I had become addicted to the USA and you would be quite right. Having "done" the usual tourist spots we felt a bit more adventurous and decided to go all the way across to San Diego, a place we had all agreed on the first tour was to be high on our dream sheet for a more thorough looksee. Our hotel was directly opposite the historical and well known Hotel del Coronado where presidents and Princes frequented, along with a few ladies who also had impact on history in the USA and the UK. Many years ago a very funny film starring Marilyn Monroe, Jack Lemmon and Tony Curtis was filmed on location at the Del Coronado. "Some like it Hot" remains a true classic even today. The film was supposed to be set in Miami but Hollywood producers are known for taking liberties with story lines and locations. Marilyn Monroe was also reputed to have had a liaison with JFK at the Hotel along with others; to the extent they named a suite after her. There was also another affair which changed history both for the US and the UK, the abdication of Edward the VII for his love of Mrs Simpson is well known but it was here in the grounds of the Del Coronado that a small bungalow was the refuge of the then Prince of Wales before it all became so public and controversial. History, like Hollywood movies, can also play sequels to past events. We were informed that the same refuge was also used by another later Prince of Wales and his lady friend before that all became likewise a public controversy prior to the tragic death of Princess Diana.

Halloween celebrations

On a lighter note, we were there at the time of Halloween, which they celebrate enthusiastically. Everyone goes all out to dress up and decorates the home and gardens with all kinds of spooky features, polystyrene gravestones and clouds of rising mists are a regular feature. We managed to stock up with a large bag of treats in readiness, but it soon ran out as dozens of children (and their parents) toured the homes and stores on the big night. The local police were always looking on but I think it was more for their enjoyment than a duty as the crime rate there was almost negligible. We were soon into November and Carole's birthday was looming. I had noticed that the Del Coronado was holding a special champagne supper in the sumptuous "Crown" ballroom on her birthday. I made some enquiries and it turned out that the event was accompanied by one of the best "big band" groups in the USA (I don't recall who). The tables were set out in groups of four or six places to a table and each table was attended by its own personal chef fro the evening. Wow, what an opportunity to out on the posh frocks and DJ threads and what an evening it turned out be. The big band group were totally superb and right on the button with their selection of memorable melodies. The staff members were falling over themselves to supply every whimsical fancy. Now to be fair I had decided that the budget would be well and truly blown out of the water, but what the hell, life is not a dress rehearsal. At the end of the evening the bill was subtly presented (how do they do that "secret slide"?) and I slid it equally secretly into my top pocket so Carole would not have a coronary. I managed to reach the concierge without her noticing and presented my plastic for final sacrifice to the slaughter. Now here is the absolute God's truth, the total bill was less that $50 for all four of us. "No mistake, Sir. We aim to please and you are most welcome" smiled the seasoned Maitre D. I smiled the rest of the evening and all the way back to our hotel, in fact I wore the same smile for a week! So did Carole, I am delighted to say. P.S. The "Crown" ballroom was named "crown" after the Prince of Wales.

I almost forgot to add that we were allowed to enjoy all the wonderful facilities of the Del Coronado because of an arrangement with our hotel which was very nice. The Del Coronado has a wonderful collection of boutiques and gift shops set in the surrounding basement walkway. Their décor and ambience give the impression of cosy village shops, very clever, very upmarket. We even found some ceramic products from David Austin Roses of Albrighton, just down the road from our home in UK. Shortly after all this excitement the phone rang in our hotel room one morning and I found myself speaking to a man from the "Nordstrom" retail outlet in "Fashion Valley". Never heard of thought I, but Carole had. He was inviting us to lunch as "special guests" because today was a wonderful opportunity to view their merchandise which is heavily discounted for today's special guests only. Our driver can call to collect and return you after. If you would like to take up this opportunity please return our call and it will be arranged. And so it was.

The driver arrived wearing a very expensive suit and led us to a very large people carrier fitted with every gismo known to man. We were whisked away to "Fashion Valley" and as the doors opened we were led to meet our "personal shopper" and escort for the day at the Concierge desk. I had never seen a department store with a concierge desk before. All our purchases were instantly sent to the concierge desk for collection. Our personal shopper was a wonderful, courteous, middle aged lady who showed us all the bargains and discounted items, ensuring we used the appropriate coupons for even further discounts. I think it was Carole's idea of true heaven! Lunch was served in the executive suite and we all got to chat with many others from local and out of town places. It was all very sociable and thoroughly interesting. The concierge at the reception desk had all the packages sorted and loaded into the limo for the trip back to the hotel. What a way to market retail. We must learn a lot from some of these methods. We did spend around $500 but it was well worth it and we did check on the regular retail prices later to find a massive saving. We still have most of the items some ten tears later so they stood the test of time and quality. The Americans, I found, do not do rubbish or poor quality.

On our visits to down town San Diego we saw local police using mountain cycles adapted for street pursuit (we have seen more versions in other countries since), it was quite an eye opener. The Bilbao Park Zoo is probably the largest of its kind in the world and we were present just after the birth of a baby panda so everyone was asked to keep especially quiet around the area. The Zoo is so large you need to take advantage of the supplied transport at every opportunity, a tiring day but so well worth it. I had heard of the Heritage Aviation Museum set in the same area so it was too good an opportunity to miss. On a gigantic plinth at the main entrance is the huge Blackbird supersonic reconnaissance aircraft. I had never seen one before so this was a real first for me. Inside the Museum they have constructed a complete flight deck of a famous aircraft carrier, complete with aircraft and animated sound effects, including a vibrating deck underfoot as the aircraft sounds of a landing come over the sound system. There is even a Spitfire and wooden dispersal hut complete with bell hanging at the doorway depicting the Battle of Britain. I was very impressed to see an entire wall area devoted to famous women aviators including those from our ATA and their American counterparts.

The Americans are very conscious of their military forces and hold them all in great respect and awe, especially the Veterans, holding a special "Veterans day" to commemorate the fallen and a tribute to those who gave so much. There is a large training base for the Navy Seals at San Diego and quite often they can be seen exercising on the beach and many local gift shops hold stocks of appropriate memorabilia to them. We managed to take a tour around the Navy yard aboard a local ferry and saw a number of submarines (though discreetly tarped over the vital bits!) and ships at anchor. Apparently you can apply to be invited to visit the base on days when the passing out parades are scheduled. As in all things American, they do not do this by halves with large brass bands, flags waving and precision drill timed to the split second. Crowds from local and tourists fill all the seats in the gallery surrounding the event and is well worth the effort of a visit.

Return to Florida a family celebration

The following year we flew to Florida for an entirely different kind of holiday. Carole's son Phillip had decided he would like to marry his lovely fiancée Jenny in the wonderful climate of Florida and preparations were accordingly put in place. We arranged to stay at a place called the Hotel Vistana which turned out to be an excellent choice. They arranged everything for us including the officiating Padre and the wedding reception. Like all American enterprises, their approach was totally professional and carried out with an almost military precision. We were equally astounded at the very reasonable outlay when the final bill came in. Phillip and Jenny hired a Harley Davidson for a trip around Florida which was equally awesome and they enjoyed thoroughly. We took in a few more sights we had missed on previous visits. I had become fairly well experienced in driving USA style, steady on the 50 mph limits which are frequent around the city outreaches, though they do climb up to 70 mph on the main highways. Whilst the police are courteous and understanding, they also do not suffer fools gladly and can be quite forceful if aggravated.

I also found to my cost on more than one occasion, that you really do need to study the route carefully before venturing out. Missing a turn on their super highways can mean a very long detour to get back to where you need to be. We found the cost of food in the usual food outlets (and the huge amounts served) was very cheap, many offering "eat all you can". We were truly stunned on one occasion at a "Wendy's" restaurant when a local American family came in. I thought we had experienced an eclipse of the sun as the daylight was obscured from the doorway by the sheer size of each member of the family group, none of whom were less than 30 stone, and I do include the three children. After their fourth circuit at the food selection display we realised why we had seen quite a number of obese families. (Sadly this has now become prevalent in many other countries we visit).

Everglades and hurricanes

We fell in love with the West coast of America so much that we returned there on a number of occasions, partly due to the fortunate discovery of a British family who owned a lovely home in Bradenton, Sarasota. I came across their advertisement in the classified section of the MOD "Focus" Newsletter, and a most fortunate find it turned out to be. Bradenton was a lovely suburb of Sarasota, within easy reach of the coast and a beautiful place called Anna Marie Island. The coastal area of Sanibel is renowned for the silver sand and the houses built on stilts to provide access for cars underneath for shade when the temperatures climb in the summer heat. It is also famous for a particular shell called a "sand dollar", which looks like a slightly miss shaped large coin, very pale cream with a slight sheen on the underside. The locals describe the posture of those collecting them as "the Sanibel stoop". While we were doing the "Sanibel stoop" one afternoon, Ann caught sight of a school of Dolphins very near the waters edge. They were so tame and appeared to be quite happy to show off, playing in the breaking waves.

We experience a bit of bad map reading on one occasion when we got very lost. It was in an area we really did not feel comfortable with as the signs at the side of the road warned you not to leave the vehicle as 'gators would be regularly moving across the highway. Not exactly the place for a picnic! We finally came across a large enclosure which appeared to be some kind of scientific research establishment and there was a serious looking security guard in attendance. We pulled up and asked for direction, showing him our local map. He looked at it quizzically and turning the map all the way around, said with a slight grin "Sir, you are in the wrong state, this is Louisiana and you are trying to read the map upside down!" It was at that moment I realised Harry was not exactly the best navigator on the planet and chose to pull over when in doubt to figure it out for myself. I do have to say that some of their signage assumes a lot of local geographical knowledge. It does not help when they change the route numbers of the highways without telling anyone! One of our excursions included a trip down to the Everglades for an airboat ride which was probably the most exiting experience of the whole holiday. Our guide was a wonderful character and took us right into the swamps where the 'gators came around to greet us, wallowing around the boat so close you could reach out and touch, if you wanted to lose a hand!

We planned for a long stay on this occasion and we also were to experience the down side of Florida's climate when we received a warning that a hurricane was brewing out at sea and we were most likely to be in its path. The warnings became more specific and soon we were advised to evacuate to a refuge centre within the next day or so. We sat tight for quite a while as no specific warning to our local area had yet been announced but then at midnight we were all rudely awakened by the local police who gave orders for a mandatory evacuation. Our neighbours across the street said they were staying because their dog would not be allowed into the refuge centre and would have to be left in the house. We discussed the situation and after reviewing the structure of the house we realised that the centre room of the house was very sturdy with solid wall so we agreed with our neighbours to stay put and prepare the room with mattresses, water bottles and some food stocks, in the event we could be hit. As it happened the hurricane missed our street and tore into the refuge centre we would have evacuated to. Fortunately there were no casualties there, but they did lose the roof and it scared the hell out of everyone. We were thankfully quite safe, but in the wisdom of hindsight when we saw the damage inflicted along the route as we travelled back to the airport a few days later, we realised we had a very lucky escape. The airport had suffered a lot of damage to light aircraft and some of the buildings. Many of the huge hoarding had been strewn over the countryside like confetti. We realised then how powerful it had been and counted our blessings.

Our fascination with the vast continent of North America did not stop there and we completed the experiences with visits to Phoenix Arizona where we saw the beautiful range of the Sedona hills carved into spectacular shapes by millions of years of wind erosion and experienced a startling helicopter ride to view the magnificent spectacle from a birds eye view. A few years later, I witnessed the incredible thunderous launch of 70 year old John Glenn from the Kennedy Space centre aboard Columbus. We spent one wonderful Christmas in Boston, took the tours around Cape Cod and Provincetown, where the first settlers landed from England. We also visited Plymouth and the recreated settler's village. I was able to re connect with my own history of John F Kennedy at the JFK Museum in Hyannis and took a trip to Martha's Vineyard, home of the Kennedy family so tragically blighted by events.

We even managed to touch the great continent of Canada which included Toronto, and the 30,000 islands scattered among the lakes like jewels on a sparkling sea. And of course the pounding volley of billions of gallons of water cascading over Niagara Falls, viewed from the famous Maid of the Mist ferry boat. I managed to overcome my vertigo sufficiently to stand on the glass floor of the CNN tower to view the ground hundreds of feet below (no mean feat for me!). I have been so lucky to have enjoyed very good health and fitness to do all these things and I do owe so much to my incredibly gifted partner Carole who made all these things possible by instilling her "can-do" attitude into my soul. I am not a religious man but I do believe that if you find the right partner then whoever is in charge up stairs, showers you with the blessings richer than any mercenary advantage.

Living in the Algarve

During the last twenty years we have also been able to enjoy our "Place in the Sun", our second home in southern Portugal. We have been able to improve and modify the interior and exterior to suit our needs and at a very conservative cost due to the skills of our local tradesmen. The end result is a compliment to their craftsmanship and skills and speaks volumes in itself. Our special friends, Bertina and Ken Andrew, were instrumental in advising and helping us to seek out the right people as they had lived in our town for many years prior to our arrival. Ken originally hailed from Stockton-on-Tees and his wonderful accent was never eroded, despite the years spent in the Royal Navy and the Merchant Navy. Bertina was born in the Algarve at St. Clara. They have three sons, Andre, who lives in France, Neville who still lives in Tunes and Charles who joined the RAF and now lives in Lincoln. Bertina is a genius at cooking and has a wealth of fantastic recipes handed down from her mother and added to over the many years. She and her family had to escape to England during the Salazar regime which had become a police state where anyone could be denounced as a threat to his "benevolent" dictatorship. She met Ken in London whilst she worked for an Arabic family as their nanny and they returned to the Algarve shortly after Ken retired in the 1989. The Salazar regime were overthrown on April 25th in 1974 by a bloodless coup of Army officers, along with the majority of the people, who had become disenchanted with the state of affairs in Government. Ken had endured a great deal of discomfort from an injury he sustained many years ago which affected his mobility. Sadly he passed away at 86 years old on March 2nd 2013. We shall miss him and his wonderful sense of humour. He was passionate about good music and greatly admired classical opera singers. It is a stark reminder that we are not immortal and time stands still for no man. It is also a stark reminder to prioritise what you want and what you really need and

Behind the Lens   355

remember that the most important things in life that no amount of money can ever buy are your health and happiness.

"Living the dream..."

The lakeside view (our UK home)

Paphos (Cyprus)

Olden (Norway)

Brissac (France)

The garden (our Algarve home)

The Malthouse Sheriffhales

Acknowledgements

To: Peter Eggleston for permission to include "Reminisces of WW2".
Roy Conyers Nesbit for extracts from "Eyes of the RAF".
Eddie Leaf for extracts from "Above All Unseen".

My special thanks also to:
The late Lord Patrick Lichfield, and Peter Kaine, his studio manager;
AVM Peter Dye, Ian Thirsk, John Francis, Al McLean, Ewen Cameron and
Ian Alder of the RAF Museum,Cosford.
The RAF Photographers Association: The committee and members;
Geoff Sellars, Ex-OC DSOP for his support in moving the Military
Photography Museum to the RAF Museum., Cosford.
Mike Mockford OBE, the Medmenham Club and members.
Jon Jarvis MA BA FBIPP, OC DSOP for his total support and enthusiasm
of this book and the current installation of the "Centenary" display at
DSOP.
Lee Barton of the Air Historical Branch (RAF) 2D.
Ian West whose illustrations included, were originally reproduced by
Kodak Ltd, in 1995, for the 80th anniversary of the Joint School of
Photography.

To my colleagues, students and associates at the Defence School of
Photography whose support was so enthusiastically given over many years.
To those whom my memory fails to recall, my sincere apologies and eternal
gratitude and to the many people I had the great privilege and pleasure of
serving and working with.

You were all simply the best!

And now to the future…

To my great relief, a few good men under the guidance of Jon Jarvis, OC DSOP including Tim Robinson, Flight Sergeant Andy Malthouse, Ian Dunning, John Freestone, and Mal Price, continue to look after the interests of the Museum of Military Photography renamed as the "Centenary Room". As time stands still for no man I have become acutely aware that my physical ability has restricted my ambitions to build empires and move mountains! I could not have chosen a better crew to hand over to the future of the historical collection. I hope to continue to play a supportive role as advisor in matters of history and reference, so I look forward to exciting new ideas from fresh eyes with the wonders of modern technology at their disposal.

My best wishes and sincere gratitude go with them.

The following publications were used for source references:

Photographic Reconnaissance.   *A J Brookes.*
Ian Allan 1975

Spies in the Sky.   *J W R Taylor; D Mondey.*
Ian Alan 1972

Aviator Extraordinary.   *R Barker*
Chatto & Windus 1969

The Air War.   *J Piekalkiewicz.*
Blandford Press 1985

Evidence in Camera.   *Constance B Smith.*
Chatto & Windus 1985. Revised 2003

World War II Photo Intelligence.   *Col R M Stanley*
Sedgewick & Jackson 1981

Aerial Espionage.   *D van der Aarl*
Airlife Publishing 1985

Eyes of the RAF.   *Roy C Nesbit.*
Alan Sutton 1996

Most Secret War.   *R V Jones.*
Hamish Hamilton 1979

Above All Unseen.   *Edward Leaf*
Patrick Stephens 1997

Sadly some of the above references are no longer in print.
I am grateful for the permissions to reproduce extracts.

Updated April 2014

The Epilogue

It has taken around five years to compile this record and I have been able to re- examine the sequence of events in my fortunate careers and place them into some semblance of order. I am not an author so I hope my record is not compared with those who are blessed with the necessary skills to create literary masterpieces. However I felt compelled to place on record, the many stories and articles I was able to gather to illustrate the achievements of those special people who gave so much. It seemed appropriate as the year 2015 is the centenary of the foundation of the training establishment which made it all possible,

On the deck of
Queen Victoria

I am deeply indebted to my friend Dave Newham an ex RAF photographer and an accomplished author in his own right. His diligent proof reading skills have enabled me to correct my original drafts into a better standard of writing.

More than twenty years have rolled by for Carole and me, as we continue to enjoy an idyllic life style in retirement. I have to award this good fortune to the expertise of my accountant, personal assistant and lovely wife Carole, who has enabled us to visit more than 20 countries, get married on Concorde, cruise on the Queen Victoria, the Queen Elizabeth and the Queen Mary, and wallow in the vineyards of the Loire Valley. We have also been able to revisit many of my old haunts at Brampton, Wyton, Wellesbourne Mountford, Germany, Cyprus, and Malta to complete the circle for me.

I have a great debt of gratitude to the Royal Air Force for allowing me in, the Civil Service for allowing me out, and to you, dear reader for having the patience to read this book. Thank you.

Dave Humphrey

13613086R00194

Printed in Great Britain
by Amazon